Graceful Exits

Graceful Exits

CATHOLIC WOMEN AND THE

ART OF DEPARTURE

Debra Campbell

INDIANA
University Press
Bloomington & Indianapolis

Publication of this book is made possible in part with the assistance of a Challenge Grant from the National Endowment for the Humanities, a federal agency that supports research, education, and public programming in the humanities.

This book is a publication of

Indiana University Press
601 North Morton Street
Bloomington, Ind. 47404-3797 USA

http://iupress.indiana.edu

Telephone orders   800-842-6796
Fax orders   812-855-7931
Orders by e-mail   iuporder@indiana.edu

© 2003 by Debra Campbell

The paper used in this publication meets the minimum requirements of American National Standard for Information Sciences— Permanence of Paper for Printed Library Materials, ANSI Z39.48-1984.

MANUFACTURED IN THE UNITED STATES OF AMERICA

Chapter 3 of the present work originally appeared as a different version in Frye and Hoagland, eds., *Feminist Interpretations of Mary Daly* (University Park: The Pennsylvania State University Press, 2000), 164–193. Copyright 2000 by The Pennsylvania State University. Reproduced by permission of the publisher.

Library of Congress Cataloging-in-Publication Data

Campbell, Debra, date
Graceful exits : Catholic women and the art of departure / Debra Campbell.
p. cm.
Includes bibliographical references and index.
ISBN 0-253-34316-X (cloth : alk. paper)
1. Catholic women—Biography—History and criticism.
2. Ex-church members—Catholic Church—Biography—History and criticism.
3. Ex-nuns—Biography—History and criticism. I. Title.
BX4667.C36 2003
282'.092'2—dc21

2003006828

1 2 3 4 5 08 07 06 05 04 03

To my mother, who taught me to cherish stories.

CONTENTS

PREFACE

A decade ago I was hired to write the centennial history of one of many nineteenth-century Catholic female academies that had transformed themselves into Catholic women's colleges in the early decades of the twentieth century. The project did not end happily. Bad omens and thwarted avenues of research clouded it, and questions of academic freedom that had always been theoretical for me suddenly became concrete and practical. I resigned from the project after devoting two years of my life to it. Leaving without submitting the manuscript left me with two strong emotions. I felt that sinking feeling that Catholic women of my generation are so quick to misdiagnose as guilt, but I also felt exhilaration at having followed my instincts instead of plodding ahead being a Catholic good girl doing work that clearly was not good for me. Walking away was incredibly liberating, a spiritually charged moment when my Catholic and feminist values and the sacredness of work became clearer to me than they had been for some time.

Synchronicities can be illuminating because they prompt us to pay attention to the Big Picture. My departure from the project, which coincided with my divorce, left me keenly aware of the spiritual benefits of departure. I knew I was supposed to feel guilty, but I had to admit that I did not. Instead, both departures evoked memories of the past, girlhood memories of confession in the early 1960s: an almost blinding clarity and the deeply scrubbed feeling of absolution. In discussions with female Catholic friends, I discovered that when they forgave themselves for not being self-abnegating good girls, they, too, found departures of various kinds exhilarating and deeply spiritual.

My new self-consciousness about departures has informed the way I teach Catholic women's narratives to my students at Colby College. We explore subterranean spiritualities celebrating departure and flight in the writings of both pre–Vatican II and post–Vatican II Catholic women. Both kinds of explorations—my own forays into the spirituality of departure and classroom investigations of Catholic women's departures as spiritual quests—have shaped and colored this book.

Anyone who sets out to examine Catholic women's departure narratives soon discovers an embarrassment of riches. I have decided to pay close attention to certain representative works rather than attempt to be comprehensive. I have chosen to focus on life-writings produced by Catholic women at their own initiative rather than interviews. The decision to write one's life constitutes a fundamental act of departure that leads to others. *Graceful Exits* intentionally casts light on texts that have achieved at least a modest degree of notoriety, texts which, in the recent past, have been more frequently cited than closely read. And yet for many Catholic women, these texts have provided maps and departure scenarios that have helped them to envision their own mobility within a Catholic culture that did not encourage women's departures and spiritual migrations.

Those who are theoretically inclined will recognize immediately that the narratives examined here lend themselves to a multiplicity of readings from the perspectives of critical theory. Rather than ground my analysis in theory, however, I have chosen to provide a carefully contextualized close reading to allow these still-neglected texts to speak to each other within earshot of the reader. This choice stems from my conviction that these texts need more attending to if we are to take seriously the idea of a still-unacknowledged tradition of Catholic women's departure narratives that has shaped and informed Catholic women's lives during the past half-century. I hope that this book represents a step toward deeper, more nuanced understandings of Catholic women's narratives. The pleasures of theory should presuppose and follow close reading and historical contextualization.

ACKNOWLEDGMENTS

This book is the result of countless conversations with former classmates, colleagues, students, relatives, and even semi-strangers. Many people have had a hand in it. Grace Von Tobel's experience and professionalism left its mark upon the manuscript at several stages in its evolution. I am deeply indebted to Marilyn Pukkila and Peg Menchen for research guidance, to Eileen Fredette for her patience and timely troubleshooting, and to several generations of Interlibrary Loan librarians who have made my working conditions so pleasant and productive. Four student assistants contributed substantially: Melissa Crawley, Michael Cobb, Sarah Miller, and Miranda Bertram. Julia McDonald brought Barbara Ferraro and Patricia Hussey to Colby at a crucial moment. Dean Rogers (Special Collections, Vassar College Libraries) and Scott Taylor (*America* Magazine Archives, Georgetown University Library) provided invaluable help tracking down archival sources. Bob Sloan, Jane Lyle, and Kate Babbitt, my editors at Indiana University Press, have patiently walked me through this first book and taught me many things.

My parents, who sent me to the Convent of the Sacred Heart, Nottingham, set the process in motion. Nikky Singh and Carleen Mandolfo believed in *Graceful Exits* and insisted on celebrating it. Mary Jo Weaver and Paula Kane provided encouragement and critiques during this project's many incarnations. My husband Doug has been there through it all, with his unfailing ear, soft shoulder, and love of irony: momentary glimpses of Grace Itself.

INTRODUCTION: FLIGHT

Flying is a woman's gesture—flying in language and making it fly. We have all learned the art of flying and its numerous techniques; for centuries we've been able to possess anything only by flying; we've lived in flight, stealing away, finding, when desired, narrow passageways, hidden crossovers. . . . Women take after birds and robbers, just as robbers take after women and birds. They go by, fly the coop, take pleasure in jumbling the order of space, in disorienting it, in changing around the furniture, dislocating things and values, breaking them all up, emptying structures, and turning propriety upside down. . . .

A feminine text cannot fail to be more than subversive. It is volcanic; as it is written it brings about an upheaval of the old property crust, carrier of masculine investments; there's no other way. There's no room for her if she's not a he. If she's a her-she, it's in order to smash everything, to shatter the framework of institutions, to blow up the law, to break up the "truth" with laughter.

—Cixous 1976, 887–888

These words from Hélène Cixous's groundbreaking essay "The Laugh of the Medusa," capture the radical and irreversible quality inherent in women's writing. The act of writing from within her own experience takes a woman back to her roots and across boundaries. It may mean leaving behind the persons, places, and things that she has loved, suffered for, and always envisioned at the center of her life. When she depicts women as birds and robbers, Hélène Cixous, an Algerian Jewish writer, is not writing with Catholic women in mind. A whole range of interested parties, from devout Catholics to secular feminists, might argue that Catholic women are too orderly and obedient to fit Cixous's description and that they represent the exception that proves the rule.

In *The Feminine Mystique*, first published in 1963, Betty Friedan initially seems to present supporting evidence for this stereotypical portrait of Catholic women. Upon closer examination, however, we see in Friedan's almost isolated example drawn from Catholic women's experience evidence that Catholic women's reputation for obedience shrouds more complex realities. Friedan interviewed a Catholic woman who had resigned from the state board of the League of Women Voters under pressure from her husband, her priest, and the school psychologist, who insisted that her political activities outside of the home were having an adverse effect on her daughter. "It's more difficult for a Catholic woman to stay emancipated," she told Friedan. When Friedan caught her on the kitchen phone hatching new strategies for the local Democratic Party, the overtly obedient stay-at-home Catholic mother admitted that she carried on a covert life of political activism by phone. She confessed that she "hid her political activity at home 'like an alcoholic or a drug addict, but [she didn't] seem to be able to give it up'" (Friedan 1983, 352). Even within the obedience of this dutiful Catholic mother, we see a pattern of transgression and flight, carefully hidden like an addiction but pursued consciously as a survival strategy.

It turns out that flight, known by many names (including escape, exodus, exile, diaspora, and crossing over), represents a central theme in the life-writings of twentieth-century Catholic women. We see images of flight not only in the works of famous renegades and resisters such as Mary McCarthy, Mary Daly, and the contributors anthologized in *Lesbian Nuns: Breaking Silence,* but also in the writings of Mary Gordon and Clarissa Pinkola Estés, who have taken great pains to remain within the Catholic fold, albeit on their own terms. Much as they need to negotiate and custom-tailor the institutions of marriage and vowed religious life to fit their own needs and special gifts, twentieth-century Catholic women need to negotiate and renegotiate their relationship to the Catholic church. Texts written by Catholic women bear witness to this often very intimate negotiation process which takes place whether or not the women choose to remain faithful practicing Catholics.

Some feminists, like Cixous and Virginia Woolf before her, insist that women's writing, the kind that truly and honestly comes from lives lived in women's bodies, always represents an exodus from the structures and conventions established by the men who make the rules governing language and life in western societies. In *Websters' First New Intergalactic Wickedary,* the radical feminist Mary Daly maintains that women's departures constitute a special virtue, the Courage to Leave, and she provides a two-part dictionary definition: "**Courage to Leave:** Virtue enabling women to depart from all patriarchal religions and other hopeless institutions; resolution springing from deep knowledge of the nucleus of nothingness which is at the core of these institutions" (Daly 1987, 69).

As Daly learned from her own life experience, even women's smallest departures require large amounts of courage. Elizabeth Evasdaughter is not exaggerating when she asserts that "a Catholic woman writing an autobiography is already a subversive" (Evasdaughter 1996, 196). Sometimes the subversiveness sneaks up on the writer herself, who is surprised to learn from readers who represent the institutional church that her personal narrative, her carefully constructed account of her own life, is unacceptable. This can happen to everyday Catholic women who do not aspire to leadership or public life in the church as well as to outspoken public figures such as Mary Daly, Mary McCarthy, and Mary Gordon. In an article on the breakdown of community in contemporary Catholicism which appeared in the Jesuit journal *America* the summer of 2000, Thomas J. McCarthy recounted his sister's painful experience seeking an annulment.

> [She] spent the better part of a year meeting with the priest assigned to her case, subjecting herself to bizarrely inappropriate questions and lectures. Told to write an autobiography, she dutifully labored over it for months, trying to be thorough and honest. She finally submitted it for review, and when she walked into the chancery office a week later to discuss it, the priest tossed her autobiography on the floor at her feet, shaking his head. "This simply won't do," he said. (McCarthy 2000, 6)

McCarthy's sister, who had begun the annulment process as a dutiful, obedient Catholic, was propelled in new directions by the official reception of her autobiography. She found herself on the margins of the institutional church, the expanding space inhabited by Catholics who no longer ask for official Catholic approval or absolution for the intimate details of their personal lives and failed marriages.

Whether she is initially aware of it or not, a Catholic woman constructing her own version of her life within the institutions of church, family, and even academia is, in fact, staging an exodus. As Cixous's metaphor suggests, such an exodus calls into question the script written for women by the Catholic hierarchy. It might even be perceived as a special kind of theft, an act of reparation, like the theft in the popular slogan "Take back the night." Catholic women writing their own lives challenge the notion of "the Catholic Woman as an abstract, clerical concept, [a being who is] naturally and inevitably subrational and sexually dangerous" and direct our attention to "real Catholic women [who] can think, are disciplined, and work in a creative way" (Evasdaughter 1996, 196).

The Catholic woman who writes her own script becomes a fugitive, a subversive, a vandal, who emerges from the shadows to spray-paint shocking, irreverent graffiti on the cherished public monuments to God and family. For that is what women have become within the official teachings of the church, public monuments to clerical values, safely enshrined upon pedestals. Like Daly's definition of the Courage to Leave, Cixous's depiction of women's nature ("If she's a her-she, it's in order to smash everything, to shatter the framework of institutions, to blow up, to break up the 'truth' with laughter.") is intentionally undiplomatic. It is a challenge, or even a battle cry for women in flight, if only in their imaginations—women willing to sacrifice public approval, and the status and perquisites that it brings, for the promise of freedom and self-love. Some might challenge Cixous's characterization of *all* women as escapees and robbers because it reduces all women to a single essential nature—and a disorderly, secretive nature at that. I prefer to embrace Cixous's carefully constructed metaphor, run with it, and let it do its work, taking us places that we could not reach any other way.

Graceful Exits explores the rich tradition of flight narratives produced by twentieth-century Catholic women and the many different aspects that flight can assume. Cixous's metaphor captures the complex and varied experiences of Catholic women, which run the gamut from memories or fantasies of stealthy exits ("We've lived in flight, stealing away, finding, when desired, narrow pathways, hidden crossovers.") to exhilarating, showy spirals celebrating newfound freedom, reminiscent of aviation shows. ("They go by, fly the coop, take pleasure in jumbling the order of space, in disorienting it, in changing around the furniture, dislocating things and values, breaking them up, emptying structures and turning propriety upside down.") Once we begin to look for images and fantasies and stories of flight in Catholic women's writings, we find them everywhere. Nonetheless, this kind of writing remains a neglected tradition, even at the dawn of the twenty-first century.

To write about flight, even tiny subtle gestures toward flight, places a Catholic woman on the margins of the church. For it entails saying the unspeakable, flouting taboos that restrict the free speech of faithful daughters of the church. This kind of speech or writing can take place only on the margins, in spaces carefully constructed for that purpose. The consciousness-raising groups of the late 1960s and early 1970s represented one prototype of this kind of protected, consecrated space. In the introduction to *Womanspirit Rising*, Carol Christ and Judith Plaskow convey what it felt like to inhabit this newly reclaimed space, the safe zone constructed by and for a new wave of robbers and fugitives:

> Women are encouraged to speak what has not previously been spoken. Often this speaking leads to the discovery of shared experiences. The woman who tearfully admits that she sometimes hates her children finds that other women feel the same way too; their experiences of

motherhood are similar. The woman who timidly ventures that she often doesn't enjoy sex hears others say, "me, too." She is not alone. The graduate student who tells how her contributions to seminar discussion are ignored by male colleagues discovers that this, too, is a common experience. Even the smartest woman has had it many times. (Christ and Plaskow 1992, 6)

Very little has been written on consciousness-raising in the Catholic community. There is evidence that the process was well underway in certain circles by the mid-1960s: a response to the widespread, free-floating expectations of change in the church generated by Vatican II (1962–1965), Catholic women's growing access to higher education, their participation in the exodus to the suburbs, and urgent questions raised by the public availability of contraceptives while the church hierarchy proscribed all "artificial" birth control methods. Sally Cunneen's pioneering study *Sex: Female; Religion: Catholic* (1968), based on replies to questionnaires sent to 4,627 subscribers to the liberal Catholic journal *Cross Currents,* shows that Catholic women of the 1960s were entertaining fundamental questions about their beliefs and experiences. Cunneen's questionnaire provided a welcome safe zone for Catholic women to publicly articulate some of their private thoughts on issues that they had been grappling with alone or with other Catholic women in convents, in college dormitories, or in each others' kitchens all across America. Cunneen's respondents spoke candidly about their hopes for the future, their evolving perceptions of their vocations, their bodies, and their responsibilities to the church and their families.

In individual respondents' voices, skillfully interwoven into Cunneen's analysis of her data, we find indisputable evidence that by the late 1960s, American Catholic women had discovered a frontier or borderland on the margins of the church, where many individual women had already staged their own small departures—sociologist Dorothy Dohen called them "working compromise[s]" (Dohen 1960, 70)—unbeknownst to family, friends, and parish priests. To the pilgrims themselves, even these small, subtle migrations revealed alternative routes and passageways that invited still other departures to the expanding territories on the margins of the church. For example, among the 317 married women who returned the questionnaire, 67 percent openly admitted using birth control. Ninety-eight women had opted for the rhythm method, then and now the only means of family limitation other than abstinence permitted by the Vatican. Sixteen supplemented the rhythm method with oral contraceptives or a device. One hundred nine used other methods, including eighty-four who used the Pill.

In the last group of eighty-four was a married Canadian graduate student who had been encouraged by her parish priest to follow her conscience. The words of this young woman, who was forthright and eloquent about her inner conflicts, illuminate the complexity of Catholic women's departures. Her conscience-driven decision to transgress Catholic norms and teachings and take contraceptives was overshadowed by her awareness of what she was leaving behind. And that abiding awareness, itself, represented a vestige of her past life as an obedient, devout Catholic, a life that would remain part of her, whatever happened in the future. She wrote:

> There are times when I am at Mass with family or friends when I would like to go to Communion because it symbolizes something very meaningful to me. To do this, the Church says I must go to confession, because I have sinned seriously against its views on love and marriage. But I cannot in all honesty confess and be sorry for these things, and so I have nowhere to turn. The Church has no place for people like myself, even though things in it still have value for us. (Cunneen 1968, 120–121)

By the mid-1960s, this young Catholic wife and graduate student, who knew that it was not the right time for her to have children and took responsible measures to avoid conception, had crossed a boundary. The safe, meaningful spiritual home and family that she had found in the church throughout girlhood and early womanhood were no longer accessible to her. Like the banished Adam and Eve, she could still see the garden and remember its pleasures and comfort, but she could not go back there. She could not return precisely because she *was* a good Catholic, acting in good faith, who could not manipulate the sacrament of penance by feigning contrition for an act that she considered responsible, the opposite of a sin. That meant that there was no place for her in the church, even though Catholic longings, memories, and spirituality would always remain a part of her.

Catholic women who can no longer find a niche for themselves in the church create a new spiritual/psychic space on the margins of the church or in a post-Catholic realm on the boundary. They build this new space on the foundations of their departure stories, in a place that transcends time and conventional notions of space. Several of the narratives examined in this book were written before the 1960s, consciousness-raising, and the outpouring of Catholic women's voices described by Sally Cunneen. Monica Baldwin, Antonia White, and Mary McCarthy wrote from a position of isolation, or rather, *wrote their way out of isolation,* by presupposing a circle of listeners, their envisioned readers, who could understand what their solitary departures meant. There is some evidence that the acts of envisioning and addressing this audience might have actually kept these three isolated women from experiencing even more severe emotional turmoil than they did during certain especially difficult moments of their lives.

As the pioneer feminist theologian Nelle Morton observed in her theological memoir *The Journey Is Home,* the emergence of an audience that cared about women's stories and really heard them has created "a new kind of seeing and hearing." The stories of flight and diaspora written by modern Catholic women are part of this new seeing and hearing, a process which had been underway behind the scenes for decades before women's consciousness-raising groups caught the attention of the media in the seventies. Morton examines the dynamics of the new seeing and hearing and reminds us that the power of women's narratives resides in the images: "Images refer to that entity which rises out of conscious and unconscious lives individually and in community that may shape styles of life long before conceptualization takes place." Morton confidently declares images "infinitely more powerful than concepts," because concepts can be "learned," "formulated, enclosed, and controlled" whereas images "have a life of their own" and frequently function "when persons are most unaware of their functioning" (Morton 1985, 17, 20–21).

This distinction between concepts and images underscored by Morton is crucial to our perception of how Catholic women's narratives function almost literally as vehicles that take them beyond the sphere controlled and ordered by the clerical hierarchy. Catholic women have sought to escape the artificial order of the ecclesiastically designed universe in which concepts and doctrines are more real than humans, especially female humans, with their untidy bodies, their needs and desires. It is not out of anti-intellectualism or the inability to comprehend theological concepts that Catholic women have turned to images, narratives, and fantasies of flight. We see this at work in the lives of gifted women such as Mary McCarthy, Mary Daly, and Karen Armstrong, who at one time hoped to "find the answers" in the mastery of theological concepts. They discovered the sterility of concepts alone in providing ultimate answers, clarity, and self-knowledge. Armed with new, often sudden, insight into the limits of the doctrines and structures of the church, individual Catholic women cross a threshold into a new place. And this crossing takes place every day, out of sight, unacknowledged, seldom assisted, always risky and brave. Reading departure narratives written by Catholic women awakens consciousness, reinvigorates memories of the crossing, and helps us to put it all in perspective.

Flight, life as a fugitive, a new life achieved after a painful separation from the old one, a new home sparsely furnished with items carefully chosen one by one, a room of one's own: these are the central realities of the narratives examined in the chapters that follow. Such experiences cannot be captured in concepts, only the concrete imagery chosen by the authors themselves explains why Catholic women have risked so much for them. Catholic women have had to struggle for control over the furnishings of their own Catholic imaginations. They have had images as well as doctrines imposed on them. This is what Mary Daly meant in her often-quoted statement in *Beyond God the Father:* "Women have had the power of *naming* stolen from us. We have not been free to use our own power to name ourselves, the world, or God" (Daly 1985b, 8).

Imagery provides a focal point for women's often-unspecified needs and desires. Reading concrete details and metaphors depicting other women's departures prompts Catholic women to question their identity and status as good daughters of the church and ask themselves honestly what they want and need. A friend told me about a retreat for Catholic women that she attended in the mid-1990s under the guidance of a wise and well-trained sister associated with the local Newman Center. In preparation, the participants had been asked to read Anne Tyler's *Ladder of Years* (1995). In Tyler's novel, the protagonist, Delia Grinstead, a 40-year-old suburban wife and mother, surprises herself and shocks family and friends by simply walking away from it all one sunny afternoon during the annual vacation at a Delaware seaside resort. The women at the retreat, themselves wives and mothers in their 30s and 40s, were asked to envision what their lives might be like were they to leave their families behind, set out alone, and start a new life. What if they could change the structure and purpose of their lives and choose a new space in which to live with only themselves in mind? What would this new life look and feel like?

My friend reported that while some of the women found it exhilarating to think about themselves and their lives in new ways, others refused to participate. The women in the latter group were appalled at being asked to imagine (collaborate in?) their own departures and balked at the prospect of envisioning a new life alone, as if the mental exercise was a form of judgment on them, their families, and the lives they currently led. Leaving family behind, even momentarily, in the privacy of one's own imagination, was taboo. It required crossing a threshold and risking the hard-earned mantle of respectability which shields and protects a dutiful Catholic wife and mother. Cixous's remarks about women and birds and robbers shed light on this taboo against leaving, which extends even to *imagining* a life focused on oneself.

Cixous and Tyler tap into the strong attraction that stories and images of flight, departure, and transgression hold for women, even the most obedient, responsible Catholic women. Those at the retreat who refused to imagine their own departures were tacitly acknowledging the power and potential attraction of flight. In Tyler's novel, Delia Grinstead's departure is prompted by her husband's old habit of leaving the scene in the midst of an argument. On this particular occasion on the beach, Delia, who had been toying with escape fantasies for a few weeks, initially responded in her habitual way and opted for a brisk walk to clear her head. But then her older instincts, birds' and robbers' instincts, took over, and she indulged her escape fantasy. Her espadrilles beat out the rhythm of an old song entitled "Delia's Gone" that her father had sung to her as a girl. She envisioned her location on a map of the East Coast, "an irregular strip of beige sand dotted with tiny humans, a wash of blue Atlantic next to it." She saw herself transformed into "a dot in motion, heading south," a dot endowed with the freedom and mobility denied to wives and mothers. In her fantasy, she "would keep on the move, like someone running between raindrops, and they would never, ever find her" (Tyler 1997, 89–92).

Partly because they are forbidden fruit, partly because they appeal to a side of us that is "natural" and familiar to women from memories of girlhood and adolescence, stories of flight and life on the lam hold a strong attraction for modern female readers. For Catholic female readers, they are superimposed on other images of flight drawn from film and literature. Among the most famous is Sister Luke's departure from the convent in the film version of *The Nun's Story* (1959). Here an ingeniously rigged "exit wing" permits the ex-nun to leave her former life, hermetically sealed from any incidental human touches. We see a process carefully constructed to isolate the sister who has stepped out of line and made a definitive choice about her own future. After Sister Luke signs three copies of the letter of secularization—for the order, the papal archives, and herself—she is told to go to the portress's room for further instructions. It feels like a Cold War spy scene. The almost-ex Sister Luke must go to Room 12, take off her habit, and put on the secular clothing laid out for her. Then she must press the button that unlocks the exterior convent door with a loud mechanical snap. She walks out, leaving no witnesses, except for us, the film viewers, who watch her proceed alone down the cobblestone road toward the canal, out of sight, and into her new life with the Resistance. The bells toll.

What a contrast between this and probably the most familiar convent exit scene enshrined in Catholic popular culture: Sister Maria's second and final exit from the abbey in the blockbuster musical *The Sound of Music* (1965). Maria, the former novice turned governess, returned to the convent when she could no longer deny that she loved her employer, Captain von Trapp, and had reason to believe that he returned her love. To win the captain, however, she had to vanquish an unscrupulous baroness who was capable of exploiting Maria's lack of confidence and experience with men. The thought of competing with the baroness sent Maria back to the security of her girlhood plan to become a selfless cloistered nun in the abbey, for which she was totally unsuited. The omniscient Reverend Mother told her simply: "Maria, you have to live the life you were born to live." So Maria departed from the abbey again, no longer a gawky girl in a country dirndl, but instead a confident woman. Buoyed by the words and power of the Reverend Mother's rendition of "Climb Every Mountain," she put her faith in a convent maxim: "When the Lord closes a door he opens a window." Through the window Maria finally saw clearly who she was and how to live her life.

These two departure scenes span the distance between the two extremes established by Cixous: between "stealing away, finding, when desired, narrow passageways, hidden crossovers," and "flying the coop, taking pleasure in jumbling the order of space." Catholic women have these and many more models for telling their stories of flight. There are almost endless permutations: accounts of leaping over the wall from the convent or the church itself, migrations from the constraints of a Catholic home or marriage to the world beyond, a world on the margins of the church. Departure narratives themselves, as well as the movement they describe, extend the boundaries of the Catholic world and point to the existence of a post-Catholic world constructed by and for women.

Catholic and post-Catholic women move to the margins or across the boundary with at least some Catholic baggage in hand. The need and desire to bring this baggage along puzzles those who have never made the passage themselves. It might even confuse those they have left behind in the safety of the fold. Friends, lovers, and colleagues who encounter these spiritual refugees after they have launched new lives—even explicitly post-Catholic lives—on the boundaries cannot begin to understand them if they do not take this (often invisible, unspoken) baggage into account. It is a part of who they are. It clings to their evolving selves even as they embrace new visions of selfhood and explore their fundamental affinities with birds and robbers.

Rose Fuchs Ebaugh, a sociologist and ex-nun who has written two important studies of the process of role exit, uses the term "role residual" to denote the baggage, or leavings, remaining from a previous stage of life after one has departed it. Ebaugh draws a fruitful analogy between role residual and nostalgia, which Fred Davis (*Yearning for Yesterday* [1979]) describes as the "sometimes pedestrian, sometimes disjunctive and sometimes eerie sense we carry of our own past and its meaning for present and future" (Davis 1979, 33, cited in Ebaugh 1988, 173). This preoccupation with the past and its strong grip on an individual's present and future bleeds through and complicates the plot of even the most lighthearted departure narratives written by Catholic women.

Nonetheless, Catholic women's attraction to flight and its many meanings and implications is extensively documented in their personal narratives. Catholic women's penchant for flight does not represent a contradiction of their religious training and spirituality, although this may be how it is perceived from within the institutional church and even by friends and families. As Mary Jo Weaver maintains in *Springs of Water in a Dry Land,* images of exodus and exile are fundamental to the Catholic tradition. The two sets of images have a great deal in common, and they leave modern Catholic women committed to their own spiritual survival in roughly the same place. Weaver explains:

> Exile or exodus, it is still a desert we are in as we search for ways to understand the deepest centers of our lives. Whether we eventually "go home" or finally move to a radically new place is not altogether important. What are we going to do *now*? Where do we look for clues? What does it mean to use women's experience as a norm against which to measure religious language, textual traditions, and the needs for communion? How do we forge a new spirituality in the context of our own particular time and place? (Weaver 1993, 118)

Examining stories of flight constitutes one promising way to begin to answer Weaver's questions. This process might also illuminate still other related questions about commonality and difference: What is it that makes Catholic women's imaginations and life experience distinctly different from those of their non-Catholic contemporaries? Can we find instances of overlap and intersection, places where modern Catholic women's experiences and imaginings appear similar, or at least analogous, to those of non-Catholic women living in the same times and places? Do Catholic women read other Catholic women's flight narratives differently than they do those of non-Catholics? Does this explain some of the divergent readings of Mary McCarthy's *Memories of a Catholic Girlhood*? Do Catholic women read non-Catholic women's exodus stories differently than non-Catholic women? Does this at least begin to explain the mothers at the retreat who refused to envision themselves in Delia Grinstead's espadrilles?

Catholic women's personal narratives can be intimidating to readers, even female readers. It is not merely the content, which breaks taboos about women leaving their proper place and absconding from their natural duties. Nor is it the careful assembly of powerful imagery, which can be unnerving to readers when it touches them where they are most vulnerable. The act of writing departure narratives prompts Catholic women to resort to forms of discourse that they might not otherwise choose, forms heavily laced with irony and humor. Discovering the power accessible in irony and humor takes Catholic women, writers and readers, across new boundaries. When such writing cuts too close to the bone, it is apt to be denounced and dismissed as neither serious nor truthful. This powerful negative reaction frequently confirms that the writer's words have hit home.

Depending on one's perspective, Catholic women's use of irony might be viewed either as a *vade mecum,* sustenance for the journey, or as a stealth weapon intended to destroy the structures and values that bolster traditional Catholicism. Either way, it can only be appreciated, seen, and heard for what it is by those who can participate in it. For others, it represents a barrier, even a blasphemy. Northrop Frye defines irony as "a technique of appearing to be less than one is, which in literature becomes most commonly a technique of saying as little and meaning as much as possible." Practically speaking, irony entails "[turning] away from direct statement or its own obvious meaning" (Frye 1957, 40). It is easy to see how irony, and humor, which results from flouting or reversing established conventions, have become staples in Catholic women's narratives. Female Catholic writers have found it useful, indeed sometimes unavoidable, "to appear to be less than they are," and using irony as a rhetorical strategy, they have devised codes with which to convey to sympathetic readers truths that remain inaccessible to others. Even intelligent female readers find fault with these codes. In a review of the most recent English reprint edition of Monica Baldwin's mid-twentieth-century memoir *I Leap over the Wall,* Penelope Fitzgerald vented her impatience with the author's use of humor and irony. She concedes that "the jokey self-deprecation is a defence, perhaps even a form of generosity." Still, she finds it disheartening and concludes her review with the question "Why must women go on coruscating, and will there ever be an end to their apologies?" (Fitzgerald 1987, 16).

There is another way to view humor and irony in Catholic women's narratives. James Joyce calls irony the enchantment killer. In narratives written by Catholic women, the enchantment that is killed is the magic conjured by the promise of salvation through self-erasure, absolute, body-denying asceticism, and submission to reason and authority: the foundational teachings of a traditional Catholic girlhood. During the first half of the twentieth century, these foundations were buttressed by the specific examples of holy women, such as Mary, the mother of Jesus, and St. Thérèse of Lisieux (1873–1897), women saved by dint of their own selflessness and submission. These two concrete examples themselves became abstractions, the Blessed Virgin and the Little Flower, purged of their particular identities but retaining their own power to enthrall Catholic girls bent on self-perfection. Mary Gordon captures a crucial aspect of early-twentieth-century Catholic girlhood with her recollection that "In my day, Mary was a stick to beat smart girls with" (Gordon 1982, 11). Gordon's writings, starting with her first novel, *Final Payments* (1978), show that irony and humor can be the smart girls' revenge. In the personal narratives, we see how irony and humor provide the resources for women to conceive and act on fantasies of flight and how they become central components of new lives and identities launched on the boundaries of the Catholic world.

Sometimes humor and irony can arrive unbidden, like the grace that they signify and actually convey. There was a moment during the proceedings of the Vatican Birth Control Commission in the mid-1960s when Patty Crowley, one of three female members of the Commission, discovered how this works. Crowley had been laboring to make the celibate clergy on the Commission confront the pain and frustration of the married American Catholics she had surveyed. A conservative Jesuit dismissed her testimony with the age-old objection: "What then of the millions we have sent to hell, if these norms were not valid?" Crowley responded instantly with her own question: "Do you really believe God has carried out all your orders?" Only when the others laughed did she see the humor (Stourton 2000, 77). It was a transforming moment for Patty Crowley and other Commission members. Catholic women's stories are full of such moments.

To be truly effective, irony requires restraint that is itself a kind of asceticism. Nothing is wasted; asceticism modeled after the life of the Little Flower can be recycled in carefully staged departures and the stories commemorating and perpetuating them. The girlhood goal of perfection, a Trojan horse that contains the goal of self-erasure, or at least the removal of any traces of individuality, can give way to the woman's goal of exploration and migration, self-love reflecting divine love. If girlhood years spent imitating the Little Flower actually prepare Catholic women to pursue the ironies of their experience in the church, time and energy devoted to emulating more worldly adventurous saints such as Teresa of Avila and Joan of Arc can pave the way for the heroic reversals on which some departure narratives hinge.

In the latter narratives, humor and laughter can function almost as an explosive, providing an escape route where none existed before. Mary Daly maintains that women are addicted to "false love," carefully rationed by pimps, abusive husbands, and priests. This addiction makes them "prisoners of the serious," for whom humor and laughter are both taboo and inaccessible. Like Cixous, Daly endorses the explosive quality of laughter: "The more women Laugh Out Loud, the more women Hear ourSelves Laughing, the bigger the cracks in the masters' mirrors." Daly also examines other useful properties in the humor that produces women's laughter: "Humor implies *seeing through* which requires distance/detachment" (Daly 1985e, xxii–xxvi). Laughter produces the detachment and insight necessary to envision departure in the various forms explored in the chapters that follow: diaspora, boundary-crossings, renaming, recycling, and reversals.

Catholic women's departure stories, replete with irony and humor, develop new forms of asceticism and detachment especially suitable for modern women's spiritual migrations. It has become a feminist convention to refer to the spiral shape of women's journeys. They are not straightforward linear movements from Point A to Point B. Neither are they merely circular routes back to the exact point where they began (or where things started to go wrong). The migrations examined in the chapters that follow spiral onward into new territory, the new suburbs of the church that were once considered the wild and dangerous frontier. Even as they spiral onward, they include side trips to old familiar places revisited by the authors. It is perhaps startling to realize how important physical spaces and actual places are in the personal narratives of generations of Catholic women conditioned to consider themselves "resident aliens" in the City of Man and permanent citizens of an otherworldly City of God. This realization constitutes one of the core spiritual truths within Catholic women's stories of flight. They are all about departure and movement, but the journey is home.

As we explore the bumpy terrain of Catholic women's departure stories, it is helpful to fall back on (and enter into) conversations already underway among feminists studying women's autobiography. Shari Benstock has called attention to the "internal cracks and disjunctures, rifts and ruptures" that determine the shape and structure of women's narratives (Benstock 1988, 152). Leigh Gilmore has coined the term *autobiographics* to distinguish women's strategies of self-representation, concerned with "interruptions and eruptions, with resistance and contradictions," from the classic treatment of (male) autobiography, modeled on Augustine's *Confessions* (Gilmore 1994, 42). It is comforting for Catholic women to hear non-Catholic feminist scholars asserting the need to break free from Augustine's towering, defining presence and especially his rendering of the anatomy of spiritual progress.

It is not that we remain unmoved by Augustine's testimony. We know whole passages of the *Confessions* by heart. Many of our female students naturally gravitate toward these same passages, which seem disproportionately concentrated in Book X ("Memory"):

> Late have I loved you, beauty so old and new: late have I loved you. And see, you were within and I was in the external world and sought you there, and in my unlovely state I plunged into those lovely created things which you made. You were with me, and I was not with you. The lovely things kept me far from you. . . . You called and cried out loud and shattered my deafness. You were radiant and resplendent, you put to flight my blindness. You were fragrant, and I drew in my breath and now pant after you. I tasted you and I feel but hunger and thirst for you. You touched me, and I am set on fire to attain the peace which is yours. (Augustine 1992 [trans.], 201)

> But when I love you, what do I love? It is not physical beauty nor temporal glory nor the brightness of light dear to earthly eyes, nor the sweet melodies of all kinds of songs, nor the gentle odour of flowers and ointments and perfumes, nor manna or honey, nor limbs welcoming the embraces of the flesh; it is not these I love when I love my God. Yet there is a light I love, and a food, and a kind of embrace when I love my God— a light, voice, odour, food, embrace of my inner man, where my soul is floodlit by light which space cannot contain, where there is sound that time cannot seize, where there is a perfume which no breeze disperses, where there is a taste for food no amount of eating can lessen, and where there is a bond of union that no satiety can part. That is what I love when I love my God. (Augustine 1992, 183)

The latter passage captivated Dorothy Day even before her conversion to Catholicism. It brought her both comfort and a mandate to move to a new spiritual plane, to reexamine her life (Merriman 1994, 35–36, 236n29). It is ironic that Augustine, known for his restlessness, his spiritual and intellectual experimentation and mobility, has come to represent the male establishment in autobiographical writing and the norm of the stable identity and consciousness (Benstock 1988, 152). Many women, like the young Dorothy Day, might find Augustine's words poetic and inspiring, but this does not alter the fact that the author of *Confessions* is a convert and bishop who advocates keeping one's mental, physical, and spiritual restlessness firmly in check. Women in diaspora may find much that is useful to recycle in Augustine's *Confessions,* but feminist scholars are also justified in challenging Augustine's text as the prototypical autobiography.

Augustine's formula for spiritual perfection, "our heart is restless until it rests in you" (Augustine 1992, 3), requires careful explication. Restlessness, and the instinct for flight, should not be condemned or considered symptoms of spiritual immaturity. To Augustine, as well as to the women whose narratives are examined in the chapters that follow, they brought wisdom, maturity, and a new synthesis of faith and experience inconceivable before their spiritual migrations had taken place. Whether the speaker is Augustine or Mary Daly, the decision to "throw [one's] life as far as it would go" (Daly 1992, 41) is always a leap of faith that reaps its own spiritual rewards.

Graceful Exits

1

"I LEAP OVER THE WALL"

> Picture to yourself, then, my excitement when, on withdrawing myself in horror from my surroundings and slamming the door of my interior citadel, I discovered therein, bubbling and seething like a witches' cauldron in the depths of what I believe is to-day known as the subconscious mind, something which obviously just couldn't wait another minute for its release.
>
> There was only one way of effecting this.
>
> I sat down, took up my pen and began to write.
>
> —Baldwin 1950, 279

With these words Monica Baldwin traced the origins of her memoir *I Leap over the Wall,* a book written throughout the 1940s in other peoples' guest rooms and bungalows and in rented flats by a woman desperately in need of a room of her own. Baldwin's memoir is about leaving "the cold, clean spaciousness" of the cloister which "breathed silence and consecration" (Baldwin 1950, 35; unless otherwise specified, all subsequent references in this chapter are to this source) and explores how that pure, uncluttered, unowned sacred space had inscribed itself on the author's mind and heart and even the way she experienced her own female body during the twenty-eight years (1914–1941) that she had spent as a contemplative nun in England. It is a book about leavings in both senses of the word: about mustering the Courage to Leave, in this case the convent, and how certain aspects of the abandoned life in the cloister cling to a woman long after she leaves the convent precincts. Despite its suggestive title, *I Leap over the Wall* is not a sensationalist book, a lurid exposé of life behind convent walls. It is a candid personal narrative which describes the spiritual and emotional journey undertaken by a woman with the courage to confess, after almost three decades as a cloistered nun, that she had made the wrong decision. She was "a Square Peg in a Round Hole" (vi). Baldwin's memoir depicts a middle-aged upper-class Englishwoman and her attempt to put together the jagged pieces of her identity: to reconcile her strong, and intellectually sophisticated, commitment to the Catholic religion with her intense desire for the personal space in which to discover at 50 years of age what it means to be "free to be *yourself*" (83).

Undoubtedly, what captured most readers' attention when Baldwin's book first appeared was the author's exotic past, or rather, the absence of a past life. Monica Baldwin was a latter-day female Rip Van Winkle. A reviewer in *Time* magazine called Baldwin "Thomas Merton in reverse . . . a nun who went back to the world" (January 30, 1950, 90). Readers in the early 1950s could appreciate the taboo-breaking qualities of Baldwin's memoir in ways that their counterparts a half-century later cannot. Baldwin's book stood out as an anomaly. There were plenty of books and magazine articles describing why sophisticated modern men and women were turning to the Catholic church for spiritual sustenance, enough for some people to speak of a postwar Catholic revival.

Baldwin's memoir, accompanied by Mary McCarthy's *Memories of a Catholic Girlhood,* provided evidence of a countervailing movement, Catholic women's flight from the church and from the constraints of Catholic institutions such as convents or convent schools. The latter trend continued and escalated throughout the second half of the twentieth century, and, even more disturbing within the Catholic fold, some of the women went public, writing personal narratives to chronicle, and perhaps to justify, their departures. These departure narratives assumed a variety of forms and generated considerable controversy. Baldwin's departure story belongs in the company of Antonia White's *Frost in May* (1933), Mary McCarthy's *Memories of a Catholic Girlhood* (1957), Mary Gordon's *Final Payments* (1978), and Barbara Ferraro and Patricia Hussey's *No Turning*

Back (1990). Like these and other exodus stories, several of which automatically placed their authors on the late-night talk-show circuit, Baldwin's memoir broke taboos by daring to speak in a public forum about Catholic women's agency and mobility. Baldwin's emphasis on the spiritual significance of Catholic women's prerogative to change their minds, as well as their vocations and locations, led readers, Catholic and non-Catholic alike, to see Catholics in a new perspective. This explains why Baldwin's book enjoyed a brief flurry of controversy when it first appeared in print on both sides of the Atlantic.

Understandably, the title of Baldwin's book, *I Leap over the Wall,* invited confusion and a false identification with another kind of convent-departure story, epitomized by Maria Monk's soft-porn classic *Awful Disclosures of the Hotel Dieu Nunnery in Montreal* (1836). The confusion could be cleared up immediately, however, simply by reading a few chapters of both books. *Awful Disclosures* is anti-Catholic propaganda, co-authored by a former priest and a handful of Protestant abolitionist clergymen. It is, in the words of Jenny Franchot, a "story of female victimization, partially written by and for men." It is "a 'masculine' tale that registers middle-class 'feminine' concerns with domesticity" (Franchot 1994, 154). *Awful Disclosures* hinges on the acts of violence that occur within a convent, frequently, but not exclusively, at the hands of visiting priests. It was part of the Protestant backlash against escalating Catholic immigration to the United States during the 1830s and has remained in print intermittently since then, catering to the needs of a mixed academic and anti-Catholic audience. A woman, a prostitute who had spent time in a Magdalen asylum, may have helped with the narrative of *Awful Disclosures,* but it is not, by any stretch of the imagination, a Catholic woman's narrative.

Baldwin's title actually comes from her own family history. It is the English translation of the Latin motto *Per Deum meum transilio murum,* adopted by one of her sixteenth-century ancestors, Thomas Baldwin of Diddlebury. The earlier Baldwin, imprisoned in the Tower of London for collaborating in a plot to free Mary Queen of Scots, carved the motto in the wall of Beauchamp Tower before his escape. In her post-convent years, Monica Baldwin claimed the motto as her own, and for clarity's sake, added that "the wall that I leapt over was a spiritual and not a material obstacle" (v).

Unlike Thomas Baldwin, Monica did not plan a surreptitious leap over the wall. She patiently followed the proper ecclesiastical procedures to procure a dispensation from her vows. In so doing, she turned her back on almost three decades, her entire adult life, which she had lived as a cloistered nun. She suddenly found herself, in her mid-40s, "a being without a background" (7). Baldwin's memoir is simultaneously very discreet and surprisingly candid. In contrast to Maria Monk's *Awful Disclosures,* which only pretends to break taboos by recounting, in salacious detail, the Protestant middle-class version of the Catholic minority's "hidden sins," *I Leap over the Wall* represents a genuine act of transgression.

The convent wall is by no means the only boundary Baldwin crosses. She confirms with her own personal experiences the aptness of Cixous's comparisons of women, birds, and robbers. Baldwin shows that even a woman of faith whose role and behavior has been fixed by ancient rule and tradition, a woman who has passed through several probationary stages and taken final vows, can still "fly the coop," and "take pleasure in jumbling the order of space." Even a woman whose life should be utterly predictable can find herself actively engaged in "emptying structures." Baldwin's age (close to 50) and class status (upper-class) only renders her carefully planned leap over the wall all the more shocking and unspeakable. Monica Baldwin was not an ingénue, nor was she a feisty working-class woman whose poverty might excuse her unconventional behavior.

I Leap over the Wall does not even concentrate on the leap itself. That might be excusable—no one in her overwhelmingly Protestant social or family circle had quite understood why she had entered the convent in the first place. The most shocking aspect of Baldwin's memoir is her decision to tell the truth about herself at long last. Baldwin's narrative assumes the "confessional form" that scholars have come to associate with women's life-writing. As Leigh Gilmore maintains in *Autobiographics,* "Autobiography's roots in the confession—spiritual and juridical—continue to mark it as a form in which it is both possible and necessary to tell the truth." As Gilmore explains, truth-telling in personal narratives remains complicated because the emphasis within autobiographies shifts from the truth to "*telling* the truth" (Gilmore 1994, 121). Gilmore's words apply directly to Baldwin's memoir, in which the author describes herself as the midwife to the truth within her, a truth whose time has come and which demands to be released. The process of telling her truth and the discovery of a voice in which to tell it are of primary importance to Baldwin. She does not see herself as a professional writer but as a woman seeking to tell the truth about herself after many years of denying and suppressing that truth.

Since mid-century, when Baldwin published her memoir, we have seen an efflorescence of women's personal narratives, many of which hinge on the theme of flight as depicted by Cixous. Baldwin's memoir represents one popular subgenre which focuses on midlife departures and reversals, stories of apparently normal, even dutiful, middle-aged women who decide to abandon the conventional scripts they have followed for decades and instead improvise, follow their gut instincts. We have already seen how this theme works in Anne Tyler's *Ladder of Years*. Latter-day women's departure narratives derive their popular appeal, in part, from the taboos that they break and the ways in which they have given contemporary female readers permission to speculate on what they have been conditioned to consider the unthinkable as they listen to characters who risk saying the unspeakable.

Baldwin's memoir, published long before the proliferation of women's departure narratives, secular or religious, displays uncanny similarities to later flight narratives (Catholic and non-Catholic) that emerged under the influence of the feminist movement in the 1970s and 1980s. The resemblance is especially remarkable given the Rip Van Winkle plot that Baldwin herself places center stage. Insights, which in later narratives we might be inclined to attribute to the pervasive influence of the feminist movement, must ultimately be traced to the workings of Baldwin's own unique and unusually sheltered life experience and her imagination grounded in that experience. As we shall see, Baldwin's voice actually gains strength from the isolation from which she speaks. She is forced to rely almost entirely on her own inner resources, but in order to do that, she must first discover and tap into them.

Baldwin's story and her distinctive voice took readers of the 1950s and 1960s by surprise and made her a persona non grata in the pre–Vatican II Catholic church. It is not a coincidence that *I Leap over the Wall* was the book that 17-year-old Karen Armstrong read the night before she entered the convent on September 14, 1962. Reading Baldwin's book constituted a last act of willfulness, a kind of last fling for Armstrong, her version of the last few brandies and cigarettes, sometimes found in stories of more worldly young women entering the convent. In her own convent-departure narrative *Through the Narrow Gate*, originally published in 1981, Armstrong called Baldwin's book "legendary": "The nuns at school had always spoken of it in tones of dire disapproval mixed with a kind of pity. 'Poor woman,' they had always said, 'it's so obvious that she hadn't got a vocation'" (Armstrong 1995, 2).

Armstrong read Baldwin's book despite the warnings of nuns she deeply respected and sought to emulate. She treated it like the forbidden fruit that it was: "Somewhat guiltily I had bought a copy and devoured it in the privacy of my bedroom. It was my last chance to read it and I felt compelled by furtive curiosity" (Armstrong 1995, 2). From Armstrong's own personal narrative, we learn that she need not have been so furtive. Her parents, who had strong misgivings about her vocation to convent life, would have been comforted to know that she was reading Baldwin and at least considering the reasons why one woman had ceased being a nun.

Armstrong the ex-nun writes with clarity about how she read Baldwin's memoir when she was a 17-year-old woman, soon to be a postulant: "I say I read it, but I skipped large chunks. I wasn't interested in the author's adventures after leaving her convent. I wanted to know what had happened to her inside" (Armstrong 1995, 2). Here, in the reference to the large chunks skipped, Armstrong acknowledges that Baldwin's book is not primarily about what happens inside convent walls. *I Leap over the Wall* is about interiors, but not convent interiors. It traces the contours of the inner life of the narrator herself and how she painfully sought and eventually found her own spirituality in the world outside of the convent. In this sense it is the precursor to an emerging genre of women's literature, one in which a female narrator with an identity and niche that has been carefully defined by an institutional church (which could be Catholic, Mormon, or conservative Protestant) writes herself out of that identity and the formal space associated with it. In the passage quoted above, Karen Armstrong inadvertently distinguishes the genre of *women's* departure narratives from the ex-nun exposés written, Franchot reminds us, "by and for men." For the former are not primarily about escape and do not dwell at length on the particularities of the place that the protagonist is leaving. Instead, they are about the narrator herself, and more broadly, about Cixous's woman in flight, who might resemble a robber or a bird but whose goal is to survive intact and move on.

Perceptive readers have noticed the resemblance between women's departure stories and more traditional Christian conversion narratives (Brereton 1991, 102–121). One specialist in religious autobiography, John Barbour, has coined a new term, deconversion, to describe the process he sees at work in narratives depicting the "loss or deprivation of religious faith." Barbour explores what he calls the "paradoxical ways in which narratives of lost faith mirror conversion stories." After examining a wide variety of deconversion narratives, Barbour concludes that these works have "potentially, deep significance for readers who may never record their lives in a literary text but who struggle in similar ways to find meaning in the loss of faith and in the uncompleted search for a better understanding of what is truly ultimate" (Barbour 1994, 2–4, 216). As Barbour suggests, the movement through and beyond faith might well be an extension of the boundaries of faith. Similarly, women's movement through and beyond particular institutions sanctioned by church and society, such as convents, religious schools, and marriages grounded in religion, might be seen as a genuine conversion to a new spiritual perspective or the deepening of faith that comes with maturity and growth.

Although Baldwin's memoir is not precisely speaking a deconversion narrative, it shares certain features of that genre. Barbour's description of the spiritual benefits of writing, and, by extension, reading autobiography applies to *I Leap over the Wall*. He asserts that when "a writer reflects upon the ultimate concerns that required him or her to reject a particular community and its benefits," the process can bring spiritual growth (Barbour 1994, 216). This is what happens in Baldwin's convent-departure narrative. Monica Baldwin's memoir presents flashbacks of a whole series of subtle interior preparatory gestures of the mind and will that paved the way for her official move out of the convent in October 1941. Because she found most of her friends and family highly unsympathetic to the religious life she embraced and painfully left, Baldwin devotes considerable attention to an explanation of Catholic theology and religious communities. In so doing, Baldwin the ex-nun reaffirms her Catholic faith repeatedly as she forces herself to confront the complexity of her evolving relationship to the church.

We discover that Monica Baldwin's faith has not been lost; it has been expanded, reconstituted, recycled. *I Leap over the Wall* is a remarkable text, a neglected narrative which explores fundamental issues pertaining to women's lives, bodies, and spiritualities with a freshness and originality that we do not associate with Catholic women's writings in the postwar era. The courageous honesty with which Monica Baldwin addresses her own alienation, aging, loss of physical beauty, sense of invisibility, and yearning for her own sacred space takes readers by surprise. Baldwin, an English debutante who had entered a contemplative convent just as the First World War broke out, struggled, first in the convent and then outside convent walls, with the whole array of "women's issues" that we have come to associate with the feminist revolution of the 1960s and 1970s. Yet Baldwin encountered these questions alone while reading St. Augustine, Huysmans's *St. Lidwine of Schiedam,* and assorted works on the mystical body of Christ. Part of what made convent life excruciating for her was the utter isolation that she found within her community of sisters. There was no one with whom to discuss these questions, the spiritual contraband that she had brought into the convent and could not find a way to discard. Baldwin's ascetic attempt to live out her vocation while suppressing her instinctive knowledge that she was unsuited for the cloister almost destroyed her health.

When she finally left the convent, Baldwin embarked on her own intensive and necessarily random course of self-education through the wireless, the cinema, and a voracious reading of modern publications of all kinds. She read through several volumes of *Illustrated London News* at the public library. She prowled about London scrutinizing the street life, the new buildings, the clothing, and the shops, and thought deeply about what the changes of the last few decades signified. Upon the advice of friends from her pre-convent days, she doggedly sought out "Experience of Life" (124) that might fill in the blank spaces in her personality and development left by her long sojourn in the convent. She tried to correlate what she learned from an intensive reading of Noel Coward, Evelyn Waugh, Aldous Huxley, Rachel Ferguson, and her cousin Angela Thirkell with the truths that she had gleaned in the convent library from a reading of Augustine, medieval and early modern saints and mystics, and an assortment of modern Catholic writers such as François Mauriac, Joris Huysmans, and Robert Hugh Benson (33–34, 165, 253).

Baldwin understood that she had a monumental task of reorientation before her. Toward the beginning of her memoir she clearly articulated the goal that had taken decades of floundering and depression in the convent to formulate: "For twenty-eight years I had lived with my outside turned inwards. Now, swiftly and violently, I had, so to speak, to reverse engines and start trying to live with my inside turned out" (8). This statement became Baldwin's guiding principle and top priority during her post-convent years, starting in the early 1940s. It suggests five themes at the center of Baldwin's memoir and other Catholic women's flight narratives: reversals, boundary-crossings, diaspora, renaming, and recycling.

Reversals

Reversals, played out in endless permutations, represent the central plot and concern in all women's departure narratives. It is the irreversibility of certain potential actions that keeps a woman in her place. Lost virtue, lost virginity, lost family honor, lost beauty, lost trust, lost fertility: Even the threat of these kinds of changes can foreclose a woman's future options permanently. Women are taught and socialized to believe that nothing is worth taking this kind of risk. *There is no going back:* This is the message that patriarchal religions continue to convey to women even as the women themselves begin to find other messages in their own spiritual lives.

Popular literature has experimented with the traditional axiom that women who step out of line and challenge inherited social and religious conventions find that there is no going back. Anne Tyler's novel *Ladder of Years* explicitly raises the question of reversals. When Delia Grinstead gives in to an uncontrollable bird-like impulse to fly away and find a new nest, her sister Eliza sends her a letter containing a warning couched in their Great-Uncle Roscoe's favorite maxim: "Never do anything you can't undo." From a distance, Delia recognizes, perhaps for the first time, how paralyzing this kind of patriarchal homespun philosophy can be for women like her, good daughters brought up to be responsible and unselfish. Her inner response to Eliza's reminder displays her newfound resistance to the avuncular wisdom that was so plentiful in the home that she has recently left. *"But if you never did anything you couldn't undo,"* she reasoned to herself, *"you'd end up doing nothing at all"* (Tyler 1995, 144).

Delia Grinstead, the fictional Baltimore mother on the run in the 1990s, and Monica Baldwin, memoir writer and English ex-nun at mid-century, share a common imaginative landscape despite the many differences that separate them. They inhabit a place where middle-aged women can experiment with the possibility of undoing acts that they and those around them had once considered irreversible. Like her fictional counterpart Delia Grinstead, Baldwin discovers that the cost (or reward) of risking a reversal is displacement, becoming a pariah. Once out of "her place," Baldwin loses the virtual invisibility that she had achieved during her convent years, an invisibility that is at least analogous to that acquired by respectable doctors' wives such as Grinstead. After the initial flurry of attempts to talk her out of joining the convent, Baldwin the nun became invisible to her family and friends and almost succeeded in becoming invisible to herself. Ann Tyler elaborates on Grinstead's invisibility when she describes a newspaper article about her disappearance. The article reflects the sad truth that none of Grinstead's loved ones had taken a close look at her for years. When she happened on the article, Grinstead was stunned: *"Fair or light brown hair . . . eyes are blue or gray or perhaps green.* For heaven's sakes, hadn't anyone in her family ever looked at her?" (Tyler 1995, 121).

Unlike Delia Grinstead's invisibility, which took her by surprise, Baldwin achieved invisibility by dint of her endless efforts at mortification and custody of her senses during her early years in the cloister. It represented one of the benchmarks of her success in following the path to holiness charted by her spiritual advisors at the convent. Detachment was the ultimate goal. Baldwin dutifully sought to disengage herself from the physical world by turning her outside inward:

> Instead of observing, remembering, deducing, reflecting, my whole energy was employed upon effacing from my memory every kind of impression almost before it was received. Indeed, as a novice, my custody of the eyes was so rigorous that I must have been a menace to the community, for I remember constantly bumping into people who happened to be coming my way. (12)

Baldwin was rewarded for her efforts with momentary flashes of understanding (interpreted as gifts of the Holy Spirit) and mystical ecstasy ("sweeping me up out of myself on to a completely different plane"). She experienced "real positive [spiritual] adventures, of a kind about which [she] had hitherto never even dreamed" (276–277).

Still, beginning in her late 20s, after about ten years in the cloister, Baldwin began to have doubts and gradually accepted the fact that she had "made a dreadful and tragic mistake." Try as she might to dismiss these suspicions as temptations, the doubts grew into convictions over the next eighteen years. Baldwin painfully recalls: "The intense dislike I felt at this time for the life I had undertaken can really hardly be imagined. From dawn to sunset, almost every detail of it was savagely against the grain. Even now, after all these years, when I look back upon it, my soul is plunged in gloom" (301).

Monica Baldwin entered the convent with the knowledge that she would need to turn her back on the friends and social pleasures of her previous life. But her efforts remained "savagely against the grain." Something deep within her never adjusted and violently recoiled from convent life. Nonetheless, the life made its mark on her so that her departure from the cloister and her energetic efforts to re-acclimate herself to the outside world still required a fundamental reversal of all that she had been and done in her twenty-eight years as a contemplative nun. When *Time* magazine called her "Merton in reverse" it captured a crucial aspect of the process depicted in her memoir.

Thomas Merton's best-selling memoir *The Seven Storey Mountain* (1948) appeared the year before the English edition of *I Leap over the Wall* and two years before the American edition. It provided spiritual clarity and a sense of direction and purpose for a whole generation of American Catholic men and even converted some other young men to the Catholic faith.

Merton's life story, about a bright, young, financially comfortable but restless man who explored every fashionable intellectual current of his day before he submitted to God's will and entered a monastery, constitutes a modern remake of St. Augustine's conversion story in his *Confessions*. Merton and his predecessor Augustine produced texts that would be considered prototypical male spiritual autobiographies in the Catholic tradition. In these classic texts, "The self is presented as a stage for a battle of opposing forces, and . . . a climactic victory for one force—spirit defeating flesh—completes the drama of the self" (Mason 1998, 321).

Baldwin's memoir, in which an obscure middle-aged nun rethinks her adolescent decision to submit to God's will by being a cloistered contemplative and leaps over the wall to face a world of uncertainty and fragmentation, reverses the storyline in the famous texts by Augustine and Merton.

I Leap over the Wall is a concrete illustration of Shari Benstock's description of the uneven, asymmetrical contours of the female autobiography (Benstock 1988, 152). Baldwin's memoir shows how, despite disruptions and reversals and often because of them, women's personal spiritual narratives can achieve their own kind of integrity. Monica Baldwin's life story is built on reversals. Her original decision to enter the convent flouted the family's expectations that she marry a suitable man from her own social class and assume the family responsibilities that she acknowledges in her memoir but refuses to name. Her decision to leave the convent at midlife and reenter the world also confused family and friends. Baldwin wryly notes: "Oddly enough, it was just those who had reproached me most bitterly for Going In in 1914, who expressed the sternest disapproval of my Coming Out in 1941. Some people are curiously hard to please" (17).

Baldwin's memoir provides one more example of the "moratorium," a pattern in women's life-writing examined by Carolyn Heilbrun in *Writing a Woman's Life* (1988). Heilbrun draws on her study of the life and writings of Dorothy Sayres when she suggests that sometimes young women deviate from society's expectations of them to provide themselves with an opportunity to pursue "a talent felt but unrecognized and unnamed." For women such as Sayres and Baldwin, "marked by a profound sense of vocation, with no idea of what that vocation is," unconventional life choices provide time and immunity from the pressures of social approval and convention. Sayres's decision to have a child out of wedlock and Baldwin's choice of the cloister without any family support were not self-conscious efforts to make room for unusual life choices, but they ultimately had that effect on both women (Heilbrun 1988, 49–59).

Baldwin could reverse directions, but her experience of grappling with convent living against the grain was a part of the very fiber of the woman who leapt over the wall in the autumn of 1941. In fact, she later found that the only way to explain her unconventional ways was to disclose her past life as a nun, which seemed to help others to interpret her otherwise inexplicable personal traits and disconcerting lack of a personal history and baggage. The moratorium in the convent gave Baldwin an opportunity to pursue the fundamental questions that haunted her as well as something within herself to accept and resist simultaneously. Both the acceptance and the resistance helped form the complex woman that she became during and after her convent years, a strange mixture of shocking inexperience and lack of confidence and the kind of inner strength that can only come with maturity and self-knowledge.

Baldwin's memoir sought to make sense of both her adolescent self, the one that entered the convent as an act of obedience to God and disobedience to family and social conventions, and her later self, the anomalous middle-aged ex-nun, and to achieve harmony between the two. At 17, as a student at a convent school, she was drawn to the cloister which she considered "a sublime object," a "life of absolute perfection," which was actually "within [her] reach." This life, "discussed in an atmosphere of thrills and trepidation" at her school and directly associated with the charisma of the headmistress, who was "held in the highest esteem and affection by the girls," became an obsession for the young Baldwin. The call to religious life came in the form of an intense longing, the renunciation of which "would have cost [her] more than giving up all of the delightful things that . . . [she] should have to leave behind." Answering the call had practical benefits as well, for the act freed Baldwin from "certain responsibilities which [she] dreaded and disliked."

Ten years as a nun killed every bit of her longing for the cloister. After a decade inside the convent, she found herself plodding onward "by sheer dogged force of the will" (299–301). Baldwin's thwarted vocation never damaged her faith in God or her Catholic identity, both of which appear to have strengthened and become more nuanced amid the trials and the deep depression of her convent years. Monica Baldwin concluded the "melancholy and depressing story" of her twenty-eight years in the convent with words of advice deeply grounded in traditional Catholic moral theology:

> The actual career which one selects is in itself of only secondary importance. The thing that apparently matters to God is one's motive for embracing it. A ballet-dancer may be—and I cannot help believing often *is*—quite as pleasing to God as a nun. The important thing is that one should take reasonable means to "fit in" to the jigsaw puzzle of life in exactly the spot where God wants one. (302)

This responsibility to find one's niche in the puzzle of life cannot be abdicated simply because one has made a decision one considered permanent. Reversals, based on a clearer perspective, are sometimes a necessary step in assembling the puzzle. These reversals, then, become a responsibility, not an abdication of responsibility. One ringing affirmation in *I Leap over the Wall* is that there are no standard-issue answers to the fundamental questions about finding one's way and one's place in the world, not even for Catholics brought up on the catechism's question-and-answer format. Elaborating on the advice quoted above, Baldwin added that "if one drifts, or forces oneself into a place for which one was not intended, one not only spoils that particular bit of the picture but defeats the whole purpose in life for which one was made" (302).

Boundaries

I Leap over the Wall chronicles Monica Baldwin's exodus across boundaries of time and space. The text itself constitutes a boundary-crossing, produced when Baldwin finally stopped suppressing the truth and wrote down the story that demanded to be told. With the truth that insisted upon its own disclosure came the disclosure of Baldwin's evolving self. Very early in her first chapter, Baldwin explicitly addresses the theme of boundary-crossing when she describes her departure from the convent on an "appropriately . . . cold and frosty" October morning in 1941.

> Now we were on the threshold.
> As I crossed it, two thoughts occurred to me. One was that the door which at that instant was being locked behind me was not a door but a guillotine. And it had just chopped off from me, utterly and irrevocably, every single thing which, for twenty-eight years, had made up my life. Henceforth I was a being without a background. And no one who has not actually experienced that sensation can know how grim it is.
> The other thought flashed in upon me with the urgency of a commandment:
> *Thou shalt not look back!*
> And I knew instinctively that if I wanted to keep my balance on the tight-rope stretched before me, I must slam the door behind me and keep looking straight ahead. Otherwise I should have to pay the penalty. (4–7)

This early sequence provides a preview into the complexity of Baldwin's post-convent identity and experience. It conveys two conflicting emotions that gripped Baldwin tightly, even viscerally. First, the act of departure for which she had been longing for decades had suddenly chopped off her entire adult identity, leaving her "a being without a background." Along with this "grim" sense of sudden deprivation, even violation, came a second, comforting assurance of deliverance. A woman with Baldwin's experience and education could not use the commandment "Thou shalt not look back" without intending a clear reference to the passage in Genesis 19 where the angels saved Lot's family from annihilation. Baldwin left the convent traumatized and afraid, aware that she was leaving large portions of her own life and failed efforts to achieve "absolute perfection" behind. She also left with a new certainty that she would be spared and delivered to a new safe place, if only she did not look back.

The rest of the memoir explores what these two combined sensations, the guillotine experience and the promise of deliverance, meant to Baldwin during the years of wandering documented in her narrative, roughly 1941 to 1948. Monica Baldwin remained marginalized, "a being without a background," in the radically altered English society to which she returned. Her only option was to move forward and reconstruct who she was from the fragments of the past and present that she could piece together. Baldwin discovered a metaphor that captured the interlocking set of challenges that she confronted: to rebuild her life, to live with her changing female body which she had been admonished to deny during her convent years, and to cross the boundaries that separated her past in the convent from her present situation in wartime England. She found it in the mundane but monumental experience of changing clothes.

Baldwin thoughtfully reflects on the unsettling experience of dressing herself in street clothes, a reversal of the elaborate clothing rituals that accompany the various stages of probation in the convent. When sisters receive the habit, they accept a new identity and a new name and make solemn promises binding them to their new life. Baldwin never mentions the clothing ceremony itself or her religious name, but they must have been in her mind at this pivotal moment when she tried on another strange period costume symbolic of her new life outside the cloister. Her description of her departure from the convent on October 26, 1941, represents yet one more clothing ritual, one more rite of passage in her life. Her new street clothing was just as strange to her as her habit, based on a fourteenth-century prototype, had been when she had first tried it on as a young woman.

The "scratchy serge" shift worn next to the body, the stays "shoulder-strapped and severely boned [to conceal] one's outline," the two serge petticoats and the heavy "habit-coat," and the eight layers of tight-fitting starched cloth that kept the veil anchored in place: These had been intended to help her to "keep her outside turned inward." The garments that her sister Freda brought for her departure gave her a visceral premonition of the intimidating task that lay ahead, the reconstruction of her identity at midlife. Dressed, with Freda's brusque guidance, in a 1940s-style corset, brassiere, sheer stockings, and high heels, Baldwin felt "top-heavy, self-conscious and slightly indecent" (4–13). At first she could not relate to the other women she saw in shops or on buses. As a young debutante on the eve of the First World War, she had internalized the feminine ideal commonly embraced in her social circle, "rounded faces; large melting eyes, soft mouths and low-piled hair." Now she had trouble placing herself in the same category with the women she met on her daily rounds: "These women appeared to belong to a different civilization. They had narrow faces, high cheek-bones, wide, heavily-painted mouths and slanting eyes. Their chins jutted. Their noses were strong and short. Their hair—invariably waved or curled—hung loose on their shoulders. And most of them had terrible, claw-like, purple-painted nails” (16).

Baldwin did not consider herself part of womankind as she first encountered it in the autumn of 1941. Part of the problem was that she felt alien to herself. Living under layers of serge with closely cropped hair, doggedly attempting to turn her outside inward, she had distanced herself from the changes that had taken place in her own body from age 17 to her mid-40s. It was as if she had moved directly from the dawn of womanhood to menopause. When she entered the convent she had been beautiful: “Eyes had a way of straying round in my direction and of returning there over and over again.” Even after her protracted attempts at self-mortification in the convent, she still remembered what “eye-homage” felt like and cherished that memory.

When she crossed the threshold and left the convent, her body once again became part of the public landscape, and her cherished memories of life before 1914 reproached her. She stood out in a crowd and felt isolated in social settings. People were far too polite to gawk at her, but this, too, made Baldwin uneasy. “*Now* nobody ever bothered to glance at me. Or if they did, they looked away again so swiftly that it was almost worse than not being scrutinized at all.” Monica Baldwin reclaimed her female body when she leapt over the wall, bravely reversed engines, and turned her outside outward. Still, she felt cheated. She was no longer beautiful and could no longer expect the eye-homage she had taken for granted as a debutante. She was almost invisible, but not quite. She still attracted public notice because she did not fit neatly into people’s expectations; strangers did not know what to make of her appearance. She almost looked like the maiden aunt that she was, but not quite. After she left the convent, she had permission to pay attention to her body again, but she did not know how. Given her generation and sheltered upbringing, it is not surprising that, for all of her candor, Baldwin does not directly mention menopause. Still, it almost certainly made her transition to life in the secular world more painful and complex. She was left mourning her losses: “I Went In [to the convent] young and good-looking. I Came Out elderly and plain. And I disliked this. Very much indeed” (233–234).

Immediately upon reentering the world, Baldwin became painfully aware that not all processes were reversible. Turning your inside outward turned out to be more complicated than an exercise of the will. Moreover, it was not only the biological or cosmetic changes that were irreversible. There were inner changes analogous to the loss of physical beauty. In her teens, Baldwin had nurtured a keen interest in ballet. She had been “enraptured” by Pavlova and Nijinsky when they had danced in London before the Great War. In her 40s, she found the performances of Margot Fonteyn and Robert Helpmann "heart-breaking." She discovered that she "had grown incapable of apprehending ballet emotionally." Ballet "reached me no longer through the senses but *drily* . . . through the mind." With sadness, she had to accept the fact that "through repression and disuse, certain sections of my being had simply withered and died" (241).

Happily, Baldwin had the opposite experience listening to music. The radio became an important mentor as she sought to embrace the new world that greeted her outside the convent gates. On one of the first nights after her departure from the convent she turned on the radio and tuned in to an old favorite, one of the last songs that she had heard before entering the cloister in 1914, Tchaikovsky's waltz from *Eugene Onegin*. Her response was immediate and sensual: the waltz "[billowed] about me and over me in wave after wave of wild, romantic music, stirring my strangely and awakening poignant long-forgotten memories" (18). Baldwin rejoiced at this experience, which would be repeated and reinforced when she reread Sir Thomas Malory. She had not lost contact with the part of herself that responded so deeply and passionately to Tchaikovsky and Malory. She was reassured by the discovery that she had only to reopen certain doors that she had painfully closed during her years at the convent and many of the wild impulses of her girlhood were once again accessible to her. She could feel vibrant and alive and connected.

Although Baldwin lamented the loss of her physical beauty and her intense emotional response to ballet, she gratefully acknowledged the rekindling of her interior life. In a radical departure from her convent training, Baldwin gave herself permission to pay attention to her "Inward Urges," starting with the urge to leave the convent. She chose the term "Urge" carefully, including the capitalization, preferring it to "inspiration" because we are less likely to connect the word "Urge" with the "strictly spiritual" dimension. She wanted to underscore the secular, concrete, physical grounding of her Urges, which "usually begin to operate from a prosaic spot somewhere in the pit of the stomach." Still, these Urges were not merely physical, for they "take complete possession of one's being, impelling one to follow or refrain from, some particular course of action." Baldwin comprehensively examined her past life and concluded definitively: "All my life I have been subject to these Urges. Now and again, I have resisted them in order to follow what then sounded like excellent advice. I have invariably regretted it. When, however, I have obeyed my Urge, no matter how crazy the course of action may have seemed at the moment, it has always turned out for the best" (250). Following Baldwin's logic here, she seems to have reexamined her original decision to enter the convent and reclassified it. It was not an Urge after all, but merely "what sounded like excellent advice," almost generic advice that was dispensed widely to young Catholic women with high aspirations but was not at all appropriate to her own special gifts and inner calling.

One Urge dominates the plot of Baldwin's post-convent narrative. It took possession of her while she was walking on the familiar turf of the old cemetery off Paddington Street in London, weighed down, almost disoriented, by a deep depression. She was frustrated by her inability, despite major exertions of the mind and will, to make definitive plans for her future. Especially pressing was the question of "how and where I could— with as much decency and unobtrusiveness as possible—retire to spend my rapidly-approaching old age" (77). As Baldwin stood marveling at the transformation of the cemetery, apparently overnight, into a garden in full bloom, she was struck by the mystical quality of the light and the "adorable faint smell of spring."

She surrendered herself to "the enchantment" and her depression disappeared "as if some sea-borne wind had rushed in and whirled it away." Then something "like a burst of song" filled her "with a longing, so violent and overwhelming as to be almost unbearable." Suddenly she knew with certainty that what she needed was a home of her own, not just any house, but *her own home*, which was already awaiting her discovery of it. Baldwin describes in minute detail how her home took shape before her: "crouching . . . on a little nest of cloud, in a kind of rift in my inner consciousness, and *looking at me*." It was "the smallest imaginable mouse-trap of a cottage; with a frill of garden round it; and a cliff behind; . . . and at the gate of the garden a cat was sitting" (78). Baldwin saw all of this very clearly, right down to the breed of the cat (Siamese).

According to Monica Baldwin, this vision of home, "this tremendous Act of Wanting . . . changed everything." Baldwin knew in her guts that the vision stood for more than the cottage, garden, gate, and cat that had been disclosed to her. "The cottage—and its surroundings—were the outward and visible sign of an inward and psychological fact, which was that, by it, and through it, but—best of all—in it, I was at last, quite simply, going to be ME" (79). It is no coincidence that Monica Baldwin the ex-nun adapts the traditional definition of a sacrament ("outward and visible sign") here to underscore the significance and function of her Inward Urge and the vision that accompanied it. Nor is it mere coincidence that she improvises on the words of a liturgical formula, the words of consecration ("by it, and through it, and in it"). The sacrament celebrated and consecrated in the vision is Baldwin herself and *the possibility of being herself*. And an important aspect of the sacrament of embodied selfhood is the sanctity of place.

[17]

Diaspora

Baldwin's vision of her cottage in the clouds punctuated her life of wandering, endless and often humiliating job-hunting, and moving from one generous friend's guest room to another's. It gave all of her assorted comings and goings, which had seemed alarmingly random after the structured life of the contemplative convent, an order and a purpose. As Monica Baldwin embraced the dream centered on the cottage that awaited her discovery, her vision of her own identity, blurred for decades, finally came into sharp focus. Baldwin's diaspora, an unchosen, scattered way of life that had resulted from her one decisive move out of the cloister, assumed an entirely different aspect when seen in the light of a clear purpose, a home, at the end of her wanderings.

Life on the move, traveling light, remains a central theme in feminist literature and film in the recent past. Anne Tyler's *Ladder of Years* and the 1991 film *Thelma and Louise* are only two of many possible examples of how the theme of diaspora is explored in contemporary American popular culture. The unifying thread behind these accounts is the idea of women as a diaspora community, which is just another very different way to reformulate Cixous's depiction of women as birds and robbers. In her 1998 book *Quintessence,* Mary Daly reflects on women's propensity to flight and its complex implications:

> We want to call out to each other, but when we do, we often hear only the sounds of our own voices. We frequently feel abandoned by our most needed Sisters and companions. To Name this state of dividedness and dispersion of women under patriarchy, the word *diaspora* comes to mind. Originally used to describe the dispersion of the Jews, this word, taken in its wide sense, means "exile, scattering, migration"... [including] the exile, scattering and enforced migration of consciousness. (Daly 1998, 37–38)

Daly insists that the negative side of women's diaspora ("enforced migration of consciousness") is counterbalanced by its positive aspects. Women have developed their natural instincts for flight into a whole array of finely tuned migratory skills. They are able to be at home on the road without the comforts and accouterments of the dwellings they have vacated (Daly 1998, 75–76). They are also capable of cultivating their migratory skills at home, in confinement, before they begin their actual migrations or of migrating within their own imaginations without ever physically leaving home.

Monica Baldwin's wanderings did not begin in October 1941. They started years before in those fleeting moments in the convent when she first allowed herself—if only in her own imagination—to conceive and fully entertain the possibility of leaving. The years spent in the cloister, "working against the grain," represent the beginnings of Baldwin's exodus, her first taste of life in diaspora. There is some evidence that this first taste of the forbidden fruit of flight led to a genuine physical and emotional breakdown. This is a recurring theme in stories written by women who have tried to live the convent life against the grain. For Baldwin, who had already imagined the anxieties and guilt associated with leaving, her actual departure from the convent was a mere formality. She had been living in limbo for some time in preparation for her departure.

And in limbo she remained for years, trying out jobs and identities, force-feeding herself on the fruits of modern culture to make up for lost time in the convent, living her life vicariously, all too conscious of not fitting in anywhere. Only when she claimed her new home, the cottage in her vision, did she find a compass to guide her in her migrations. The imaginary landscape disclosed to her in her vision became the place where Baldwin went to reconstruct and reimagine her own identity that she had taken such pains to dismantle during her early years in the convent. Suddenly, when she was in her late 40s, she was almost shocked to discover that "such phrases as 'my very own' or 'exactly as I please'" had acquired "a peculiar and urgent fascination." These phrases and her response to them reassured Baldwin that she still existed after years of "[setting] one's teeth grimly and just [carrying] on by the will, without paying the slightest attention to how one felt" (83, 222). Her hopes for reclaiming her own life, identity, and future hinged on the possibility of settling down in a home of her own, a home comfortably perched on the margins of society, in the clouds, on a cliff, almost at the end of the earth.

There, in her own home, Monica Baldwin was certain that she could find (rediscover) herself through the process of carefully building a world made to her own specifications.

> The idea of possessing—actually possessing, as my own—a place (no matter how small and simple) in which I could put furniture that *I* had chosen, curtains whose colours *I* had decided upon, books and pictures that I actually *wanted* and *liked*, was almost too wonderful to be realized. And the thought of a garden of my own, with potential roses and delphiniums . . . and the knowledge that I should be able to cook my own meals, weed my own garden, say my prayers, read (and perhaps write) books, and get up and go to bed exactly when and where I pleased, was—well—so intoxicating that I hardly dared let my mind dwell upon it for too long a time. (83)

The pilgrimage that Baldwin began in her imagination during a moment of despair materialized on two different planes during the late 1940s: on paper, as a memoir, and geographically, as she became immersed in a single-minded search for a cottage (literally *the* cottage of her dreams) in Cornwall. "Places have always meant more to me than people," Baldwin confessed in *I Leap over the Wall* (257). Certain places, such as the convent during the last eighteen years and her aunt's house in the town of Hove in Sussex, brought on the severe depressions that appear to have plagued Monica Baldwin throughout her adult life. These places reinforced her perception of herself as a woman who had made all of the wrong choices and forfeited her best opportunities, a woman with nowhere to go whose Inner Urges were held in check by forces to which she had abdicated control. After she left the convent, Baldwin discovered that acting on her own Inner Urges, even the smallest gesture in that direction, kept depression at bay and transported her to a new place.

The "birth narrative" of her memoir, a book conceived during one of the dark suffocating moments that she had learned to expect when visiting her aunt in Hove, is quoted at length at the beginning of this chapter. This section of her narrative captures the distinct moment in which Baldwin seized upon the idea of writing her way out of confinement. This time Baldwin confronted the familiar sensation of helplessness and isolation with an entirely new approach. Instead of turning her outside inward and waiting out the storm, she responded to the Urge to release what was "bubbling and seething" within her by writing about it. At long last, Baldwin's Inner Urge provided the means to move beyond the dark nights of the soul that she had come to accept as a necessary and inevitable part of her personal spirituality as a contemplative nun.

Like Hélène Cixous, for whom writing a personal narrative was itself an act of departure, a *sortie,* and who wrote to find (and be) "somewhere else" (Morris 1993, 119–120), Baldwin began her memoir with the hope of leaping over one more wall. What helped, Baldwin discovered, was to "speak the truth." And in speaking the truth about herself and her own diaspora, both "behind 'high convent walls'" (281, v) and outside them, Baldwin gained the courage and energy to achieve the other kind of mobility that resulted in her move to Cornwall described at the end of her memoir.

Renaming and Recycling

Mary Daly's revolutionary statement, first made in 1973, that "women have had the power of *naming* stolen from us" (Daly 1985b, 8) illuminates the process we see at work in *I Leap over the Wall.* Daly insisted that the power to name constituted a basic human right; without it, women could not "speak humanly" or even begin to envision their own self-liberation (Daly 1985b, 8). Monica Baldwin discovered the truth behind Daly's words, which became one of the mantras of the feminist movement in the 1970s, decades earlier and without the benefit of feminist texts or mentors. Her life in exile on the fringes of English society, combined with the insights bestowed to her in the vision in Paddington Street cemetery, gave her the power to name her own experience and her needs in distinctive terms. Baldwin learned that the power to name and claim her vision of the cottage in the clouds was inseparable from the vision itself.

In an aside to readers placed directly after her description of the cottage, garden, gate, and Siamese cat that lay in store for her, Baldwin took pains to emphasize the "tremendous Act of Wanting" that had given birth to her vision in the first place. It was the Act of Wanting that had "changed everything" (79). From this point in the narrative onward, unexpected unconventional capitalization serves as a signal to the reader that Baldwin is exercising her power to name, to make language reflect—and even celebrate—her own unique Acts of Wanting and Inner Urges. Indeed, both of these capitalized expressions represent subtle recurring gestures, even manifestos, of rebellion against the world and values of the convent where Baldwin had spent so many years. Writing these phrases in her memoir was itself a public departure, a demonstration of her intention to turn her inside outward both for her sake and to communicate effectively with her intended readers.

When Baldwin names Cornwall as her destination, the place where she expects to find the cottage in the clouds, she is tapping into a whole reservoir of associations that have since been rediscovered by feminists of the 1980s and 1990s, the world of Marion Zimmer Bradley's *Mists of Avalon* (1982) and Jean Shinoda Bolen's *Crossing to Avalon* (1994). In their very different ways, Bradley and Bolen found in Arthurian legends about the mythic kingdom of Avalon a new world and a healing place for modern women on both imaginative and actual physical pilgrimages. Like Monica Baldwin, whose inner spirit responded instantly to the "secret life … intense, primeval, pagan" (293) which she discovered in Cornwall, the Jungian psychiatrist and author Jean Shinoda Bolen found in the area around Glastonbury access to Avalon, her Home in the deepest sense of the word.

One way to comprehend the personal attraction of Baldwin and Bolen, two extremely different women living in different worlds a half-century apart, to the same mystical forces in the Cornish landscape is to recall an image invoked by still another contemporary female Jungian psychoanalyst, Clarissa Pinkola Estés. Estés recalls a dream in which she became aware, in the midst of telling a story, of someone patting her feet as she spoke. She was standing on the shoulders of an old woman who was "steadying [her] ankles and smiling up at [her]." When she prevailed upon the older woman to stand upon her younger, stronger shoulders instead, the other woman demurred, insisting that "this is the way it is supposed to be." Gradually Estés understood that "the telling moment of the story draws its power from a towering column of humanity joined one to the other across time and space, elaborately dressed in the rags and robes or nakedness of their time, and filled to the bursting with life still being lived" (Estés 1995, 19).

The link between Baldwin, the deracinated ex-nun who rediscovered her girlhood attraction to the myths of Avalon during one of the loneliest periods of a lonely life, and Bolen, a successful Jungian therapist and author of *Goddesses in Everywoman,* who likewise found herself turning to Avalon in a time of solitude and transition, resides in Estés's image of the "towering column of humanity." Baldwin and Bolen responded to the stories and site of Avalon in moments of isolation and were similarly nurtured and empowered by the experience. Arthurian legend provided both women with access to an otherwise imperceptible community composed of the women who had shared the same stories throughout the ages. Baldwin and Bolen become the mediators between their readers and the towering column of women standing on the shoulders of their foresisters that was described by Estés.

Baldwin set her sights on Cornwall after a friend reintroduced her to Malory's *Morte d'Arthur,* which she had devoured at 15 during the few unscheduled moments at her convent school. At first, she hesitated to reread Malory for fear that it, like ballet, might have lost its magic for her. Instead, Malory turned out to be a bridge that led her back to her girlhood and her younger self. She called the *Morte d'Arthur* "a door that opened into an enchanted world." Its humor and pathos reawakened something in Baldwin that she had tried hard to extinguish during her novitiate, the part that responded to magic and enchantment. Malory showed Baldwin that her emotions and imagination were not dead but merely asleep, another aspect of the Rip Van Winkle state she had been in for so long. Baldwin cherished her renewed bond with Malory most of all because "its closely printed pages positively effused romance" (168), and she discovered through rereading its familiar pages that she was still able to respond to the romance, with even more passion and depth than she had as an adolescent.

In this section of Baldwin's memoir, we see at work the healing process at the center of Jean Shinoda Bolen's personal narrative *Crossing to Avalon*. Bolen draws on both personal and clinical experience in her description of "stone mother depressions": "If [a woman] has become numb and 'turned to stone,' no longer feeling anything for the people she remembers loving, she may feel guilty as well as dead. She needs to be reunited with her own inner young self, who, like Persephone, will bring back spring and with it the return of greenness to the wasteland" (Bolen 1994, 187). This might seem to be merely a generic application of present-day therapeutic popular culture were it not such an accurate description of what both Baldwin and Bolen gained from their own exposure to Arthurian legend at a painful, critical juncture in their late 40s.

Bolen found solace in Marion Zimmer Bradley's feminist retelling of the grail legend in the voice of King Arthur's half-sister Morgaine. Baldwin found deliverance (and the familiar "witchery," even "ecstasy") in Malory's text itself, which she compared to "meeting old friends from whom I had been separated for too many years." She spent an entire train trip engrossed in Malory, and as she steamed into her station in London, "the Thing happened": "Cornwall, like a lovely sleeping sorceress, bestirred herself, sat up, stretched forth a long, slim, beckoning hand and, in a voice like the sound of fairy harps across deep water, commanded me to come" (170).

None of this really surprised Baldwin. She had remained subliminally aware of this hidden side of herself all along, even as she had tried to subdue it as a novice, even as she had prematurely mourned its death in the anxious and frustrating months after she had left the convent. She knew that her attraction to Cornwall and all that it stood for was the part of her that Reverend Mother could never condone. It was the part that had made her a failed nun. "In Cornwall, one had always felt subconsciously aware that something was brewing which, in a world stupefied by civilization, could no longer be experienced." The landscape of Cornwall, which Baldwin came to recognize as the site of the cottage in her dreams, rekindled her "passionate longing." Although she was on a slender budget, Baldwin made several cottage-hunting trips to Cornwall. In the "warm, flower-scented hollow of the hillside" in Trevelioc, she sensed a promise of deliverance: There "I could find solitude and open my soul wide to the secret things that were floating like gossamer spells among the rocks and trees." Yet even as she was transported by the rocks and trees of Cornwall and their own mystical powers, Baldwin could not help but wonder "what Reverend Mother's reactions would have been if she could have glimpsed what was going on inside my mind" (292–293).

There were other magical sensations as well, and Baldwin, in her newly empowered and reinvigorated state, does not shrink from naming them. Sometimes the "very air seemed filled with strange and hidden presences" and "it was as though I had slipped back into contact with some experience that I had undergone in another existence long ago." She was "enraptured," even though she knew by instinct that her growing intimacy with the land and spirits of Cornwall "was also just a little creepy." This was all part of the wildness she sought and found in Cornwall, a wildness whose absence from the cloister and the drawing room had left her for three decades with a palpable sense of deprivation and longing.

At one moment Baldwin is standing at the window of a Cornish cottage at bedtime, listening to waves lapping the shore and staring at "an enormous biscuit-coloured moon." The next moment, propelled by memories of another night spent staring at the same kind of moon, she recalls standing at the window in her cell at the convent embroiled in an inner struggle, "wondering how long it would be before I could make up my mind to break with the life for which I now knew myself so unfitted, and go back again to the world." Baldwin's goal in writing her memoir was to "speak the truth," and frequently that meant that she had to repudiate false stereotypes of the religious life that were cheerfully embraced by her friends in the secular world. She argued consistently that there is nothing wrong with convents and monasteries, but they aren't for everyone. The problems arose when people like her, people without religious vocations, joined the convent for their own selfish reasons (297–298, 281, 301).

Monica Baldwin continued to attend mass after she leapt over the wall, and she embraced the same Catholic faith that she had as a nun. Her faith was an especially sophisticated version of Catholic belief centered on the mystical body of Christ as she heard it described in an address by Robert Hugh Benson, a priest-theologian who popularized the doctrine in the English-speaking Catholic world at the turn of the century. Baldwin's explanation of the mystical body in her memoir, inserted into an account of a post-convent conversation with her doctor, shows that even years after her exodus from the cloister, she remained thoroughly convinced that the prayers of contemplatives represented "the white-hot centre of the furnace: at the very source of that Infinite, Absolute Force that created and preserved the world." She was similarly adamant about the strength and importance of St. Thérèse of Lisieux and how poorly she was understood by the church at large (253–258, 180–181).

Baldwin the ex-nun remained a faithful Catholic in touch with the most important currents of Catholic theology at mid-century. This did not mean that she shrank from admitting, based on her own experience, that convent life could lead to deep depression and could also infantilize some sisters who sincerely thought that they were striving for holiness and spiritual perfection. Nor was Baldwin hesitant to discuss the limitations of the priests who had served as chaplains at her convent (123, 182–188). Finally, although she could argue persuasively that contemplative nuns were at the center of the salvation process, she confessed that she had left the convent with such a strong distaste for nuns that she crossed the street to avoid passing them. Moreover, even though it was one of the few jobs for which she was clearly qualified, she categorically refused to consider teaching in a girls' school. She explained her efforts to avoid encountering sisters in public at some length, lest she be misunderstood: "As a class, I hold nuns in the highest esteem. But the sight of those starched wimples, long dark habits and low-heeled shoes rouses memories I've no use for. And that is why, when nuns show themselves on the horizon, I dart up side streets, averting my eyes as though Gorgons lurked beneath their veils" (242).

There is a sense in which Monica Baldwin's memoir belongs in the category of inspirational literature. In her candid and painfully honest recollections, we look on as a bright, mature, middle-aged woman finds her voice and the courage to say out loud and on paper what she wants and expects from life. We also see Baldwin find a way to break through the patina of piety and gentility learned in her convent school and in preparation for her social debut, which had obscured her ability to see and say what she wanted from life. This is why her decision to cross the street to avoid encountering sisters can be seen as a personal victory, not a snub. Monica Baldwin records that little victory along with the more stunning moments, such as her departure from the convent and her vision in the Paddington Street cemetery. They are all of a piece, threads in the same tapestry, Baldwin's magic carpet on which she still rides at the conclusion of her narrative, for her pilgrimage remains a work in progress.

Baldwin's memoir is about desire, about how she learned to want things, to name and pursue the desires that made her who she was. She shows us, the readers, that her failure to fit into the social world of upper-class English drawing rooms and country houses was ultimately a failure of desire. When she refused to give up on her dream of finding a Cornish cottage where she could simply be herself, her refusal was based on an instinctive belief in her "power to 'want.'" Invoking the popular wisdom that she had taken such pains to acquire in the years immediately after she left the convent, Baldwin developed her own axiom concerning desire. "As everybody knows, if you fail to get what you want, it is simply because you have not 'wanted' it with sufficient passion and intensity" (289).

At first glance, this might appear to be a hard-boiled Becky Sharp type of observation, the kind one found in the society novels written by Baldwin's cousin Angela Thirkell. Baldwin makes it clear, however, that her emphasis on desire is actually a recycled version of the most important lesson that she had brought with her from her convent years. Life in the cloister, especially her spiritual struggles to achieve perfect holiness, had taught her "the tremendous importance of knowing how to 'want' things." As a nun, she sought the life of perfection and mystical union with God that her novice mistress considered dangerous and "practically taboo." The novice mistress told her precisely what (and how) to want: "the only safe way to divine union . . . through humility and faithful performance of God's will" (289).

Years later, Baldwin vividly recalled that her deep-felt unspoken response to the novice mistress's admonitions was "Oh, how I hate safe ways!" Rebuffed by the novice mistress, Baldwin saved her practical questions about how to achieve mystical union for the Benedictine priest who was to give the next retreat. When she asked the priest whether it was wrong to want to be united with God as the famous mystics were, he took her seriously and replied with genuine compassion: "Good heavens, child, no! Blessed Angela of Foligno declared that the surest and quickest way of reaching it was to go on and on beseeching God to grant it, 'humbly,' 'continually,' and even 'violently' . . . until He gave it" (291).

Perhaps the best way to understand Monica Baldwin's Inward Urge to make Cornwall her home is to consider it the culmination of her lifelong quest for mystical union. What living "against the grain" in the convent had taught her was that her life as a mystic should not be a temporary escape from an unbearable daily routine structured around obedience to duly appointed spiritual authorities who cordoned off the safe route to God's love and favor. For Monica Baldwin, the mystical life was about wanting those things toward which she felt an irrepressible Urge. It was as easy and natural as her response to Cornwall when it appeared to her as a sorceress and made a request that it was not in her power to refuse.

2

FALLING AWAY

OR CROSSING OVER?

Something's, like, crossed over in me and I can't go back. I mean, I just
couldn't live.

—Thelma in *Thelma and Louise* (Khouri 1996, 161)

Everything was the same—the smell of beeswax, the red lights of the
sanctuary, the words that the small children were whispering beyond the
altar screen. But Nanda knew that whatever might happen in the future,
nothing for her would ever be the same again.

—White 1992a, 221

My own chief sensation was one of detached surprise at how far I had
come from my old mainstays, as once, when learning to swim, I had been
doing the dead-man's float and looked back, raising my doused head, to
see my water wings drifting, far behind me, on the lake's surface.

—McCarthy 1985, 123

I thought of Sister Scholastica who always said to the debating team
before we went to another school: Remember who you are and what you
represent. I no longer knew whom or what I represented, and I became

absorbed in the word itself. What did it mean, to represent? . . . It meant being connected to something so strongly that people could not think of you without thinking of that thing. What if you represented nothing but were only yourself?

—Gordon 1979, 165

The accepted euphemism for the gradual, half-willed, half-passive departure from the church is "falling away." Like other euphemisms, this one never even approaches the concrete powerful reality of the experience that it signifies. The phrase "falling away" sounds as if it was concocted by church authorities to denote other people's lapses of faith as they are perceived by superior beings, believers, safe within the fold, those who have never doubted or been tempted to leave. It captures the perspective of staunch Catholics who stand still, firmly grounded in an unwavering (or unquestioned) faith and watch others "fall away," victims of some mysterious spiritual avalanche that is comprehensible only within the infinite wisdom of God.

The experience of Catholic women who act on an impulse to distance themselves from the church is distinctly different from the standard depiction of "falling away." It is far closer to what Thelma, in the controversial female friendship film *Thelma and Louise* (1991), means when she talks about "crossing over." At a pivotal moment in the film, Thelma and Louise, friends in their early 30s who have been close since high school, find themselves at a point of no return. It is not something that they have planned, but neither is it something that has simply happened to them. Faced with an ultimatum, they have chosen themselves and flight over trusting the system.

What starts out as an impulsive decision to take a "girls only" fishing trip without consulting Thelma's controlling husband and Louise's feckless boyfriend turns into a fatal encounter with a would-be rapist outside an Arkansas night spot. In a few intense days on the run in Louise's 1969 red Chevrolet Impala convertible, Thelma and Louise confront themselves and choices that have kept them, or parts of them, locked in a post-adolescent state just short of adulthood. For Thelma, it was her marriage to Darryl at 17. For Louise, it was a sexual assault in Texas many years before, when she was victimized first by a rapist and then by the legal authorities.

Somewhere on their pilgrimage on the back roads between Arkansas and Arizona both Thelma and Louise cross over. Thelma, whose arrested development has been most obvious up to this point, suddenly emerges as the leader, the one who is capable of taking charge and articulating what their recent transgressions, such as killing her assailant and standing up to an abusive trucker, and their short life on the lam have done for them. She is also the first to recoil openly at the thought of turning themselves over to the authorities and hoping for a plea bargain. Thelma asks Louise whether she plans to "make a deal" and return home to her boyfriend. She is relieved to hear that Louise, too, knows that going back is "not an option."

It is at this point, as they make their way into the Arizona desert, their last refuge, that Thelma realizes "something's crossed over" in her; there is no turning back. She elaborates, grasping for words to explain to Louise this sudden, definitive, unintended boundary-crossing: "I feel awake. . . . Wide awake. I don't remember ever feelin' this awake. Everything looks different. . . . You know what I mean. I know you know what I mean. Everything looks new. And I feel like I've got something to look forward to. Do you feel like that? Like you've got something to look forward to?" (Khouri 1996, 161–164).

In Callie Khouri's screenplay, "crossing over" remains a mysterious process, not really understood, much less controlled, by Thelma. Still, we see signs of human agency and choice absent in the various images evoked by the expression "falling away." "Crossing over" is a personal achievement, strangely unforeseen until it happens, an almost mystical combination of Mary Daly's Courage to Leave and grace. Once realized, however, it changes everything.

Monica Baldwin's *I Leap over the Wall* shows how much flexibility there is within Thelma's metaphor. Baldwin "crosses over" in the Paddington Street cemetery. Her exodus was from the convent and the emotional and spiritual constraints that she had grappled with unsuccessfully for so many years. Her post-convent struggles showed her that it was not only Catholic structures but also the social and political institutions of wartime and postwar England that she sought to move beyond. Baldwin did not "fall away" in the conventional sense, but she did "cross over" when she began to envision and create a new space that could contain her recently recovered, partially recycled spirituality, which still had strong roots in her convent years. She first conceived and then constructed a new place for herself *within* Catholic spirituality, a space not available to her in the convent or during the years of diaspora that immediately followed her departure.

The expression "crossing over" conveys the Harriet Tubman aspect of the exodus experience that many Catholic women's narratives describe. The destination need not be a physical place, such as Monica Baldwin's cottage in Cornwall. It can be a new psychic and spiritual space more suitable for one's evolving Catholic (or post-Catholic) identity. This chapter explores three Catholic women's personal narratives about adolescent experiences of "crossing over" written by Antonia White (1899–1980), Mary McCarthy (1912–1989), and Mary Gordon (1949–). It concentrates on three classic treatments of Catholic girlhood and young womanhood: White's *Frost in May* (1933), McCarthy's *Memories of a Catholic Girlhood* (1957), and Gordon's *Final Payments* (1978). These three works range from autobiography sometimes mistaken for fiction (McCarthy) to autobiographical fiction (White) to fiction deeply grounded in personal experience (Gordon). All three narratives tell the truth about Catholic women's lives and show, in meticulous detail, what "crossing over" means and—just as important—how it feels. All three provide an opportunity for readers to participate in the protagonists' border-crossings. They represent part of an underground tradition within Roman Catholicism that acknowledges the need for departures and migrations as necessary rites of passage for women who hope to survive and move beyond Catholic girlhood and reach emotional and spiritual maturity.

Read together, the narratives by White, McCarthy, and Gordon take us into the still-unmapped territory of Catholic girlhood. They depict a landscape often invoked in bitter or humorous reminiscences but rarely examined by historians bent on exploring the evolution of Catholic girlhood over time or the place of departure in Catholic women's writings. One critical aspect of Catholic girlhood that historians cannot penetrate without the help of personal narratives (both nonfiction and fiction) is the emergence of a sense of spiritual mobility and personal agency that necessarily precedes adult life as a woman. The instinct for flight described by Cixous assumes different forms in these three narratives by White, McCarthy, and Gordon, which take place in three distinctly different historical eras and cultural settings. Still, there is a family resemblance among these texts and many others written by Catholic women about girlhood and adolescence, attempted flight and ties that cannot be severed. All three books are about crossing boundaries between the safe, carefully delineated world that pre–Vatican II Catholic priests, sisters, and parents envisioned for daughters of the church and the many tempting, forbidden worlds that have presented themselves to the imaginations of Catholic girls in the process of becoming women.

Antonia White

Although it is not widely known or read among either Catholics or feminists in the United States, Antonia White's first novel, *Frost in May,* was respected and controversial in England during the decades after it first appeared in the small run of a new and struggling publisher in 1933. Forty years after its original publication, it was rediscovered and became the first book issued by Virago Press, founded in 1972 "in an attic on Wardour Street [London], specializing in forgotten female masters of the twentieth century" (Chitty 1985, 181). Carmen Callil, the founder of Virago, was working for a publishing firm in London in the 1960s when a colleague gave her a copy of *Frost in May*. Callil, who was educated in a series of convent schools in Australia starting in the early 1940s, including Germaine Greer's alma mater, Star of the Sea Convent in Gardenvale, Victoria, responded viscerally to *Frost in May*. She recalls being "absolutely suffused with misery and agony and fury" while she read it.

Callil fled Australia directly after university in Melbourne in part to escape from the scene of her Catholic girlhood. Nonetheless, she believed that White's convent-school novel, which had dredged up all of the old feelings that she had worked so hard to overcome, should be required reading for the emerging generation of young English feminists who needed to understand what they were trying to move beyond. White's novel captured the "suffering" and "the feeling of mindless repression" that had colored Callil's own convent-school experience (Callil in Bennett and Forgan 1991, 55). What made Frost in May such an apt choice for the first Virago book was the way in which it provided readers with access to the all-female world of Lippington, White's fictional convent school run by the Sisters of the Five Wounds, modeled after her own experience at Roehampton Convent of the Sacred Heart near London.

In her introduction to the 1948 edition of *Frost in May*, the Anglo-Irish Protestant novelist Elizabeth Bowen noted that a convent school like Lippington was "a world in itself—hermetic to a degree possible for no lay school" (Bowen 1992, viii). White's protagonist and alter ego, Nanda Grey, remained ever conscious of living on the margin throughout her five years at Lippington. As a convert and one of the least affluent students, she was constantly reminded that she could never completely fit in with the school elite, born Catholics from aristocratic English and European families. She later recalled feeling "as conspicuous as a sparrow in a flock of canaries" (White 1954, 35). Yet even when she was most conscious of being an outsider, Nanda could not help but find the atmosphere at Lippington intoxicating and irresistible. Her descriptions of Lippington, its ambiance, the complex pedagogy adopted by the nuns, and the intense joys and sorrows of convent-school life resonated with generations of similarly educated women from all over the world. White captured the timeless quality inherent in a convent school. She told an interviewer that after *Frost in May* was first published in 1933, she received letters from two alumnae of Roehampton, one who had left in 1883 and another in 1927, "both . . . quite certain from my description of the convent that I must have been their contemporary. The fact that I left in 1914 is irrelevant" (Bennett and Forgan 1991, 1).

Nanda Grey is a guileless, bright but average girl who is not afraid to record her impressions honestly, without euphemism or exaggeration. *Frost in May* is written in the third person, entirely from Nanda's perspective. We know only what she knows and experience what she experiences. Bowen compares the narrative voice in *Frost in May* ("precise, clear and unweighty") to that of Jane Austen and of Joyce in *Portrait of the Artist as a Young Man* (Bowen 1992, vii). Through the use of this voice, White provides many female Catholic readers with an opportunity to reenter the scene of their girlhood. When Nanda observes that "in [Lippington's] cold, clear atmosphere everything had a sharper outline than in the comfortable, shapeless, scrambling life outside," former convent-school girls know exactly what she means. When she compares life at Lippington to a stint in the navy ("the scrubbed boards and whitened walls," "the scantiest of personal belongings stowed away in the smallest possible space," the uniforms, obeying orders to the letter [White 1992a, 190–191]), convent-school alumnae are transported back to what that rarified life meant to them at one time. Almost inevitably, readers are moved to ask the next question, the one that captivated the writer Antonia White: Can we see traces of that life and the self-consciousness it engendered permanently inscribed on the selves that we have become?

Elizabeth Bowen clarifies the distinction between the "school story" written for children and adolescents and the "school novel" intended for an adult audience (Bowen 1992, v–vi). *Frost in May* falls into the latter category. The focus may be on convent-school experience but the questions being addressed are primarily of interest to adults who want to understand the permanent impression made by a convent education on impressionable girls and young women. In the introduction that first appeared in the 1980 edition of White's reconversion story, *The Hound and the Falcon* (1965), Sara Maitland locates a complex, even ominous strain in Nanda Grey's voice. It is "not solely, or even predominantly, a nostalgic longing for the sweet security of childhood." Maitland identifies in Nanda's voice "a note I have heard from other lapsed Catholics and nowhere else." At the risk of shocking the sort of reader that might be interested in the story of White's return to the church, Maitland draws an analogy between the voice of the pious convent-school student Nanda Grey and voices she had heard at a shelter for battered women. Both Nanda and the battered women spoke "with a knowledge that they had been hurt and would be hurt again which could not totally outweigh the passionate longing to be involved again in that relationship which was the source of all emotions—positive as well as negative" (Maitland 1992, vii–viii).

Frost in May is a memoir thinly disguised as fiction. Even the protagonist's name, Fernanda (Nanda) Grey, taken from a character in Henry James's *The Awkward Age*, is a play on the author's pen name Antonia White. The plot line closely follows the experience of the author, whose given name was Eirene Botting, during the five years (1909–1914) that she spent at Roehampton. Eirene Botting was a convert, brought into the church at age 7 by her convert father, a classics master at St. Paul's School in London. She was precocious, reading in English at 4 and in Greek not long after. Like Nanda Grey in the novel, Eirene Botting was intellectually gifted and spiritually devout. When *Frost in May* explores the ways in which the protagonist's intellectual gifts and spiritual fervor brought her both positive and negative recognition, the story is taken directly from Eirene Botting's clear memories of Roehampton. Precocious young Nanda could see that Lippington constituted a special form of girl-centered Catholic culture with its own authority structures, language, customs, rituals, and forms of community life. She set out to master that culture, starting with the fundamentals, for example "the elaborate technique of dressing according to Christian modesty so that at no time, even in the privacy of her cubicle, was she ever entirely naked" (White 1992a, 45). After the first difficult week of adjustment, Nanda quickly learned the many rules governing life at Lippington and set out to excel. She earned the pink and green ribbons awarded to the school leaders. Her academic gifts were openly acknowledged. Yet she experienced sudden reprimands and disciplinary actions that took her by surprise.

Early in the first term, Nanda discovered that "being good was surprisingly easy, there seemed so little time to be anything else" (White 1992a, 48). Right before she received her pink ribbon for eight straight weeks of exceptional behavior, her teacher, Mother Frances, took her aside and accused her of having serious spiritual flaws masked by her exemplary behavior:

> The trouble with you, my dear, is that you don't seem to have any normal, healthy, natural naughtiness about you. God doesn't care about your namby-pamby goodness . . . ; he wants the real hard goodness that comes from conquering real hard faults. I don't mean you haven't got faults. The trouble with your faults is that they don't show. You're obstinate, you're independent, and if a child of nine can be said to have spiritual pride, spiritual pride is your ruling vice. (White 1992a, 49)

This was Nanda's first exposure to the Lippington pedagogy, which centered on the goal of breaking the girls' wills. "True education," Mistress of Discipline Mother Radcliffe once told her, means that "every will must be broken completely and re-set before it can be at one with God's will" (White 1992a, 219). This particular pedagogy proved to be the catalyst for Nanda's attraction to acts of transgression, from choosing her own friends, eccentric and upper-class girls rather than the more conventional middle-class students the nuns had designated as more appropriate for her, to reading and writing forbidden works of literature. These transgressions led to her departure from Lippington at 15 in the wake of a traumatic confrontation with two looming authority figures, Mother Radcliffe and her father.

One of the most vivid, memorable characters in *Frost in May*, Nanda's best friend Léonie de Wesseldorf (closely modeled after the author's Roehampton schoolmate and lifelong friend Charlotte d'Erlanger), provided White with a vehicle to convey the social, emotional, and spiritual complexity of her convent-school experience. Léonie, who proved her loyalty and deep affection for Nanda on several occasions, never forgot the distance that separated them. The distance was not defined by Léonie's considerable wealth and Nanda's relative poverty, a disparity dismissed by Léonie despite the pain that it caused Nanda. Financial inequities were almost trivial. They could be remedied by a sudden windfall or a loan. What separated Nanda from Léonie had far deeper roots, which became apparent in Léonie's casual explanation of the unequal treatment of the pair by the nuns:

> "It's funny, Léo," mused Nanda. "You say the most extraordinary things; you're awfully slack about prayers and all that, you've even got a copy of *Candide* bound up as a missal, and I believe the nuns know, and yet you get away with everything. Yet if I do the slightest thing, I'm punished."
>
> "Because they're not sure of you yet. You're a nicely washed and combed and baptised and confirmed little heathen, but you're a heathen all the same. But they're sure of me. In ten, twenty years I'll be exactly the same. It's in the blood. . . . And when I die, my great uncle Cardinal de Wesseldorf and my great-great aunt the Carmelite Abbess de Wesseldorf, who had an affair with Napoleon before she entered, will say to the recording angel: 'My dear sir, you can't seriously send a Wesseldorf to hell,' and into heaven I shall go." (White 1992a, 122–123)

Léonie, for whom Nanda felt "pure admiration, the feeling of page for prince, too cold and absolute to be called love" (White 1992a, 80), represents an entirely different breed of Catholic girl from Nanda, one more likely than Nanda to survive Lippington unscathed. What made Léonie (Charlotte) and Nanda (Eirene) understand and express their Catholicism so differently was a potent mixture of elements, ranging from their divergent class backgrounds, girlhood experiences, and temperaments to the profound, still unexplored, differences separating born Catholics from converts. As Sara Maitland observes, Léonie embodied a way of being Catholic that Antonia White recognized as healthy but did not have the capacity to emulate. Léonie displayed "a high level of loving self-irony and inner confidence, plus an amused delight in ritual and cultic imagery" which allowed her to "take [Catholicism, including the Lippington version] lightly—practice but not get knotted up about it" (Maitland 1992, xiii). Both her confidence based on class and wealth and her inner resources made it possible for Léonie to laugh heartily at the prospect of pulling strings to get into heaven. The same qualities helped Charlotte d'Erlanger to lapse comfortably in her later years, while Antonia White struggled against the grain to be reconciled to the church.

While the fictional Nanda and the writer Antonia White recognized the desirability of Léonie's confident and ironic spirituality, it was not within their reach. The power of Nanda's narrative derives from her pure, almost photographic, rendition of her impressions and experience. Maitland states bluntly that "Antonia White cannot take religion like [Léonie] because she has no sense of humor about herself and—riddled with guilt and awe—absolutely none at all about God or the Church" (Maitland 1992, xiii). We see clear evidence of this lack of irony and humor in a diary entry written on November 21, 1961, when she was 62 years old, on the fiftieth anniversary of her First Communion.

> I lay awake in the night, finding I still felt bitter against Mother D'arcy for not letting me make my First Communion with the others on Corpus Christi—and I still do not think it was justified to do that—with no warning and no chance to appeal—just on the grounds that I had "talked too much in the corridors"! . . . I had been wanting to make my First Communion since I was 9 and did not make it till I was 12. I can't help feeling, if I'd been an Ambassador's daughter she wouldn't have so cruelly disappointed both me and my parents. (Chitty 1993, 56)

Antonia White first questioned the authority of the nuns (and the Catholic church, which they represented) when she believed that they acted unjustly, abusing their authority and favoring the girls from rich, powerful families. Mother Frances's abstract and frivolous reprimand couched in spiritual counsel and the sudden postponement of Eirene's first communion are but two examples of the kind of injustice operative at

Lippington/Roehampton. White underscores the relationship between her discovery of injustice and her first hidden, interior gestures toward departure from Lippington's prescribed model of Catholic girlhood in an episode in *Frost in May* in which Nanda rises to the defense of the class underdog, Monica Owen. All of the girls knew that Monica, the daughter of "a struggling doctor in a provincial town," was a charity student. She was given the worst seat in class, the stubbiest pencils, already-used exercise books, and feast-day dresses made of old, yellowed nun's veiling while the others wore new dresses of pure white fabric. She was routinely humiliated for her poor grasp of Christian doctrine. At Christmas, when all of the girls in the Junior School were assigned animals near the manger, Monica's was placed the farthest from the Christ child (White 1992a, 65, 152). Monica's one known talent, her passion for drawing dogs with "oddly human faces" endeared her to girls like Nanda. When a routine desk inspection unearthed an exercise book full of dog caricatures of nuns, Monica was expelled.

Monica was not her best friend, but when Nanda heard of Monica's fate, something snapped. She disregarded all of the Lippington rules and customs and went straight to the mistress of discipline to protest. She insisted that Monica, who had been in solitary confinement in the retreat house, had been punished sufficiently and that the nuns knew that they were sending her home to a strict father and a cruel stepmother. Nanda finally confronted Mother Radcliffe with an accusation: "I thought Catholics were supposed to be charitable." She was summarily dismissed by the nun, who never looked up from her paperwork to acknowledge the substance of her charge (White 1992a, 152–155).

Monica's expulsion represented a watershed for Nanda:

> A small core of rebelliousness which had been growing secretly for four years seemed to have hardened inside her. Outwardly her conduct was perfectly respectable: she no longer giggled or talked at forbidden times, she worked fairly hard and generally comported herself as a green ribbon should. But she delighted in asking awkward questions in the Christian Doctrine class and smiled with the complacent cynicism of thirteen when her mistress was temporarily flustered. (White 1992a, 156)

Although White tells us that Nanda's resistance was "directed entirely against the Lippington methods" and did not affect her Catholic faith, the narrative suggests otherwise. The Monica incident paved the way for other departures from the prescribed path for Catholic girls and women. Almost systematically, Nanda began to dispense with the spiritual practices fostered by her teachers. She stopped writing *Ad Majorem Dei Gloriam* on the flyleaf of her exercise books. She fled the "flowery ecstasies of the Garden of the Soul" and found that even the "colder, more solid prayers of St. Augustine and St. Thomas Aquinas" did little to keep her focused on devotions. A dedication to art and beauty gradually displaced religious devotion. She began to compose "labored little lyrics about spring and the sea, with a tardy reference to God in the last verse, and elaborate fairy-tales with saints for princes and devils for dragons." She started a novel about "a brilliant, wicked, worldly society . . . composed of painters, musicians and peers, . . . [in which] all her characters [would] be sensationally converted in the last chapter" (White 1992a, 157–158).

Meanwhile, another episode further catalyzed Nanda's detachment from Lippington and Catholicism. Léonie prepared to play Beatrice in a school adaptation of Dante so skillfully performed that rehearsals moved Nanda to tears. Suddenly, for no apparent reason, Léonie was replaced by a much less talented actress. Léonie, stifling back tears, found the usual relief in heavy irony. To Nanda's apoplectic question, "Surely they can't take away your part just because you liked playing it?" Léonie responded with her best parody of Mother Radcliffe:

> Didn't you observe that I enjoyed myself? Didn't you observe that I took a wilful and sensuous pleasure in the performance? Had that pleasure anything to do with the glory of God or the honour of this sanctified school? . . .
>
> Have you forgotten that we are not here to acquire vain accomplishment but to form our characters? And don't you realize that there's nothing worse for the Catholic character than to do something it really enjoys? (White 1992a, 169)

Léonie's words verbalized Nanda's growing discomfort with the limitations that girls at her school were required to place on art and beauty, which were always supposed to be in the service of God and the church. Thanks to Léonie, Nanda finally found the words to express her displeasure and register her objection to the official Lippington spirituality: "I'm sick of all this beastly cant. Why can't we for once do something for its own sake, instead of tacking everything on to our own eternal salvation. One can't even get dressed or have a bath or eat one's bacon and eggs without keeping an eye on eternity. I am prepared to be as devout as you like, if I can only have a little time to myself" (White 1992a, 169).

Nanda needed time and space to explore her attraction to beauty in art and literature and her desire to become a writer, both of which were becoming a kind of spirituality in themselves. Upon reflection, she realized that her passion for the play had less to do with friendship than with art. She needed an opportunity to concentrate on "the thing itself" and could no longer tolerate the Lippington requirement that "poetry and pictures and things . . . be messages from God" (White 1992a, 170).

The letter Nanda received from her class mistress Mother Percival during the following Christmas holidays only intensified her uneasiness with the mandatory Lippington spirituality, which the nuns portrayed as the only road to salvation. Mother Percival reminded Nanda, who had recently received a special prize for English, that natural gifts are far less important than what one does with them. "It is a hundred times better to knit a pair of socks humbly for the glory of God than to write the finest poem or symphony for mere self-glorification." Before closing, Mother Percival added a caveat about Nanda's choice of friends "for such superficial attributes as cleverness and humour" and admonished her that "the healthiest friendships are those between people who share the same background." Like Mother Frances before her, Mother Percival lost control of her tone as her remarks wore on. "Schoolgirls are notoriously uncritical," she assured Nanda. She predicted that "in the world you may find that Nanda Grey does not seem the clever, fascinating little person she appears to a small circle at Lippington" (White 1992a, 180–181).

Jane Dunn, Antonia White's biographer, treats *Frost in May* as an accurate rendering of Eirene Botting's experience at Roehampton. She maintains that Antonia White's lifelong struggle with feelings of insecurity and insignificance had its roots in the pedagogy and spirituality of her convent school, where "her individuality [was] constantly under attack." To illustrate her point, Dunn quotes a letter that White sent in 1955 to her good friend Emily Coleman where she confessed that "it took me a long time to realize that I existed!" (Dunn 1998, 39–40).

Each head-on confrontation with the Lippington pedagogy left Nanda stunned, but with each one she crossed a threshold, however unwittingly and unwillingly. White records each crossing in Nanda's clear meticulous voice. Mother Percival's letter was an unwelcome invasion into her already haunted childhood home where the shadow of her overscrupulous and probably abusive convert father eclipsed all other bodies. The letter had the desired effect. It claimed all of Nanda's time and space, even the holidays and her girlhood home, for the totalizing project undertaken by the nuns at Lippington on behalf of each girl. Upon reading Mother Percival's letter, Nanda saw the formerly warm, familiar world of her childhood home suddenly turn "unfriendly." "Even the room that had been inviolably hers until now had been polluted. There was no privacy anywhere" (White 1992a, 182).

The climax came suddenly on Nanda's 14th birthday, which happened to fall on Easter. On Holy Thursday, Nanda had given Léonie her unfinished novel to read—reluctantly, because she respected Léonie's opinion above all others and she had yet to add the mandatory Catholic ending in which all of the sinful characters were miraculously converted. On Good Friday, while the girls were in chapel, Mother Radcliffe scheduled one of her random inspections and seized the manuscript, folded inside a French exercise book, from Léonie's desk. Nanda spent the weekend in limbo; devotions and festivities seemed to take place in slow motion, grinding toward an inevitable crisis. The dreaded interview with Mother Radcliffe and her parents took place on Easter afternoon in the unaccustomed, off-putting surroundings of the nuns' parlor, where Nanda's parents had been reading her novel. Her father's face, "stiff as a death-mask," and his icy voice prepared Nanda for the worst. When she addressed her father in the usual fashion, calling him Daddy, he interrupted: "I would rather you did not use that name."

As if by prior arrangement, Mother Radcliffe and Mr. Grey played "good cop/bad cop" while Nanda sputtered and her mother tried fruitlessly to temper her husband's reaction. Mr. Grey asked if the novel was entirely Nanda's work, and Nanda confirmed that it was. Pounding his hand on the nuns' plush-covered table, he replied, "If a young girl's mind is such a sink of filth and impurity, I wish to God that I had never had a daughter." Neither Mrs. Grey's attempts to comfort her nor Mother Radcliffe's suggestion that she be moved to another school run by the order softened the blow Nanda suffered from her father's denunciation and his insistence that Nanda leave Lippington immediately: "Nanda's last thread of self-control snapped. She burst into a storm of convulsive, almost tearless sobs that wrenched all her muscles and brought no relief. The whole world had fallen away and left her stranded in this one spot for ever and ever with her father and those awful words" (White 1992a, 215–216).

One might be tempted to dismiss this scene as an overdramatized girlhood crisis, but it was written faithfully from experience and turned out to be the pivotal moment in the author's life. Very few of the details were changed in the novel, which was begun shortly after Botting left Roehampton in 1914 but remained unfinished until the early 1930s. Eirene Botting was 15, rather than 14, on the climactic Easter Sunday. The real confrontation was with her father; there were no nuns present. Aside from these almost cosmetic changes, Antonia White was careful to record the scene with her father accurately. This is the moment to which Antonia White returned again and again in her diaries and in analysis. For Antonia White, this moment, understood in connection with a prenatal trauma (possibly a marital rape a few months before she was born), represented the key to understanding her struggles and her unique way of being in the world. In denying his daughter, her novel, and the reputation (intellectual, moral, and spiritual) that she had worked so hard to earn at Roehampton, Eirene Botting's father, Cecil, had done all that he could to erase the part of her that had not turned out as he had hoped.

After the interview in the nuns' parlor, Mother Radcliffe told Nanda that she should leave Lippington because she had now learned the primary lesson that the nuns hoped to teach their students: Her will had been broken "before [her] whole nature was deformed." Still, to the end, Mother Radcliffe applied the Lippington pedagogy in her dealings with Nanda. Like Mother Frances, Mother Radcliffe could deliver praise and affection with one hand and pain and denunciation with the other. She explained that even having learned her lesson, even with her will successfully broken, Nanda belonged to the spiritual and moral category analogous to the population that doctors called germ carriers: "People, harmless in themselves, who can be a source of danger to others." Then, in the next breath, she said, "But I want you always to think of yourself as one of us. . . . Come back and see us often—and write to us—pray for us as we shall pray for you" (White 1992a, 219–220).

Immediately after this conversation Nanda made her final visit to the Lippington chapel. That experience is described in the quotation at the beginning of this chapter. Nanda had begun her departure from Lippington in her mind long before the Easter that she turned 14. Her crossing took place not in the confrontation with her father, but in her own reflections on its meaning. In the chapel the night before she left the school for good, Nanda crossed over. She was endowed with the double vision that sometimes signals the experience of crossing over: the profound, bittersweet realization that "everything was the same," but "nothing *for her* would ever be the same again" (White 1992a, 221; my italics).

Even before the confrontation with her father in the Roehampton parlor, White (then Botting) had had intimations of the changes that were in store for her. Her daughter Lyndall Hopkinson insists that these changes were more than the "shock," "terror," and "shame" that accompanied puberty. (Like many sheltered Edwardian girls, Botting associated the growth of pubic hair and other physical changes with punishment for unspecified sin.) The most significant inward change documented in her first two novels was the emergence of a new private self, a "mysterious stranger" beyond the control of her father (Hopkinson 1988, 33). Hopkinson calls attention to her mother's treatment of this important inner change in a passage in White's second autobiographical novel, *The Lost Traveller,* originally published in 1950. When Clara, the protagonist, is chastised by her father after he has surreptitiously witnessed her first kiss, her reaction, captured when she looks in the mirror, surprises her. "Bewildered and resentful as she was, there was one clear point in the confusion of her mind. Some part of herself seemed to have broken loose and to judge differently from the rest. Had he beaten her, the original Clara could not have felt more humiliated. But someone else . . . was it the girl in the glass? . . . had the strangest sense of triumph" (Hopkinson 1988, 33; White 1993, 78).

One way in which White eventually confirmed and embraced the double vision that had accompanied crossing over was by renaming herself. Her new name, Antonia (Tony) White, was constructed from a girlhood nickname given to her by her mother and her mother's maiden name. Later, she would gradually realize that renaming herself was her attempt to move beyond her father's control and be her own person. Antonia White was more than a pen name; it was a new identity. In an unpublished diary entry written two years after *Frost in May* first appeared in 1933, White explained her need to leave her given name behind. She believed that she had no choice but to rename herself for "with such a name could I ever be anything?" (cited in Dunn 1998, 9).

The account of Nanda's painful final years at Lippington and her departure from the Eden of Catholic girlhood made *Frost in May* a cult classic. The novel was twice reborn: first in 1978, when it was reprinted as a Virago classic, and again in 1982, when the BBC broadcast a miniseries that combined *Frost in May* with its three sequels: *The Lost Traveller* (1950), *The Sugar House* (1952), and *Beyond the Glass* (1954). Antonia White both acknowledged and lamented that *Frost in May*, her first book, remained her most highly regarded work. The only other work that even approached its sales and reputation was *The Hound and the Falcon* (1965), a collection of letters reflecting on her return to the Catholic church, after fifteen years' lapse, in 1940.

White's actual departure from the church was far less easy to document than the first steps away, which are so faithfully preserved in *Frost in May*. Just as Nanda insists that her discovery that nuns could be cruel and unjust did not affect her Catholic faith (White 1992a, 157), White maintains that her belief in Catholic doctrine outlived her disenchantment with Roehampton. In a long diary entry written May 12, 1941, she reports that her Catholic faith survived the nervous breakdown that put her in Bethlem Royal Hospital from November 1922 through August 1923 and the abortion that followed in 1924. She refers to the "[Jim] Dougal episode," an acquaintance rape by a duplicitous married man that led to her first abortion, and asserts that the incident and the abortion "left [her] perfectly serene and unguilty." She maintains that she "practiced [her religion] again afterwards but in a much cooler and more formal way" (Chitty 1992, 175–176).

Only later, under the influence of her second husband, Eric Earnshaw Smith, who was also her intellectual mentor, did White begin to doubt Catholic doctrine and gravitate toward Smith's secular spirituality, which was informed by the writings of Santayana. In the same 1941 diary entry, she recalls: "I did not so much deliberately leave [Catholic belief and practice] as let it drop away gradually, bit by bit. . . . I suppose I gave up finally about 1926 or 1927 when I began to go in for promiscuous love affairs" (Chitty 1992, 176). Gradually, White realized that her departure from the church in her late 20s was more complex than she had acknowledged on paper to herself, even after her return to the church on Christmas 1940. In an essay written in 1954, White maintains that "it would be impossible, apart from lack of space, to determine all the complex and overlapping causes which led to my lack of faith." She confesses: "I reached a stage where I was convinced it was intellectually dishonest to believe in God." Acknowledging her lost faith had been costly, however. Her newfound freedom and pride in having "faced up to the truth" had been tempered by "a sense of emptiness." To some extent, at least temporarily, the void had been filled by a secular spirituality: "There was an austere beauty in this world where everything acquired a peculiar intensity and poignancy precisely because all that was beautiful or true or good could only be perceived and enjoyed during the span of human life" (White 1954, 38).

In 1962, twenty years after she had returned to the church, White was short of cash and agreed to transcribe *Frost in May* for an interested manuscript dealer. She was struck by "how all the themes of my life are there— my father and religion" (Chitty 1993, 66–67). White's diary and *Frost in May* present a very consistent portrait of the author's troubled relationship with her father and its direct bearing on her relationship to the Catholic church. White's relationship with her father was complex. Her eldest daughter, Susan Chitty, editor of her diary, states that "it is hard not to suspect that Cecil [Botting] may have, even if only to a small degree, sexually abused Antonia as a child" (Chitty 1993, 9). Moreover, White's father had sought to control every aspect of her life, from her reception into the church at 7 to her education at Roehampton, where he hoped that she would meet Catholics from good families. He had already determined what her future held: a good secondary school, Cambridge, and a teaching career in modern languages or classics.

In her diary, White explained the link between her father, who appeared to love her only when she pleased him, and the theology implicit in her training at Roehampton. Both her father's style of parenting and the

Roehampton pedagogy contributed to White's growing revulsion at "the idea of an omnipotent being who only loves you when you *please* him and is exceedingly angry with you when you don't and, if you are not careful, will punish you not only in this world but eternally in the next" (Chitty 1993, 159). White made an intriguing, if disturbing, connection between her father's rejection of her first novel and his response to her pregnancy as a result of the Dougal affair in 1924. On June 25, 1938, toward the end of a period of Freudian analysis with Dr. Dennis Carroll, she wrote:

> My impulse to write a novel began in the year following the beginning of menstruation. My father, as it were, killed the child. He thought of it as *having been conceived in sin.* Just about ten years later, I conceived a real child, about the same time of year, this time definitely "in sin" and to my father's horrified disapproval. This time my father wants me to have the child, in very distressing circumstances, *as a punishment.* . . . I suddenly remember something I had forgotten—I cheated him over the money [for the abortion]. (Chitty 1992, 139)

Mary McCarthy

Mary McCarthy's biographers do not mention any connection between her and Antonia White. There is no evidence that the two ever met. White's life in literary and advertising circles centered in London and McCarthy's peripatetic career in literary and academic circles centered in, but by no means confined to, New York, Paris, and the major cities of Italy were analogous rather than overlapping. Still, these two authors had much in common. Both secured their literary reputations with autobiographical works about boundary-crossing and transgression during their Catholic girlhoods, books that constructed their girlhoods from the perspective of middle age. (White was 34 and McCarthy 45 when their respective memoirs appeared.) Both launched their writing careers with the support of literary husbands who believed in their talent, perhaps before they did, and urged them to write by imposing deadlines for them. Both spent time in mental hospitals in their 20s and subsequently lived conspicuously promiscuous lives that included multiple marriages, multiple infidelities, and multiple abortions. Both married gay men. And neither of them lived down their Catholic girlhood, which shadowed each woman to the end of her days.

These similarities are even more striking given the different contexts in which White and McCarthy wrote their girlhood narratives. White belonged to a small vocal minority within a minority in England. She was an English Catholic convert author. *Frost in May* caught the attention of the London literary elite, both Catholic and non-Catholic. English readers and reviewers were, for the most part, attracted rather than repelled by her account of the complexities and struggles of her convent-school years. *Frost in May* afforded White a place of honor in the English literary world of the 1930s, and in its next incarnation four decades later, it won her the affections of English feminists, including Catholic feminists. Mary McCarthy's memoir of growing up Catholic in America about a decade after White provoked mixed reactions from American readers and reviewers. Some were deeply moved, while others insisted that McCarthy was lying and blaspheming.

There is no real consensus among American feminist historians and critics about what is to be done with *Memories of a Catholic Girlhood.* McCarthy gave her feminist contemporaries no reason to mistake her for a fellow traveler. When, in an interview originally published in *The Nation* in 1984, McCarthy told Carol Brightman that she believed that "feminism is bad for women, [because] it induces a very bad emotional state" she was expressing a position that she had espoused consistently in the preceding decades. She decried "the self-pity, the shrillness and the greed" that characterized most of the feminists she had observed. She questioned the intellectual foundations of feminism and pronounced Simone de Beauvoir "a good 'B' student somewhere in the intellectual world, maybe not even a 'B' student" (Brightman 1984, 616–617).

McCarthy was not without her admiring fans, a group that included priests and missionary sisters as well as feminists such as the literary critic Beverly Gross, who has examined in print the reasons why so many have labeled McCarthy a bitch. "There may be much to dislike in McCarthy," Gross maintains in her essay "Our Leading Bitch Intellectual," "but there is much to admire in her capacity to break the mold of female expectations, subservience, politeness, and respectability" (Gross 1996, 33). We gain insight into the vast spectrum of reactions to McCarthy's writings, including her personal narrative about her girlhood, when we examine the context in which McCarthy's memoir first appeared. *Memories of a Catholic Girlhood* contains recollections of McCarthy's life from age 6 to age 17 (1918–1929), which were preserved in stories written when the author was in her late 30s and early 40s and hastily revised as a memoir during the fall and winter of 1956, when the author was 44.

In her memoir, McCarthy does not pretend to be depicting the girlhood of some abstract Catholic Everywoman. The uniqueness of McCarthy's experience is presupposed at every turn. *Memories of a Catholic Girlhood* illuminates American Catholic life in the 1920s in two distinct settings, a parish and parochial school in Minneapolis and an exclusive Sacred Heart convent school outside Seattle, as remembered by a precocious orphan girl from an upper-middle-class background. In so doing, *Memories* explores what this period of increasing visibility and prosperity for American Catholics meant within the microcosm of a Minneapolis Irish-American family that had amassed considerable wealth at the turn of the century selling grain and grain elevators. It also examines the impact of the stifling insularity of the American Catholic community on Mary McCarthy during her highly impressionable preadolescent years.

This insularity, deftly examined in *The Survival of American Innocence* (1980), William Halsey's pioneering study of American Catholic culture between the world wars, promoted—virtually mandated—Catholic alien-ation from the artistic ferment of the 1920s and the political radicalism of the 1930s. It also cast its shadow on the training of girls at convent schools and Catholic women's colleges. In a frequently quoted letter to Wilfred Parsons, S.J., editor of the Jesuit journal *America*, dated October 15, 1927, Mary McGill, associate editor of *The Catholic Girl*, displays a startling awareness of Catholic insularity and its byproduct, self-righteousness, in her own times. "No one but a well-instructed Catholic appreciates Catholicism, and no matter how *broad* our friends on the outside say they are, I find them quickly sensitive. We are so SURE. That characteristic would hurt me, if I didn't believe. I think I would hate people who are so certain and set apart, if I were not so favored with our *Supreme Gift*" (*America* Magazine Archives). McGill's remarks, those of a staunch believer, a mature woman, and a professional Catholic female journalist, remind us not to dismiss lightly Mary McCarthy's observations about Catholic insularity.

Mary McCarthy had explored aspects of her Catholic girlhood in fic-tional and nonfictional works since her college days at Vassar (McCarthy 1985, 82–83). In her study of Catholic girlhood narratives, Elizabeth Evasdaughter calls attention to the pun in the title of *Memories of a Catholic Girlhood:*

> "Catholic" refers literally to the contrasting Catholic situations she expe-rienced in childhood. McCarthy shows that she did not entirely join any one Catholic group in her family. Her mother and father identified with the loving and festive Church, her grandmother Lizzie McCarthy with the sectarian Church, her great-aunt Margaret Shriver with the totalitar-ian or disciplinarian Church, and the Madams of the Sacred Heart in Seattle with the Romantic and infallible Church. . . . McCarthy herself identified, however gradually, with the eclectic Church. (Evasdaughter 1996, 218)

"No virtue is more intimidating than truth-telling," Phyllis McGinley asserted in her review of *Memories of a Catholic Girlhood* in the *Saturday Review*. "For truth, no matter how plain or unvarnished, is also so multiple-faced that few can see it whole." McGinley maintained that Mary McCarthy "seems to have come as near the truth as is rationally probable; and she has contrived a new technique for doing so" (McGinley 1957, 31). Perhaps it is precisely the "multiple-faced" quality in Mary McCarthy's recollections of her Catholic girlhood that impressed her admirers and sometimes startled her fans and critics alike. In her memoir and the autobiographical stories that preceded and evolved into it, Mary McCarthy dared to examine many unattractive, even threatening, faces of Catholicism as she had encountered them. In so doing, she shattered cherished myths about Catholic girlhood and the nature of the American Catholic church that many of her contemporaries were fighting hard to preserve.

In the prefatory section of *Memories* addressed directly to the reader, McCarthy insists that the chapters that followed were not mere stories but personal recollections in which only certain names, like those of her teachers and fellow students at her convent and boarding schools, had been changed. Names of family members, neighbors, friends, and servants remained unaltered, as did the intimate details of McCarthy's childhood. "This record lays a claim to being historical," she asserts, and adds, "If there is more fiction in it than I know, I should like to be set right" (McCarthy 1985, 4–5). What follows is a narrative so vivid and detailed, so engagingly written, that its neglect by Catholic social historians can only be interpreted as intentional.

In *Memories of a Catholic Girlhood,* McCarthy provided all of the facts about her first six years (1912–1918) that she had been able to uncover. She and her three younger brothers were the pampered and beloved children of an invalid father, Roy McCarthy, and his attractive younger wife, Tess Preston McCarthy. During most of this period, they lived in Seattle, Tess's hometown. The family was always in debt because of the parents' extravagant tastes and Roy's recurring illness. McCarthy's recollections of her first six years are Proustian: little diamond rings, an ermine muff and necklace, birthday cakes, ice-cream molds, peaches consumed in mounds of sugar, May baskets, a hyacinth plant, Easter-egg hunts, parties with grab bags and fish ponds, chocolate and cambric tea made by Tess in the afternoons on the little electric stove (McCarthy 1985, 10). Tess, the daughter of a Protestant father and a Jewish mother, converted to Catholicism at the time of her marriage. Mary McCarthy's first impressions of what it meant to be Catholic came from the warm and exuberant spirit in which she saw her mother embrace her new faith.

She was proud and happy to be a convert, and her attitude made us feel that it was a special treat to be a Catholic, the crowning treat and privilege. Our religion was a present to us from God. Everything in our home conspired to fix in our minds the idea that we were very precious little persons, precious to our parents and to God, too, Who was listening to us with loving attention every night when we said our prayers. (McCarthy 1985, 13)

Mary McCarthy's whole world fell apart when her family was called back to Minneapolis in the middle of the influenza epidemic of 1918, ostensibly so that they could see Roy's younger brother Louis, on furlough in Minneapolis, but probably because Roy's lifestyle in Seattle was costing his father too much money. The trip, combined with the epidemic, proved fatal to Roy and Tess and left Mary and her brothers orphans. The three boys were sent to live down the street from the McCarthy mansion in a more modest dwelling with their Great-Aunt Margaret Shriver and her husband Myers. After an interval of a few weeks during which she lived with her grandparents and received weekly shock therapy to erase any troubling memories of her past life (McCarthy 1985, 38–39), Mary was sent on to join her brothers. Among the senior McCarthys and the Shrivers, Mary McCarthy saw several more of American Catholicism's many faces, which stood out in sharp relief from her first impressions of the faith gleaned from her mother during the early years in Seattle.

One aspect of Catholicism that made a permanent impression was Grandmother McCarthy's "blood-curdling Catholicism," which was focused on the extermination of Protestantism. McCarthy describes her paternal grandmother as "an aggressive churchgoer," completely lacking in mercy, whose "piety was an act of war against the Protestant ascendancy." Young Mary McCarthy, deprived of books and magazines by her aunt and uncle and hyperconscious of reading opportunities, discovered that the religious magazines next to her grandmother's chair provided "not . . . food for meditation but . . . fresh pretexts for anger; articles attacking birth control, divorce, mixed marriages, Darwin, and secular education." Grandfather McCarthy put yet another face on Catholicism. When he was not engaged in his successful grain business, he attended to his rheumatism, "as though to a pious duty." Grandfather McCarthy's affliction, which "set him apart" and blessed him with "the mark of a special vocation," sent him on therapeutic "pilgrimages to Ste. Anne de Beaupré and Miami" and exempted him from the physical and emotional demands that his wife's bellicose faith might otherwise have made on him (McCarthy 1985, 50, 31–34).

A very different strain of Catholic spirituality dominated in the house down the street, presided over by the Shrivers and Aunt Mary, the third sister of Lizzie McCarthy and Margaret Shriver: a "totalitarian" effort to "[destroy the children's] privacy" (McCarthy 1985, 70–71) so that the house was run along the lines of an orphan asylum or a strict religious order. Uncle Myers was a nonpracticing Protestant, but his dedication to corporal punishment as a means of eradicating all traces of pride and affectation in the McCarthy children actually promoted aspects of this particular strain of Catholic piety. The dangers and attractions of this "house spirituality" became apparent to Mary McCarthy in an episode so emblematic to her that she examined it first in a play that she wrote while at Vassar, then in a *New Yorker* story, and finally in the third chapter of *Memories*. The story concerns a missing tin butterfly, a Cracker Jack prize that belonged to Mary's youngest brother, Sheridan, who was Myers's favorite. After asking Mary to look for the butterfly several times, her aunts finally confided to her that Uncle Myers believed that she had stolen it.

When the butterfly turned up under the tablecloth at Mary's place at the dinner table, she was once again accused and eventually dragged off to the lavatory for the inevitable beating with the razor strop. Uncle Myers tired before Mary confessed her guilt. When Aunt Margaret took over with the hairbrush, she urged Mary repeatedly: "Say you did it, Mary Therese, say you did it." Mary, a bright, competitive student, almost a celebrity at St. Stephen's parochial school, had by this time become a "flaming young Catholic" (Brightman 1992, 29). She outlasted her aunt and uncle and refused to give in, despite the "intercessory note" in Aunt Margaret's entreaties, which had come to assume the cadences of a prayer. "I finally limped up to bed," McCarthy recalls, "with a crazy sense of inner victory like a saint's, for I had not recanted, despite all that they had done or could do to me." She was a bit apprehensive the next morning, wondering what the day would bring, but these misgivings were eclipsed by another set of emotions. When they did not touch her or even allude to the previous evening's punishment, McCarthy confesses that she "walked on air, incredulously and, no doubt, pompously, seeing myself as a figure from legend: my strength was *as* the strength of ten because my *heart* was pure!" She adds that she was subsequently beaten for other offenses "in the normal routine way," but implies that with this victory, she crossed a threshold and her uncle and aunt never attempted to beat her into submission again (McCarthy 1985, 77–78).

The reference to McCarthy as a "flaming young Catholic" calls to mind the third face of Catholicism during her Minneapolis years (1918–1923), encountered in her interactions with the priests and sisters at St. Stephen's

Parish Church and School. McCarthy connects this kind of Catholicism with her mother's faith, "on the whole, a religion of beauty and goodness, however imperfectly realized." She suggests that it was all the more welcome and important to her because it was practiced in such close proximity to the Catholicism that she associated with Grandmother McCarthy's parlor: "a sour, baleful doctrine in which old hates and rancors had been stewing for generations, with ignorance proudly stirring the pot." In 1929, after having spent her adolescent years in Seattle in the care of her Preston grandparents, she stopped in Minneapolis en route to Vassar College. Grandmother McCarthy invited the parish priest, Father Cullen, to meet Mary, expecting clerical support for her view that Vassar, like other non-Catholic women's colleges, was "a den of iniquity." Although she was a self-proclaimed atheist by the time she went to Vassar, McCarthy was nonetheless deeply grateful to Father Cullen, who defended the interests of truth and beauty and the "rare intellectual opportunities" available at Vassar, even in the stale air of Grandmother McCarthy's parlor (McCarthy 1985, 21).

At the end of her prefatory remarks written for *Memories* late in 1956, McCarthy explains why she is "not sorry to have *been* a Catholic." Here she examines vestiges of her Catholic upbringing that remained important to her as a writer and a woman who lived and wrote her conscience, even in her post-Catholic years. Most of the references in this section point to her convent-school years (1923–1925), but some acknowledge the fundamental importance of her prior experience at St. Stephen's (1918–1923). She maintains that it had made a crucial difference to her that she had learned about the lives of the saints and church doctrine as a child "for the glory of God," not as a graduate student intent on unlocking the key to an Italian painting or a poem by John Donne (McCarthy 1985, 26). She expressed gratitude for the Catholic memories of her girlhood that had become part of the fiber of her being:

> the sense of mystery and wonder, ashes put on one's forehead on Ash Wednesday, the blessing of the throat with candles on St. Blaise's Day, the purple palls put on the statues after Passion Sunday, which meant they were hiding their faces in mourning because Christ was going to be crucified, the ringing of the bell at the Sanctus, the burst of lilies at Easter— all this ritual, seeming slightly strange and having no purpose (except the throat-blessing), beyond commemoration of a Person Who had died a long time ago. In these exalted moments of altruism the soul was fired with reverence. (McCarthy 1985, 26–27)

The woman who wrote these words was a far cry from the "flaming young Catholic" who had spontaneously composed a sad, prophetic poem about the pope's death at age 8 ("Alas Pope Benedict is dead, / The sorrowing people said.") and kept it in her desk for a year until the papal death called for an elegy (McCarthy 1985, 62–63). In fact she was the woman who only a few months before had been deflecting the amorous advances of the Harvard theologian Paul Tillich in the card room of the ocean liner *Christoforo Columbo*, "to the tune of pseudo-scientific conversation about sadism, beatings, and biting, and Greek Gods," while Tillich connived to get into her stateroom so that he could see her feet (Brightman 1992, 390–391). McCarthy had moved far beyond the world of St. Stephen's, but she still capitalized "Person Who had died" and she still cherished the almost ineffable aspects of Catholic spirituality that one could only discover from the inside.

It must have been as early as St. Stephen's when McCarthy, precocious as she was, first internalized what she later acknowledged to be "the final usefulness of her Catholic training," that is, "a conception of something prior to and beyond utility," a tolerance for "sheer wastefulness" that non-Catholics found so repellent when they encountered baroque Catholic churches side by side with poverty and slums. From the inside of St. Stephen's Parish Church, between the ages of 6 and 11, McCarthy had seen the saving quality of "sheer wastefulness" (McCarthy 1985, 26). When McCarthy affirms that "it was religion that saved me" from the cruelty and squalor and emptiness of Grandmother McCarthy and the Shrivers, she is not referring to the Catholic church in general but to the priests and sisters of St. Stephen's and the sanctuary provided by the parish church and school. In the school, her gifts and talents were praised: She proudly recalls that she was the outstanding student in her class, as well as the best athlete, the most effective speaker, and the "second most devout." In the parish church, which she only later appraised as ugly, she discovered aesthetics. The mass, litanies, Latin hymns, altar, rosary, ornamented prayer books, votive lamps, and holy cards, which were frequently "cheapened and debased by mass production," were for young Mary McCarthy "the equivalent of Gothic cathedrals and illuminated manuscripts and mystery plays" (McCarthy 1985, 18–19).

McCarthy underscores the importance of competition at St. Stephen's. It was the means employed by the sisters to motivate students: competition with fellow students; with the Protestants at Whittier, the local public school; and with themselves. She speculates that it worked so well, in part, because many of the students were immigrants whose parents were urging them to perform well to get ahead. At St. Stephen's, competition, which extended to devotions, was not only for the sake of personal achievement and status but also to glorify God and show gratitude for the gifts one had received. McCarthy's successes in the various competitions at St. Stephen's bolstered her self-esteem and determined the shape of her dreams. In her memoir *How I Grew*, written when she was in her 70s, McCarthy revisits her Minneapolis years and provides us with a vivid portrait of what it felt like to be a flaming young preadolescent Catholic in the American Midwest in the early 1920s.

> In my case, dreams substituted for thought. The bits and pieces of history and legend I was picking up were fuel for my dreams, going up like bonfires, rather than building blocks for a picture of the world. I dreamed of becoming a Carmelite nun, like the great St. Teresa, who was half my name-saint; it was the reputed harshness of the discipline that appealed to me. For me, excess was attractive almost per se: not to be a mere nun, but to be a *cloistered*, silent, non-teaching nun, in rope sandals with a rope around the waist, continually fasting, and praying two hours a day in her cell. At the same time, not fully satisfied with this effaced, selfless, brown-clad vision, I pictured myself an abbess. Under my able administration were devoutly girded nuns singing the offices and at my right hand a chaplain, like Teresa's St. John of the Cross. (McCarthy 1987, 19)

Given her two name-saints, one can see how and why McCarthy dreamed of following in Teresa's, rather than Mary's, footsteps. At St. Stephen's, Mary showed herself to be on the "Teresa track": She was smart and devout, disciplined, and even powerful in her own way, able to withstand the attacks and temptations doled out by the Shrivers without recanting. I have dwelled on this period in McCarthy's life because it is important to remember the kind of Catholic girl McCarthy was at age 11, when she left Minneapolis and St. Stephen's to live with her maternal grandparents in Seattle. Only then can we appreciate what she means by her statement in *Memories:* "When I left the competitive atmosphere of the parochial school, my religion withered on the stalk" (McCarthy 1985, 19).

In 1923, McCarthy's maternal grandfather, Harold Preston, brought her back to Seattle to the comfortable upper-middle-class life that his successful legal career made possible. During the next two years, the Prestons sent Mary to the Convent of the Sacred Heart at Forest Ridge, north of Seattle, where she was a five-day boarder. McCarthy's experience at Forest Ridge in the mid-1920s was strikingly similar to that of Antonia White at Roehampton roughly a decade before. Subjected to the intense atmosphere and pedagogy of the Society of the Sacred Heart, both girls felt like aliens. At the same time, the religious of the Sacred Heart awakened something in both girls that would encourage them to become writers. Both faced their own moments of crisis and learned important lessons about transgression and flight, which provided them with rich material for very successful memoirs. Two *New Yorker* stories, "The Blackguard" and "C'est le Premier Pas Qui Coûte," examine McCarthy's life at Forest Ridge in painstaking, and frequently humorous, detail, and these stories appeared in revised annotated form in *Memories*. These two stories and a third chapter in *Memories* entitled "Names" depict yet another face of the American Catholic church in the 1920s: the world of the elite boarding schools run by the Society of the Sacred Heart, which, McCarthy quickly discovered, bore almost no resemblance to her past life centered on St. Stephen's Parish in Minneapolis.

Many Catholics have been offended by McCarthy's stories of Forest Ridge. The *New Yorker* heard from this constituency immediately after the publication of the first installment, "The Blackguard" (October 12, 1946), which explores her reaction at 11 to a Jesuit's sermon on the damnation of Protestants that was delivered at a Forest Ridge retreat. Teachings that had been considered unassailably orthodox among Catholics of the 1920s, even the 1930s, became suspect after the Second World War and the GI Bill made Catholic-Protestant interactions more frequent, and, to most upwardly mobile Catholics, more desirable. One such teaching, associated with a letter of St. Cyprian in the third century, was the ancient formula *extra ecclesiam nulla salus:* outside the church there is no salvation. "The Blackguard" depicts McCarthy's younger self grappling with the implications of that teaching for her Protestant grandfather, whom she loved dearly. It tells the truth about her perceptions of the doctrine as a precocious girl while employing irony and humor to convey her adult perspectives on the doctrine and her younger self.

When the Jesuit's sermon made her anxious about her grandfather's salvation, Mary sought the advice of the Mother Superior, Madame MacIllvra, who seemed to anticipate her visit and her questions. This nun, sitting at the pinnacle of authority at Forest Ridge, gently suggested to Mary that "[the sermon], doctrinally, perhaps correct . . . had been wanting in delicacy." She conceded that "the fiery Jesuit," might have been "a missionary celebrity," but he had "lived too long among the Eskimos." McCarthy, who was liberally educated in European history from her convent-school days through Vassar, was familiar with the connection between the Jesuits and casuistry. Drawing on her academic knowledge and her recollections of the true pecking order at Forest Ridge, she playfully—and accurately—reversed the authority structure of the church to place Madame MacIllvra on a higher plane than the Jesuit missionary and made the nun, rather than the Jesuit, a casuist. It was the nun who declared the Jesuit's sermon sound but inappropriate and the nun who found the

loophole not acknowledged by the Jesuit. Full of confidence, the preadolescent Mary McCarthy in the story insists: "Surely this lady, the highest
authority I knew, could find a way out for my grandfather. She could see
that he was a special case, outside the brutal rule of thumb laid down by
the Jesuit" (McCarthy 1985, 88).

Here McCarthy captures the voice of a true child of the Sacred Heart
and the underlying spirit of Sacred Heart convents throughout the world,
which are rarely known for cultivating deference to priests and bishops.
The solution to Mary's problem, and her grandfather's salvation, was
explained to Mary a few days later in a solemn conference that included
Madame MacIllvra; the prefect of studies, Madame Barclay; the convent
librarian; and the chaplain. It was found in a passage in St. Athanasius that
outlined the doctrine of invincible ignorance: No one could be damned
for insufficient knowledge of the church's teachings. Hence, Mary's task
was not, as she had previously thought, to convert her grandfather but
rather to preserve the status quo: her grandfather's long-standing attachment to the Presbyterian Church, his reputation for "a kind of rigid and
fantastic probity," and his fundamental ignorance of the fine points of the
Catholic faith (McCarthy 1985, 91, 89).

Despite, or even because of, its playfulness, the story touched a nerve
in the Catholic community, which had only recently been forced to reexamine its former posture of superiority and separatism vis-à-vis WASP
America. In the italicized comments added to the story when it was repub-
lished eleven years later in *Memories,* McCarthy provided the context for
her critics' adverse reactions to the original story. She reminded readers of
the so-called Boston heresy case, which had been front-page news in the
New York Times and had also warranted articles in *Newsweek, Life,* and
Time during Holy Week 1949. Father Leonard Feeney, S.J., affiliated with
the St. Benedict Center in Cambridge, Massachusetts, and his newly constituted religious group, the Slaves of the Immaculate Heart of Mary, had
caused public disturbances at open-air meetings on the Boston Common,
and even in classes at Boston College, by preaching that there was no salvation outside the church. The official letter from the Holy Office in
Rome (August 8, 1952) that was intended to resolve the controversy
sounded more than a bit like Madame MacIllvra's approach to the Jesuit's
sermon and the thorny issue of Mary's grandfather's salvation. It reaf-
firmed the orthodoxy of *extra ecclesiam nulla salus* and then added a loophole, albeit a different one than Madame MacIllvra had originally
suggested to Mary. The papal letter reminded Catholics that one did not
have to be Catholic to be "in the church." "Implicit desire," rather than full
membership in the church, provided an alternative avenue to salvation for

those who had insufficient knowledge of Catholic belief and practice (Massa 1999, 21–37; Silk 1988, 70–86).

In *Memories,* Mary responded to the protestations of many readers who wrote to her and to the *New Yorker* insisting that the sermon in the story was a fabrication. McCarthy conceded that "it could not be preached here today—not since the Father Feeney case brought matters to a head," but even as a self-proclaimed post-Catholic, McCarthy felt the need to say more to clarify the church's position. She pointed out that in traditionally Catholic countries such as Spain, and even in America in 1957, priests were still free to cling to a strict constructionist position on Cyprian and "believe privately that Protestants are damned, good and bad alike" (McCarthy 1985, 99). Even in a memoir intended to explain why she was no longer a Catholic, McCarthy bore the earmarks of the "flaming young Catholic" she had become at St. Stephen's shortly after she reached the age of reason.

Precisely because McCarthy appeared to care so much about clarifying what Catholics believed and what she had received from the church during her girlhood years, her most explicit departure story, "C'est le Premier Pas Qui Coûte," published in the July 12, 1952, issue of the *New Yorker,* came as a rude shock to many upper-middle-class Catholic readers. In "The Blackguard," McCarthy had paved the way by suggesting that the boundaries of the church were not as clearly defined as they might appear, nor was its clerical authority structure unavoidable and unassailable. "C'est le Premier Pas Qui Coûte" took the next step and related in meticulous detail, with grace and humor, how and why McCarthy had left the church at age 12. McCarthy begins her second memoir, *How I Grew,* published exactly thirty years after her first, with the statement: "I was born as a mind during 1925, my bodily birth having taken place in 1912" (McCarthy 1987, 1). The birth of McCarthy's mind and her adult post-Catholic identity trace their origins to a brief period on the cusp of adolescence toward the end of McCarthy's second year at Forest Ridge (1924–1925).

"C'est le Premier Pas Qui Coûte" is one of the stories that has been cited as an example of McCarthy's lack of veracity, her confessed habit of public lying. It has given some critics an occasion to dismiss her as a bitter ex-Catholic who has relinquished her right to speak from or for the church. But if we think of McCarthy's life-writings as a kind of *Pilgrim's Progress,* a guide for readers seeking to understand the spiritual and intellectual journeys required of some Catholics earlier in the century, then another approach to this controversial story opens up for us. "C'est le Premier Pas Qui Coûte" is the story of how McCarthy learned to fashion her own truth and construct her own public identity as she sought to negotiate safe passage from the comfortable world of St. Stephen's to the intimidating, often intractable world of Forest Ridge, where none of what she had learned at St. Stephen's made any sense at all. McCarthy's arrival at Forest Ridge meant crossing a threshold into another Catholic world with its own rules, values, and aesthetics, one that revolved around the lives and needs of Catholic girls and the women who taught them.

McCarthy's description of Forest Ridge calls to mind Antonia White's fictional Lippington: hermetic, intense, infused with "a tumult of emotion," but above all, the stage for "a great religious drama, which was also all passion and caprice, in which salvation was the issue and God's rather sultanlike and elusive favor was besought, scorned, despaired of, connived for, importuned." The nuns were powerful women: "Like all truly intellectual women, they were in spirit romantic desperados. They despised organizational heretics of the stamp of Luther and Calvin, but the great atheists and sinners were the heroes of the costume picture they taught as a subject called history" (McCarthy 1985, 92–93).

The nuns at the Sacred Heart convent at Forest Ridge, enamored of Marlowe, Baudelaire, and especially Byron, passed on these exotic tastes to their students. When Madame Barclay, a legendary nun rumored to have studied at the Sorbonne, proclaimed Mary "just like Lord Byron, brilliant but unsound" in the presence of her classmates, a whole new world of possibilities opened up for her. Forest Ridge was not a meritocracy. At St. Stephen's, McCarthy had persuaded the parish priest to confirm her ahead of her age group because of her extensive knowledge of the catechism and her endless stores of perseverance (McCarthy 1985, 94–95, 107). At Forest Ridge, the key to success and recognition completely eluded her. However much she resembled Byron to Madame Barclay, she could not win the friendship of the most popular girls or the pink ribbon awarded for good conduct. Finally, during her second year, she vowed that she would become an entity at Forest Ridge, whatever the price. As she put it: "If I could not win fame by goodness, I was ready to do it by badness." "People are always asking me how I came to lose my faith, imagining a period of deep inward struggle," McCarthy writes in her forties, with the air of someone who has frequently dined out on her Catholic girlhood. "The truth is the whole momentous project simply jumped at me, ready-made, out of one of Madame MacIllvra's discourses. I had decided to do it before I knew what it was, when it was merely an interweaving of words, lose-your-faith, like the ladder made of sheets on which the daring girl had descended into the arms of her Romeo" (McCarthy 1985, 111).

Young women were taken very seriously at Forest Ridge, so seriously that they were exposed to their teachers' intellectual tastes and passions, not merely the doctrinal party line in the catechism. They knew the respect that some of the nuns had for atheists such as Lord Byron, both despite and because he was "brilliant but unsound." When 12-year-old Mary McCarthy confided to Madame MacIllvra that she had lost her faith, the latter "*summoned* Father Dennis," the chaplain from the neighboring Jesuit college, while she prayed for Mary's faith to return (my italics). Mary saw her plan to become Somebody at Forest Ridge working so perfectly that it almost frightened her. She realized, not for the last time, that "once the convent machinery had got into motion, there was no way of stopping it. . . . It was like the mills of the gods" (McCarthy 1985, 113). So she took advantage of her isolation in her cubicle awaiting Father Dennis to construct a plausible atheist worldview without the aid of even the most fundamental reference books. Almost miraculously, she discovered that "doubts that I had hurriedly stowed away, like contraband in a bureau drawer, came back to me, reassuringly."

The first doubt that the orphaned schoolgirl unpacked concerned the afterlife: "I found that I had always been a little suspicious of the life after death. Perhaps it was really true that the dead just rotted and I would never rejoin my parents in Heaven?" From there it was an easy step to questioning the resurrection of the body, where basic biology and the existence of cannibals provided many objections that visiting priests had been unable to answer. By the time Father Dennis had appeared, "elation had replaced fear" and Mary was in the greenroom preparing to play the part of the precocious young atheist with doubts and arguments "so remarkable in one of my years." She had become a modern female atheist version of 12-year-old Jesus in the temple among the teachers; she reminded herself of Jesus in the Gospel of Luke (2:42–52): "And all that heard Him were astonished at His Wisdom and His answers" (McCarthy 1985, 114–116).

The scene in the parlor with Father Dennis combines the perspectives of McCarthy at 12 and McCarthy at 40. Father Dennis is not a powerful authority figure but Madame MacIllvra's subordinate, "a sort of spiritual factotum, like an upper servant in an apron." He looks unhealthy, "colorless and dry," "as though he had spent his life in his confessional box." When McCarthy's question about whether cannibals undermined the doctrine of the resurrection of the body was dismissed as a scholastic question for which the church had answers, Mary "began to be suspicious of him, in the manner of adolescents. What, I asked myself shrewdly, was the Church trying to hide from me?" (McCarthy 1985, 116–117).

None of Father Dennis's rhetorical strategies to trick her into submission (viz., "*Think!* Don't you know?" and "You consider Our Lord a liar, then?") had the desired effect. Mary realized that she was winning her first theological argument, with a Jesuit chaplain, no less. Father Dennis "was looking down at [her] with a grave, troubled expression, as if he, too, were suddenly conscious of a gulf between [them], a gulf that could not be bridged by words." Then, McCarthy explains, "the awesome thought struck me that perhaps I *had* lost my faith." She asked for Father Dennis's help, "aware that this was the right thing to say but meaning it nevertheless." It is at this point in the narrative that McCarthy relates a sensation frequently found in Catholic women's departure narratives, one that signals the moment of crossing over. It is the sensation of being divided in two, having the uncanny ability to experience reality as two people, one watching the other and literally *witnessing* a profound experience that will change everything (McCarthy 1985, 117–118).

One side of her looked on with genuine interest while the other side found holes in every one of Father Dennis's arguments grounded in the uniqueness of Jesus Christ, the perseverance of the Catholic faith, and natural law. The second side was on edge, "anxious and aghast at the turn the interview was taking," but still intent upon following the discussion wherever it might lead. Mary noticed with some surprise that she had developed a "comradely" feeling for her opponent and sincerely hoped to show him "the new possibilities" that her questions and doubts opened up for her. Father Dennis concentrated on diagnosing the extent of Mary's spiritual decline and putting her doubts and arguments to rest as efficiently as possible. When he finally asked whether she doubted the existence of God, she admitted that she did, "in exultant agony, knowing that it was true." Unconvinced by the argument for the unmoved mover, Mary asked, "Why can't something in matter be the uncaused cause? Like electricity?" Father Dennis surrendered and enjoined her to "give up reading that atheistic filth" (McCarthy 1985, 118–121).

After the interview, Father Dennis's stock plummeted and Mary's rose dramatically. At Forest Ridge, Mary became a personage. No longer did she fear that "the convent did not know *who I was*"; she was universally acknowledged to be "the girl that a Jesuit had failed to convince" (McCarthy 1985, 110, 121). When she left school later that year, she brought her newfound identity with her, along with a growing confidence in her own rhetorical and intellectual powers. There is a sense in which the writing of her memories, first in stories and then in the book that appeared in 1957, constitutes the culmination of the process begun at Forest Ridge. She had started out innocently enough with a natural desire for the school to know who she really was, but this had led circuitously to her own discovery of a truth and a self quite different from the one that she had so ardently wished to disclose.

Her realization that there were at least two sides to the traditional arguments for the faith that Father Dennis had articulated transported young Mary McCarthy to a new frontier inhabited by adolescent girls and women who have discovered the two-sidedness of life. In a section of her groundbreaking study *In a Different Voice,* Carol Gilligan uses McCarthy's *Memories* to explore and illustrate young women's moral dilemmas. She describes a classroom discussion that took place at a woman's college when students examined two passages, one from McCarthy's *Memories* and the other from Joyce's *A Portrait of the Artist as a Young Man.* Gilligan relates that the female college students wanted to emulate Joyce's Stephen Daedalus, who could declare courageously and unequivocally: "I will not serve that in which I no longer believe, whether it calls itself my home, my fatherland or my church: and I will try to express myself in some mode of life or art as freely as I can and as wholly as I can, using for my defense the only arms I allow myself to use—silence, exile cunning" (quoted in Gilligan 1993, 157).

Almost despite themselves, however, the college women in Gilligan's example found their deepest instincts more accurately portrayed by a quotation from "Yellowstone Park," a section of McCarthy's *Memories* devoted to her experience at Annie Wright, the Episcopal boarding school in Tacoma where she finished her education after Forest Ridge and prepared for Vassar. The quotation describes a decision McCarthy made in her teens to tell a lie in order to save the feelings of a well-meaning bystander: "I felt caught in a dilemma that was new to me then but which has since become horribly familiar: the trap of adult life, in which you are held, wriggling, powerless to act because you can see both sides" (McCarthy 1985, 189; Gilligan 1993, 156).

McCarthy's obvious pleasure in her reputation as the bad girl, "the girl that a Jesuit had failed to convince," suggests that she, like the female college students in Gilligan's study, might prefer making simple unequivocal declarations and clean breaks rather than embracing the two-sided perspective that she claimed as her fate. At Annie Wright, McCarthy, already an atheist, went to mass in the nearby town with the other Catholic students. She also studied the Old Testament in Sacred Study sessions with Mrs. Keator, an Episcopal bishop's widow. Writing thirty years later, she affirmed that the words of Micah ("And what doth the Lord require of thee, but to do justly, and to love mercy, and to walk humbly with thy God?") still moved her. So did her memories of morning and evening chapel services. She "loved the hymns and the litanies and hearing my principal intone at nightfall: 'We have left undone those things which we ought to have done; And we have done those things which we ought not to have done; And there is no health in us.'" Looking back, McCarthy realized that childhood injustices "had made me a rebel against authority, but they also prepared me to fall in love with justice, the first time I encountered it" (McCarthy 1985, 167–168).

Mary McCarthy's immediate and enduring response to the words of Micah, the comfort that she found in the litanies and hymns, her gratitude for the Catholic culture she first encountered at St. Stephen's: these components of McCarthy's identity defined her just as surely as her public atheism. Seeing both sides had some positive implications. One could *choose* to see both sides, whether or not the sides seemed compatible. McCarthy could choose to claim explicitly Catholic tastes, memories, and metaphors even as she self-consciously constructed herself as a post-Catholic. Of course, this gave some of her readers reason to hope that her loss of faith was only a stopover on a much longer pilgrimage and that she would eventually return to the fold. In the introductory section of *Memories*, McCarthy quotes a letter from John Dunne, pastor of St. Peter and Paul's Church, Wilmington, California, dated July 16, 1952. Father Dunne assured her that she would find her spiritual home, indeed that she had found it. In a section of the letter that was not quoted in *Memories*, Dunne reflected on the significance of McCarthy's protagonist's spiritual journey depicted in her *New Yorker* story "C'est le Premier Pas Qui Coûte": "She found social status by leaving it—even disdaining it. She will also find the ultimate truth of the Church (and of God) in the same way. . . . Faith and doubt are inseparable. . . . the meeting of opposites—and all that it leads to—conflicts not solved but suffered—contained within you until you become the truth distilled from them" (Series I, 13.10, Mary McCarthy Papers).

In McCarthy's autobiographical writings from her first collection of stories, *The Company She Keeps* (1942), onward, she depicts a female spirituality that is at once both vehemently atheist and undeniably Catholic. This was an uncomfortable position to maintain. In *Bare Ruined Choirs* (1972), Garry Wills describes the two options available to American Catholics of the 1940s and 1950s, the period during which McCarthy was turning her personal recollections into autobiographical stories and *Memories*. Wills's characterization of the mindset of educated American Catholics of this era, just preceding the Second Vatican Council, is pertinent here.

> A protective skein was . . . woven all around us—not forming a time capsule, since it kept us at a far remove from time; an *un*time capsule, a fibry cocoon of rites and custom in which we were to lie, a chrysalis till we broke though into promised Reality after death. . . .

For people brought up inside this total weave of Catholic life, it did seem that departure from one aspect of the faith meant forfeiting all one's connections with religion. A single authority ran through each aspect of one's upbringing. That authority stood behind every practice, endorsing them all. To doubt anywhere was to doubt everywhere. (Wills 1972, 19)

Wills maintains that some people who have been raised Catholic escape the constraints by embracing "an opposite totalism . . . belief that reality was just outside, one must flail through to it with one blow" (Wills 1972, 20). Raised in this context of either/or, Mary McCarthy discovered that her experience of her own Catholic girlhood demanded an alternative perspective: the ability to embrace two sides. This courageous and public ambivalence impressed some readers and gave hope to those, like Father Dunne, who considered McCarthy a deeply spiritual writer. Mary McCarthy, the post-Catholic author of *Memories,* purposely chose the most uncomfortable niche for herself, just as her 12-year-old self had actively constructed the crisis of faith that led to her intellectual awakening. McCarthy found her niche on the margins of the Catholic world described so eloquently by Garry Wills, a world dominated by two totalisms that seemed to occupy all available space and foreclose on the possibility of any new questions and answers (especially those posed and posited by girls and women).

McCarthy did not return to the fold, as some of her readers had hoped; however, the Catholic atheism that she embraced for the rest of her life bore traces of the church of her mother and the priests and sisters at St. Stephen's. Thanks to her Vassar education, McCarthy knew all about Pascal's wager (in which he decided to act as if God existed, just in case) and rejected it as "too prudential." "I prefer not to play it safe," she affirmed toward the end of her introduction to *Memories* (McCarthy 1985, 27). Instead, she adopted a personal ethic and spirituality that grew directly out of the Catholic education that she chose not to repudiate when she embraced atheism. It is best expressed in one of her early stories, "Ghostly Father, I Confess," in the collection entitled *The Company She Keeps* (1942). The protagonist, Meg Sargent, is an Irish-American Catholic girl with a Protestant father who publicly lost her faith as a freshman at a convent school. Years later, her Protestant husband sends her to a psychiatrist to help rid her of any residual Catholic scruples. Despite some sleight of hand with the facts—for example, the substitution of a Protestant father for a Protestant grandfather—the story is true. The part about the psychiatrist is based on McCarthy's marriage to Edmund Wilson (1938–1945).

In therapy, McCarthy's alter ego struggles with the question of whether she would have lost her faith if she had not had strong, if implicit, paternal support for the idea. Her psychiatrist, Dr. James, urges her to "stop belittling herself" because "it doesn't make any difference what you would have done under some different circumstances." Meg smiles and tells herself that once again her learned doctor has missed the point. Losing her faith in early adolescence had not been "a real test."

> That was what she feared and desired, the real test, the ordeal, the burning tenement house with the baby asleep on the fifth floor (would you rush in and save it if there were absolutely no one looking, no God in heaven to welcome your charred but purified spirit, no newspaper account the next day, YOUNG WOMAN DIES SAVING SLUM CHILD; if there were nothing in the world but you and the baby and the fire, would you say not to yourself that it was undoubtedly too late, that the baby must already have suffocated, that the fire was not serious, that the baby was not there at all but in the house across the street?). (McCarthy 1942, 273–274)

This is what being an atheist looked like to Mary McCarthy at age 30 as she took her need to ask the uncomfortable questions, first recognized at age 12, to a new level. Her stories, and especially *Memories of a Catholic Girlhood,* provide something close to documentary evidence of what the church at mid-century looked like to a former flaming young Catholic— now post-Catholic—a woman who had crossed over and found herself on the outside. The metaphor introduced at the end of "C'est le Premier Pas Qui Coûte" captures both the moment of crossing and McCarthy's perspective on it decades later. After 12-year-old Mary feigned a reconversion to the faith (in a dream to avoid giving Father Dennis "the credit") she received communion with her schoolmates, knowing that the nuns seated behind her were "rejoicing, as good nuns should, over the reclamation of a soul." But the experience of basking, at last, in the nuns' approval and belonging among the personages at her school represented only one aspect of this pivotal moment. From a completely different vantage point, from deep within herself, she heard a different voice. "My own chief sensation was one of detached surprise at how far I had come from my old mainstays, as once, when learning to swim, I had been doing the dead-man's float and looked back, raising my doused head, to see my water wings drifting, far behind me, on the lake's surface" (McCarthy 1985, 123).

Mary Gordon

Both Antonia White and Mary McCarthy wrote as an act of resistance against the traditionalism and insularity of the church and their convent boarding schools as they had experienced them during the second and third decades of the twentieth century. Mary Gordon's first novel, *Final Payments* (1978), takes place in an entirely different church than the one presupposed by the authors of *Frost in May* and *Memories of a Catholic Girlhood*. The Catholic church in *Final Payments* is radically altered, still reeling from the changes that followed Vatican II. Gordon writes from the margins of a spiritual community in which the adult members clearly recall the certainty, changelessness, and exclusive claims of the pre–Vatican II church, but these recollections are eclipsed by their awareness that whatever the future might bring, nothing would ever be the same again. By the late 1970s, when *Final Payments* was published, the American Catholic church had crossed a threshold. A debilitating "Vatican lag" had replaced the invigorating spirit of renewal, akin to time travel, unleashed by the Council in the mid-1960s. In 1987, the prominent American Catholic theologian Richard McBrien described the characteristics of the post-conciliar Catholic church:

> It has been a church marked by a weakening of its authority structure, by a decline in traditional devotional practices, by instability in marriage, by theological dissent and catechetical uncertainty, by a decrease in attendance at weekly Mass and an even sharper decline in the reception of the sacrament of Reconciliation, and especially by a precipitous dropoff in vocations to the ordained priesthood and religious life. (McBrien 1987, vi)

Gordon's ability to evoke the atmosphere within the American Catholic community during the awkward transition to the post–Vatican II church helps to explain why this first novel, a female bildungsroman, sold 60,000 copies in hardcover and more than a million in paperback. American Catholics of the 1970s experienced the truth expressed by Gordon's character Father Mulcahy, who lamented that many older Catholics felt "like someone's broken into their home and stolen all the furniture" (Gordon 1979, 103). When the novel first appeared, readers could respond viscerally to the private jokes exchanged by protagonist Isabel Moore and her two girlhood friends Eleanor Lavery and Liz O'Brien, who were born in the mid-1940s in a middle-class parish in Queens. Jokes about activist nuns "in Ship'n Shore blouses who made [them] want to join the Green Berets just to be on the opposite side" and "priests with no sense of irony losing their virginity in their forties" (Gordon 1979, 13) cemented the bonds between Gordon and her readers just as they did between the characters Isabel and Liz.

This kind of humor represents an important vehicle for understanding the nature and meaning of the departures negotiated by Isabel, Eleanor, and Liz. In the midst of the turbulence and change of the late 1960s and early 1970s, when coming-of-age metaphors were being applied to the church at large, transgression and departure were becoming harder to recognize, perhaps even harder to achieve. The spiritual journey of Gordon's protagonist Isabel Moore illustrates the ambiguity of Catholic girls' and women's departures in the post–Vatican II church. The novel opens with the funeral of Isabel's father, who had been a professor of medieval literature at St. Aloysius College from 1934 to 1962. The funeral represents a major boundary-crossing for Isabel, who has been sole caregiver for her father between his stroke in 1962 and his death in 1973. Now she is finally free at age 30 to start her own life. Like Monica Baldwin, Isabel is a female Catholic Rip Van Winkle, a woman who has endured a substantial period of seclusion within the constraints of an exclusively Catholic setting, only to emerge during a period of unprecedented social change. The personal pilgrimage of the fictional Isabel Moore parallels that of Monica Baldwin. In both cases, their long seclusion and the particular challenges they face when they return to the world are only explicable in terms of their Catholic upbringing.

Final Payments is a meditation on Catholic women's departures since Vatican II. Initially Isabel's task appears to be rather straightforward (especially to the non-Catholics she meets when she flees the old neighborhood): She must decide what she wants to do with her life, and perhaps make up for the time she "lost" caring for her invalid father. In order to do this, she must politely but firmly refuse the kind offers to find her a position that keeps her in Queens as a nurse, companion, secretary, or teacher within the Catholic community. This literal departure turns out to be fairly easy to achieve. Isabel sells her father's house, her only possession, and with Liz's help gets a short-term job assessing the effectiveness of a pilot project that uses government funds to provide care for the elderly in private homes.

Isabel's recollections, told in the first person, confirm that her physical exodus from the Catholic ghetto is by no means her first move away from the church. During her father's eleven-year illness, while many in the surrounding Catholic community considered her "an-honest-to-God saint" (Gordon 1979, 46) for caring for her father alone, Isabel only pretends to go to church. Every Sunday from eleven until noon, when she is supposed to be at mass at Assumption Parish Church, she takes the same carefully timed walk to Dwyer Park; she spends rainy Sundays at Milt's luncheonette. Skipping mass is a necessary expression of her attitude toward the tenets of the Catholic religion. Isabel left Catholic beliefs behind in high school. As if in response to an inquisitive member of the parish who suggests that she try to pray, she explains: "It is possible to pray for faith when one is grappling with a crisis of faith, but when loss of faith comes gradually, as it did to me, the issue seems plain and no longer compelling; no prayer is possible" (Gordon 1979, 16–17).

There is a crisis, shown in a flashback to a time before the action of the novel begins, but it is not exactly a crisis of faith. It is closer to Nanda Grey's moment of truth in the convent parlor in *Frost in May:* a confrontation with her adoring and implacable Catholic father who is suddenly faced with her lapse of purity and good judgment. One summer afternoon when Isabel is 19, her father finds her in bed with her boyfriend David Lowe, Professor Moore's star student. Although she is overwhelmed by her father's reaction to the event ("the waters of my act surrounded me"), she cannot and will not confess it (Gordon 1979, 20). She goes to confession under protest, but—unbeknown to her father—she omits the particular sexual sin she is supposed to confess. She does not enter a confessional for the next eleven years. Toward the end of the narrative, Isabel indulges in one of her "orgies of self-abnegation" (Gordon 1979, 56) and returns to confession. Again, she approaches the sacrament against her will, coerced by Margaret Casey, her father's former housekeeper, whom Isabel dismissed at age 13 when she realized that Margaret hoped to marry her father.

This second confession and the decision to do penance by living with Margaret, whom she abhors, are Isabel's gut response to the pain that accompanies two sexual liaisons embarked on shortly after she moves out of the old neighborhood. This time, Isabel tells the priest about the sexual sins that she is supposed to confess. Still, the effect is comic. "The comedy of Catholic life," Gordon writes in an autobiographical essay entitled "Getting Here from There," "comes . . . like all other comedy, from the gap between the ideal and the real. In my case the ideal was so high and the real was so real that the collision was bound to be risible" (Gordon 1992, 167). Drawing on her own experience of the comedy inherent in American Catholic life and worship in the 1970s, Gordon mines this confession scene for its comic potential. Ultimately, it is the irony and dark humor revealed in this incident that later reemerges and helps Isabel discern that departure from Margaret and all she represents—notably the mortal sin of excessive self-abnegation—is the only route to spiritual maturity.

Even though she is numb from the emotional travail brought about by her two messy sexual affairs and the strain of living a complex adult life after eleven years spent deferring all personal decisions, Isabel does register an immediate negative reaction to the interior of Margaret's parish church, St. Stanislaus's. Gordon uses the scene to underscore the comedy in some efforts to update Catholic worship in the wake of Vatican II and the pastoral tone-deafness behind some versions of sacramental reform. St. Stanislaus's was "built to look like [a firehouse], impromptu, unconsidered, American." There is a dark wooden statue of the virgin, but it is so much a product of the times that it appears to have been "invented yesterday." Isabel cannot bring herself to pray in the presence of that image. The sterility and banality of the church, which contains nothing inspiring or beautiful, leaves her alone with the task at hand:

> I knew what I had to tell. I knew what they wanted me to acknowledge. I would say what they wanted me to say—that I had committed adultery, that I had been away from the sacraments. But I would keep the most important thing, the only important thing, to myself. I had been selfish. I could have devoured the world with my greed. But this they were not interested in hearing. And for this I had devised my own repentance. (Gordon 1979, 273–274)

Upon entering the flimsy plywood confessional, in which the patently uncharming Polish priest's face was clearly visible, Isabel discovers that even her modest strategy of compliance with Margaret's wishes might be hung up on technicalities. The priest resents her attempts to confess while he is giving his blessing and asks Isabel not to interrupt him. He rebuffs her when she begins with the words she has always used ("Bless me, Father for I have sinned") with a gruff statement: "We don't begin like that anymore." She hopes to make things easier by pretending to agree with the priest that her absence from the sacraments for eleven years is sinful. To herself (and to readers), she explains the other side of the issue: "If I had believed and had not gone, then it would have been sinful. . . . I cannot confess my loss of faith because it is still lost to me." Slapped with what she suspects is a generic penance for the lapsed ("Think carefully about your future and say the Lord's Prayer"), Isabel concludes that the sacrament is a sham: "I understood that I had bored him and I understood his boredom. The whole exercise seemed to lack importance. . . . There was no sense of seriousness here, no sense of inevitability. I did not believe that anything had happened and I did not believe that *he* believed it" (Gordon 1979, 274–276).

Isabel perfunctorily ends with the "Act of Contrition" as she remembers it. Again, the priest interrupts her, instructing her instead to read one of the new versions printed in green on a laminated card decorated with daisies. In large print below the three updated prayers are the words *"Remember: Tomorrow is the First Day of the Rest of Your Life."* Isabel kneels at the altar saying her penance "to no one"; "I could not believe that any-one was interested in what I was saying." She had left the church behind in high school, but with the security of knowing that it was there for her if she ever wanted to return. Now she has to face the fact that the Catholic church that she had shared with her father, the one symbolized by the *Missa Recitata* and Holbein's portrait of Thomas More hanging over her father's desk, is dead (Gordon 1979, 276–277, 31, 40). She has no sanctu-ary; the only conceivable option is to continue the penance she has assigned herself and take care of Margaret for the rest of her days.

In the weeks that follow, Isabel mortifies her flesh, actively by binging on junk food until her body is repulsive to her and passively by allowing Margaret's hairdresser Dorothy Kowalski to give her an Annette Funicello haircut. When Father Mulcahy visits during Lent, he urges her to leave Margaret and not to feel guilty about reneging on the commitment that she has made, for after all, "even God breaks promises." When this line of argument proves unpersuasive, Mulcahy changes tack. He firmly advises Isabel to lose weight and get a better haircut because wasting one's beauty is a sin against the Fifth Commandment. Isabel quibbles, asking what denying one's beauty has to do with killing. Mulcahy replies that "it means slow deaths, too" (Gordon 1979, 297).

This exchange leads to a moment of truth with Margaret that brings clarity and closure and allows Isabel to break out of her father's church once and for all. When Father Mulcahy is out of earshot, Margaret, who would never confront him to his face, insinuates that it is not safe for Isabel to be alone with him after he has had a glass of wine. Isabel instinctively jumps to the defense of this gentle and vulnerable man who was her father's dearest friend and still is a second father to her. She realizes that this is the perfect moment to embrace Mulcahy's advice and suddenly, quite naturally, reverts to her adolescent self that has been lost during her years as a caregiver and a penitent, the part of her that "could have led armies" at 13 (Gordon 1979, 33). Margaret tries to reawaken the vulnera-ble, abject, self-hating Isabel who has fled her own life to care for her. That self has evaporated at the sound of Margaret's first attack on Mulcahy and has left the outspoken irreverent younger Isabel to fight the battle. Margaret's passive-aggressive reference to her own poverty and defense-lessness, which has effectively elicited Isabel's guilt and self-abnegation during the preceding weeks, no longer functions in this way. Instead, it reminds Isabel of a scripture passage from Mark (14:7) that she has not thought about in a long time: "For the poor you will always have with you."

In an aside, Isabel takes a moment to pay tribute to the Catholic edu-cation that she jokes about with Liz and Eleanor: "It is one of the marvels of a Catholic education that the impulse of a few words can bring whole narratives to light with an immediacy and clarity that are utterly absorbing." Suddenly Isabel finds herself deeply contemplating a scene with Jesus at the house of Mary and Martha. Mary opens a jar of precious ointment—called "spikenard" in the Catholic version of the Bible that she had studied as a girl—and, despite the protestations of Judas about the poor, wipes the feet of Jesus with her hair. It does not matter that Isabel conflates Mary with the unnamed woman in Bethany and confuses John 11:2, where Mary wipes Jesus' feet with ointment and her hair, with Mark 14:3, where a woman anoints his head with ointment. What matters is how the passage, dormant in her imagination for over a decade, comes alive for her at just the right moment. Isabel, who had so recently showed such contempt for her own hair and body, suddenly sees the meaning of her future inscribed within the scripture passage. "What Christ was saying, what he meant, was that the pleasures of that hair, that ointment, must be taken. Because the accidents of death would deprive us soon enough. We must not deprive ourselves, our loved ones, of the luxury of our extravagant affections. We must try not to second-guess death by refusing to love the ones we loved in favor of the anonymous poor" (Gordon 1979, 297–298).

Isabel finally understands why she left Hugh, the man she loves, and why she fled the company of her closest friends, Liz and Eleanor, to live a drab penitential life with Margaret. She wanted to be called a "saint," as she had been by Delaney, the family lawyer, and the "faceless priests" at her father's funeral. She knows how to be a saint: simply give up your self. There is "safety" and "certainty" in that course of action. One need only sacrifice love and the pleasures associated with being loved for one's whole self: mind, soul, *and body.* In this moment of meditation in Margaret's aggressively ugly kitchen, Isabel understands the power that she has given Margaret, her chosen vehicle of self-mortification. She realizes that she is being led—by scripture, by Father Mulcahy, and by every instinct that she values—to depart from Margaret and the temptation to surrender to the inappropriate demands of universal Christian love. She must return to the messy world where she is loved for her whole self and where she has the opportunity to love others passionately for themselves: "I knew now I must open the jar of ointment. I must open my life. . . . I must leave" (Gordon 1979, 298–299).

A few days later, on Holy Saturday, Eleanor and Liz come to collect Isabel, who has devised a new penance for herself, one that will honor her father's wishes that Margaret be taken care of as well as her own resolutions for the future. She writes a check to Margaret for $20,000, all that remains from the sale of her father's house. Still overweight, still wearing a bubble haircut that looks and feels like a football helmet, she is nonethe-less transfigured: "I was light now; my body was high again, and dexterous, and clever." She is beyond Margaret's power to hurt or coerce her. She rides off at dawn in the company of her best friends; their friendship is as "solid" as the laughter that envelops them (Gordon 1979, 306–307).

Final Payments is a more purely fictional narrative than either Frost in May or Memories of a Catholic Girlhood, but the departures depicted in Gordon's novel are no less true than those in the other two works. Readers have responded to the truth and consistency in Gordon's depictions of Catholic women's departures and diaspora over the years. (In fact, the response was so intense that some of her devoted readers were not ready for her third novel, Men and Angels, in which Gordon ventured beyond the Catholic counterculture.) In a 1997 interview with her former student Sandy Asirvatham, Gordon describes a core group within her audience that has been present since Final Payments first appeared in 1978: "There's a kind of reader whom I value enormously and whom I'm very touched by, and I find her when I travel across the country: a middle-aged, college-educated woman—probably not a real intellectual, but a serious reader—who feels like I'm saying things she's always had in her heart" (Asirvatham 2002, 172).

Gordon, who is never careless with her words, certainly didn't omit the adjective "Catholic" here by accident. She has made it clear that she does not wish to be considered "a Catholic writer," at least not until and unless John Updike is treated primarily as a Protestant writer (Lee 1997, 223). Still, the truth that Gordon tells in her various writings has special meaning for Catholic women, who constitute a core group within the readership described above. Catholic female readers have long recognized the importance of fiction for saying things about women that need saying in a church known for curtailing women's speech and revising or rejecting their personal narratives. Catholic women have learned that it can be more expedient to tell the truth in a story or a joke rather than a personal nar-rative, if the latter is vulnerable to expurgation and censorship. They have learned to look to (and in) fiction for the narratives that tell the whole truth about Catholic women. Catholic feminists can say things in fiction that they could not say with impunity in nonfiction. In books published by most Catholic presses, there is a great deal about Catholic women's lives that still cannot be said at all, even in the twenty-first century.

This makes the remarkable consistency in Gordon's treatment of Catholic women's departures all the more impressive. Later works, such as her autobiographical essays in Good Boys and Dead Girls (1991) and Seeing through Places (2000) and her memoir The Shadow Man (1996), help us to appreciate the depth and complexity of the departures at the heart of *Final Payments;* they do not prompt readers to doubt their truth. Like many Catholic women of her generation, who were old enough to have memories of the church before and after Vatican II, Gordon has been a flaming young Catholic, a Catholic in diaspora, and, most recently, a returnee who has come back on her own terms. This means that she incorporates in herself and her writings many different perspectives on being Catholic and a woman. In post–Vatican II Catholic women's writings, the two-sidedness that we have observed in the narratives of Baldwin, White, and McCarthy gives way to the many-sidedness of Gordon and Mary Daly.

Mary Gordon is Isabel Moore and she isn't. In real life, it is her father who dies when she is young (age 7); she is raised by her Irish-Italian American mother and a large extended family. Within that family, she had ample opportunity to be caregiver, at age 12, for both her grandmother, who lay dying after a stroke and colon cancer, and her mother, who suffered from depression and alcoholism. Isabel's attempts to cultivate a spirituality of selflessness and mortification of the flesh in her required tasks of caring for the sick is grounded in the author's own girlhood experiences. Like Isabel, Mary Gordon grew up in the Catholic ghetto. She reports that until college virtually everyone she knew was Catholic:

> The tailor and the man who ran the candy store were Jews, and the women who worked in the public library were Protestants, but you allowed them only the pleasantries. Real life, the friendships, the feuds, the passions of proximate existence, took place in the sectarian compound, a compound, like any other, with its secrets—a secret language, secret customs, rites, which I now understand must have been very menacing at worst or at the best puzzling to the outside world. (Gordon 1992, 164)

In Gordon's prose across genres and across the years, we hear Isabel Moore: ironic, vulnerable, bristling with intelligence, in love with words. These qualities were both survival skills and liabilities in the Catholic world in which both Gordon and her protagonist came of age. In a 1982 article in *Commonweal,* Gordon recalled how the example of the Virgin Mary had been invoked and recommended to Catholic girls in the 1950s:

> With the kind of smile they would give to the behavior of Margaret the wife in "Father Knows Best," they talked about *the one assertion of Mary's* recorded in the Gospel: her request at the wedding feast at Cana. It was noted that she didn't ask her son directly for anything; she merely said: "They have no wine." Making him think it was his decision. Not

suggesting it was her idea, no, nothing like that. Then, disappearing, once again, into the background, into silence. (Gordon 1982, 11, italics mine)

Neither Isabel nor Gordon could emulate the "official Mary's" silent disappearance into the background. They assert, speak their minds, often using the irony and humor that became a code within a code for Catholic girls in the compound. Gordon reached a critical turning point at age 12, when she developed from a quiet girl, a "watcher," into an adolescent with a growing circle of friends. She discovered that she was funny and that humor could be "a coin of the realm" for a teenaged girl (Asirvatham 2002, 166). Gordon tells us where she got her sense of humor. She relates how, as a pious young Catholic, she had awakened with an imprint of the cross on her chest. She ran to her mother to report that she had the stigmata, only to be corrected by her very amused, down-to-earth, occasionally bawdy mother: "You goddam fool—you've slept on your crucifix" (Occhiogrosso 1987, 65).

Throughout *Final Payments,* especially in the conversations between Isabel, Eleanor, and Liz, we see how humor healed pain, built bridges, and sustained friendships over the rough spots. In this way, it made movement to a new place within the Catholic community possible, even encouraged it. At one point, when Isabel is afraid that Eleanor and Liz are about to revert to their most unhealthy versions of their girlhood selves, Isabel jokes about one of their former teachers at Anastasia Hall to invoke the old bonds between them. She knew the inherent limitations of her jokes about an ecumenical nun with a bad pocketbook on television saying into the camera, "I am a *nun.* My business is *love.*" They launched a riff of jokes about a kitschy nuns' boutique, full of bad purses and accessories for nuns lit by vigil candles with Gregorian chant for background music. "None of it was funny, but we laughed," Isabel relates, hinting at the complexity and power of the jokes cracked within close circles of Catholic girlhood friends. The jokes made it "possible to go on living" (Gordon 1979, 126). By the end of the novel, which is set in the mid-1970s, all three women find a place on the margins of the church where they are still considered Catholic, ardently prayed for by Father Mulcahy, and yet have the freedom to construct their own identity and spirituality.

In an interview with Peter Occhiogrosso for his popular book *Once a Catholic,* which appeared in 1987, Gordon expands on her own experience in a Catholic girls' high school (Mary Louis Academy, Jamaica Estates, New York) with the two other "smart girls" who remained her best friends two decades after graduation. The single-sex environment gave them the freedom to speak up without fear of repelling the opposite sex with their intelligence. It provided them with an arena in which to test their wits. The unfailing irreverence of Liz in *Final Payments* is cultivated in this environment. Liz's sharp wit is tolerated by the parish priest but not by most of the nuns. Father Mulcahy viewed it as "an Irish tradition, a lightning rod that channeled the energy of doubt to a safe grounding" (Gordon 1979, 102). Gordon confesses that she, too, got along better with priests than with nuns during girlhood and adolescence because she was "untidy and mouthy and . . . not demure." She explains that "certain kinds of priests would like you for that, but nuns never would" (Occhiogrosso 1987, 72).

There is another dimension to the intimate bonds forged with humor and wit at Gordon's and Isabel's secondary schools, one that reappears in Mary Daly's narratives as well. Gordon told Occhiogrosso that when she went to Barnard, she had to work to regain the intellectual discipline that she had not used since age 10. She maintains that "the real tragedy" of her high school was "that there were some very smart girls in there . . . and nobody to teach them." Gordon's working-class high school has much in common with Grandmother McCarthy's upper-middle-class parlor: "They were against any intellectual achievement at all." Gordon describes an environment in which the smart girls mentor each other and sharpen their wits by exploring the humor and irony in their situation. She recalls being imbued with the consciousness that "we were the smart girls in an environment that we knew was not equal to us." Gordon and her friends were aware of being "very dependent on each other for sustenance."

> You had no clues and no help, yet you were secretly, with each other, groping for a hidden intellectual world that you sensed was out there but for which you had no map. This created a tremendous intimacy and sense of intellectual purpose and adventure. I think if there had been boys around and the social or sexual ante were upped, we wouldn't have had that sense of adventure and thrill and camaraderie. (Occhiogrosso 1987, 68–70)

In her interview with Occhiogrosso, Gordon mentions, almost in passing, that "by the time I was sexual, I was out of the Church," and therefore not particularly vulnerable as a young woman to the church's negative teachings on the female sex (Occhiogrosso 1987, 72). This admission does a great deal to illuminate the two confession scenes in *Final Payments*. One kind of departure embarked on by Isabel, and countless female Catholics who reached adolescence during or after Vatican II, is the retreat from clerical supervision of their sex lives. Isabel refuses to believe that extramarital sex, even the painful affairs with married men, are her most serious sins.

A powerful passage in Gordon's autobiographical essay, "The Architecture of a Life with Priests," recounts her adolescent intimations of the limits of the sacrament of penance and the departures that resulted.

When we compare this passage with the second confession scene toward the end of *Final Payments,* we see how Gordon transmuted a pivotal moment in her own life to produce the confession scene that becomes the prelude to Isabel's departure from Margaret and the Catholic church that she represents. In "The Architecture of a Life with Priests," Gordon recalls how, at age12, shortly after her grandmother's death, she confessed her chronic sin ("private impurity") to a young priest (Father W.) who has visited her home many times to bring the Eucharist to her grandmother. Into a house that smelled like the sickroom at its center, Father W. brought countervailing smells ("Noxzema, Old Spice") and "his immaculate young maleness" which "seemed to redeem and purify the air." Thus far she has purposely avoided this priest's confessional, not "[wanting] to stain his purity with the defilement of my constant sin." On this occasion, she has no choice and briskly begins her usual confession, only to be told—gently—that her "private impurity" was "nothing to worry about." The priest sends her forth with the words: "Think of the boundless love of God and try to love others as you have been loved. And go in peace" (Gordon 2000, 171–176).

Gordon records a whole series of reactions to this moment: She felt blinded by the light of the new world that Father W. had revealed to her and wondered whether the priest had lost his senses. As she walked home, she considered acting on the priest's advice ("Try and Make friends." "People your own age." "Have fun for a change."). She had to admit that the world looked dramatically different. "But how could I live like that in the house where my grandmother had just died? I knew then that I would have to leave the house, that I would have to leave the church, because to live with this new sense of lightness and clarity I would need a dwelling that let in the light" (Gordon 2000, 176–178).

Isabel's darkly comic second confession scene in Margaret's parish church captures some aspects of crossing over, while Gordon's account of confessing her sin to Father W. illuminates others. In both cases, a sensitive and intelligent female Catholic suddenly becomes keenly aware of not being taken seriously, and this leads to a departure. The motives and personalities of the priests in these two scenes differ greatly, as do the circumstances surrounding the two confessions. In both cases, however, the sacrament of penance and reconciliation precipitates a departure fueled by a profound sense of not being heard, of being misunderstood. Departure from the Catholic compound, with its muted light and its ritualized mis-understandings, brings true absolution.

There is a larger sense in which Gordon's two confession scenes reca-pitulate the departure narratives in White and McCarthy as well. Whether the year is 1914, 1924, or 1961, a smart girl who is beginning to understand who she is and is learning to trust her own inner voices eventually discov-ers that the institutional church sets up roadblocks in her path. Departure narratives frequently describe the journey out of the candlelit sanctuaries (wombs?) of Catholic girlhood and into an expanding landscape flooded with natural light. In the narratives by White, McCarthy, and Gordon, Catholic girls growing into women begin to trust what is natural to them—intellectual and artistic gifts, physical observations, and sexual experience. They also begin to distrust and question the kinds of know-ledge commended to them by Catholic fathers and priests and at least some nuns.

Father W. gave Mary Gordon permission, even encouragement, to pursue the natural pleasures within her grasp when she was 12. One sus-pects that most of the priests manning the other confessionals might have proffered very different advice. It is not surprising to read later in Gordon's essay that Father W. left the priesthood, married, and became a social worker on Long Island. Father W.'s mundane, practical suggestions, which had initially sounded so exotic within the sacred precincts of her parish church, must have reinforced the natural inclinations of a precocious lonely girl such as Gordon, who was just figuring out that she was funny and worthy of a close circle of friends. They opened up the possibility that there were alternative ways of approaching the most basic components of life: her house, her family, and her body. Only one aspect of her intensely Catholic girlhood escaped this reevaluation. Her father, David Gordon, a Jewish convert to Catholicism who had died when Mary was 7, remained enshrined in his daughter's memory. She left his memory in the same untouched condition that she might have left a room that had been occu-pied by him alone.

In the interview with Occhiogrosso in 1987, Gordon described her father as "a great failure in every sense, ... except that he was a wonderful, wonderful father." Like Isabel Moore's father in *Final Payments,* David Gordon "was obsessed with the decline of the modern world" and lamented the way the American Catholic church was becoming "more Protestant and more Rotarian, blurring distinctions between the sacred and the secular." So David Gordon launched conservative Catholic maga-zines and other ventures doomed to extinction; for example, his plan to market a line of "liturgical greeting cards" intended to raise the aesthetic taste of American Catholics from "Ivory Soap madonnas" to Grünwald and Goya. Even as she recognized her father's commercial failures and fundamental shortcomings as family breadwinner, Gordon romanticized him in the manner of daughters who have lost fathers in girlhood. And even when she ceased being a practicing Catholic during the years between adolescence and motherhood, Gordon preserved her memories of the devout Catholicism that they had shared. Occhiogrosso began the interview section of his chapter on Gordon with a quotation from her: "I think that the first thing that you really need to know about me is that my father was a Jew who converted to Catholicism and became an absolute zealot" (Occhiogrosso 1987, 67–68).

In her memoir *The Shadow Man,* published nine years later, Gordon relates how, in the spring of 1994, at age 44, she was researching her father's life when the realization sunk in: "I am not the person I thought I was" (Gordon 1996b, xiii). This discovery, followed up methodically and painstakingly in her memoir, was part of another departure, which has everything to do with Gordon's connection to her Catholic roots. The first stirrings of doubt concerning her father arose suddenly at age 12, the same year Father W. challenged her to absolve herself for her chronic sin of impurity. Among her dead father's things Gordon had found a copy of a magazine that he had edited in the 1920s, the decade before his conversion. In her memoir, she recalls the exact moment in vivid detail: "Stuck in a book—a volume of *The Catholic Encyclopedia?* A study of the priesthood or the Eucharist?—was a small magazine called *Hot Dog.* I knew it was my father's, so I opened it, looking for a trace of him. What I found was a photo of a bare-breasted woman, plaintively looking out at the camera. Underneath her body is the caption 'Lover Come Back.'" Gordon ripped up the magazine and flushed it down the toilet, but she could not find a way to dispose of the image emblazoned in her memory. Her father was slipping away; a sense of her own defilement remained. She had become "a daughter who had to be ashamed" (Gordon 1996b, 59; Gordon 1996a, 38).

Part of it had to do with David Gordon's Jewishness. Mary had known from a young age that her father had been Jewish before he had converted. She remembered his having told her that if Nazis should ever come to power again the two of them might be sent to a concentration camp but her mother would not (Gordon 1996b, 18). After her father's death, Mary suffered—but not enough, she sometimes felt—for her Jewish lineage. Family members invoked her Jewishness as a slur, knowing that it would hurt all the more because of her dead father. They blamed her faults on her

Jewish blood, but they also traced the intellectual gifts that placed her above them to her Jewish ancestry. Someone even suggested that the sin that preoccupied her, impurity, stemmed from her connection to her Jewish father (Gordon 1996b, 189).

In twentieth-century America, Jews frequently gravitated toward leftist political activism, but David Gordon had taken the opposite route. He converted to Catholicism and embraced the conservative flank of the American church in the 1930s and 1940s. Chapter 2 of *The Shadow Man*, "Reading My Father," traces the efforts Gordon made as an adult, a professional writer and literary critic, to understand her father's mind through a systematic and self-consciously objective reading of his published works. The process began in the 1970s on a steamy summer day at the Vassar College Library and, after a hiatus, gained momentum twenty years later in the mid-1990s, when she was researching for her memoir. Reading her father's writings could be an exhilarating experience; it was a pleasure to discover that she had inherited certain features of her father's prose style; for example, his fondness for colons and semicolons. There were hidden treasures, like the sentences in her father's articles that Gordon, who had followed in his footsteps and become a professional writer, "would be proud to have written" (Gordon 1996b, 58, 54).

There were also more uncomfortable discoveries, such as the article published in *The Hibbert Journal* in 1920 in which her father misconstrued the spiritual meaning and semiotics of Francis of Assisi in an attempt to dress him in modern clothing. This prompts Mary Gordon to ask whether it is her responsibility to tell her father that he has it all wrong and that she "[knows] more than he does." Gordon's reaction here parallels her memory of her father dipping the wrong finger in the holy-water stoup at St. Patrick's Cathedral. Even as a young girl, she had responded to her father's lack of church protocol with a mixture of superiority—for her innate, born Catholic's knowledge of such things—and affection for her father's personal style of worship ("like a foreign accent or spats") (Gordon 1996b, 36; 1996a, 40). These moments, when she must admit that she knows more than her beloved deceased father, for whom knowing all about the church was at the center of his post-conversion identity, constitute small painful departures for Gordon. Somehow she must leave her father's church and much of what he claimed to know about the church and move on if she wants to recognize the truth about David Gordon and somehow reclaim him and her adult self.

At times, when reading her father's words on religion and politics, Gordon slips through discomfort all the way back to the revulsion that she felt at 12, suddenly face to face with the nude model in *Hot Dog*. Reading David Gordon's references to "the Reds" in a journal called *The Children's Hour*, from the early 1950s, she recalls her father's belief that the Rosenbergs were justly executed (Gordon 1996b, 69). She is alarmed by her father's chosen clerical mentors: Father Charles Coughlin, the popular radio preacher who blended populism, xenophobia, and venomous tirades against Roosevelt and the Jews, and Leonard Feeney, who had preached a gospel so exclusive to Catholics that even the Vatican of the early 1950s had singled him out for censure. Gordon's quest for her father within his publications is complicated by mixed emotions; she begins to dread what she might find. "If only I could keep from knowing these things about my father! That he supported Mussolini and Franco, and reviled the Lincoln Brigade because it was full of Jews. And, more terrible, that he saw no difference between the Nazis and the English and (was he insane?) defined the worst work of Hitler as closing Catholic schools in Bavaria" (Gordon 1996b, 78–84).

Part of the shock that accompanied investigating her father's writings when she was a mother, a woman in her mid-40s, stemmed from all of the emotional and spiritual ground she had covered since she had left the church behind in adolescence. As she read her father's writings at Butler Library at Columbia University in the mid-1990s, she could not help remembering how definitively she had moved beyond his beliefs and politics when she went to Barnard in 1967. From the library window she saw the site of demonstrations against the Vietnam War in which she had participated. She knew that her father would not have approved of her school, her politics, or her lifestyle. "I stood on the steps of Low Library, nineteen and not a virgin. I was shouting, 'Ho Ho, Ho Chi Minh, N. L. F. is gonna win.' I didn't allow myself to think of my father" (Gordon 1996b, 55).

At 19, Gordon was not the woman that her father had hoped she would be. Nor did she grow into that woman. Writing *The Shadow Man* helped her to clarify what her father had had in mind for her when he taught her to read at 3 and the Latin responses for mass at 5. He had wanted her to become "his partner: someone who would get his jokes and help him with his work." Anna Gordon, Mary's mother, shared his piety but was not fitted for this role, nor would she have chosen it. Mary Gordon had tried, between the ages of 7 and 12, to become what her dead father wanted, but she could not.

She outgrew her father's aspirations for her. She discovered the notes that he had hidden for her to find in books that he hoped would help shape the woman that she would become. In time-bound Catholic classics of the 1920s, such as Christopher Hollis's epistolary novel *With Love, Peter* and *The Life and Letters of Janet Erskine Stuart,* he had written comments intended to guide her down the right path in adolescence. "Never lose your Catholicity, my daughter," he had written, "it's the one thing no one can ever take from you" (Gordon 1996b, xix, 50). Ironically, this was one bit of advice she took to heart. She spent the years between puberty and motherhood in diaspora, on the margins of the church, but she never lost *her* Catholicity. Her relationship with her dead father might have been "marked by reversals and undoings, moments of frozen incomprehension, shutting my eyes, turning away" (Gordon 1996b, xvi), but her Catholicity stayed with her through it all.

After her father's death, she improvised, experimenting with ways to connect her Jewish and Catholic roots with her own emerging identity. At 10, she asked a priest who had been her father's friend and confessor whether her father might be the prophet Elijah (Gordon 1996b, 17). That would give him a purpose, significance, and a fate that she could under-stand. At one point, she thought of converting to Judaism. At Barnard, she remained alienated from the church, primarily because of its teachings on women and sex, but like many Catholics of her cohort group, she found a good substitute for the devotional Catholicism of her girlhood in the anti-war movement and the search for justice in the world. She described her Barnard years to Don Lee in an interview for *Ploughshares:* "There was such a sense of possibility—that you could change the world, and that the poor were important and were your concern, and that others were your concern, and you had a vested interest in making the world better" (Lee 1997, 220).

This perspective functioned as a genuine spirituality for Mary Gordon and other Catholics in diaspora during the 1960s and 1970s. It prepared her well for the role she began to play when she resumed being a practic-ing Catholic in the 1980s. Like her father, she has chosen a vocal and prophetic stance within the church of her time, albeit one on the other end of the ideological spectrum from his. She knows and accepts the chasm between her father's church and her own. She concedes: "There is much about me he would have hated. He didn't want a daughter who was a fem-inist, a leftist, divorced and remarried, the media's usual suspect when they need the insider's rap sheet on the Catholic hierarchy or the pope" (Gordon 1996b, xix). But she has reached a place from which she can see that her relationship to the church has little to do with how she conforms to what her father (or the fathers of the church) want from her. In order to reach that place, she first had to come to terms with her father.

Mary Gordon's familiarity with the experience of crossing over and her recognition of the many habitable places within the Catholic church (and its periphery) place her in good company with Antonia White and Mary McCarthy. The sense of mobility that all three understood and claimed as their own has Catholic roots, along with the spirit of protest against injustice that they first learned within the church and later applied directly to Catholic institutions. These three women show how the departures made during Catholic girlhood are complex and never finished: There are always more boundaries to be crossed.

3

BE-ING IS BE/LEAVING

The sermon was dedicated to the subject of Bingo, and as I gazed around at the blank-faced, lily-white congregation in easter attire I experienced an overwhelming desire/need/decision to leave.

We were sitting near the front. Just as I stood up and strode alone down the long aisle to the exit, the organ began to play. Unbelievably, the hymn that resounded through the church as I departed was "Daily, Daily, Sing to Mary"—that paean which my teacher had found it amusing to tease me with in my childhood. I had considered the joke unfunny and boring. At this Moment of Be/Leaving, however, I Heard the hymn take on dimensions of cosmic hilarity. For years I had been struggling to avoid church. This, however, was a Great Departure and Debut. I was Moving Out—Leaving/Leaping further in this First Spiral Galaxy of Outercourse.

—Daly 1992, 94

M ary Daly, the self-proclaimed Radical Feminist Pirate, has made a career of writing about leaving. There is a sense in which her entire corpus deals with departures of one kind or another. Some of Daly's departure narratives, such as the account of Easter 1968 quoted above, could have happened to almost anybody. (Didn't most Catholic feminists lose patience with traditional worship services during the late 1960s?) Yet even the narratives that start out as almost anybody's story can take a wild turn in midstream when Daly revisits her past and reinterprets it, using insights gained from the moment under examination and later discoveries. Then we encounter Be/Leaving as only Mary Daly experiences it. A formerly irksome traditionalist hymn gives way to a cosmic joke; an impulse to leave an embarrassing sermon becomes a theophany; a mundane walk down the aisle of a St. Petersburg parish church ends in a new mode of be-ing.

Daly's many stories about leaving fit into a larger framework, her own highly idiosyncratic discourse on life as a Be-dazzling Journey, Outercourse, a "Voyage of Spiraling Paths, Moving Out from the State of Bondage" (Daly 1992, 3). This framework, which Daly constructed in stages in her later works *Gyn/Ecology* (1978), *Pure Lust* (1984), *Outercourse* (1992), and *Quintessence* (1998), encourages and empowers readers to enter the New Time and New Space that Daly has found and embraced on the Boundary in a realm beyond the confines and constraints of patriarchal social, political, and ecclesiastical institutions. Daly maintains that it is only on the Boundary that women can realize their Power of Presence and their Archaic Futures (Daly and Caputi 1987, 84). The central axis around which Daly's spiraling pilgrimage and the New Space and Time on the Boundary revolves is Be-ing: "the Final Cause, the Good who is Self-communicating, who is the Verb from whom, in whom, and with whom all true movements move" (Daly and Caputi 1987, 64). In order to embark upon the Be-Dazzling Journey, however, one must cross a threshold, the first in the endless series of boundary-crossings encountered on the voyage. These boundary-crossings constitute acts of Be/Leaving (Daly 1992, 94, 121), the performance of Originally Sinful Acts that question and challenge the patriarchal order and display "a Prude's Self-centering Lust" (Daly and Caputi 1987, 86). Spelled with a slash in the only two references to the word in the index of *Outercourse* (Daly 1992, 94, 121), Be-Leaving can also be hyphenated, because it is part of a whole network of related words associated with women's participation in Be-ing, such as Be-Falling, Be-Longing, and Be-Monstering (Daly and Caputi 1987, 63–64).

Mary Daly is the incarnation of Cixous's vision of women "flying in language and making it fly." In their tone, content, substance, and syntax, Daly's published works convey her "pleasure in jumbling the order of space, in disorienting it, in changing around the furniture, dislocating things and values, breaking them all up, emptying structures, and turning propriety upside down" (Cixous 1975, 887). Like Monica Baldwin, whose use of language and capitalization became unpredictable in the course of her journey beyond the convent and the drawing rooms of her aristocratic friends and family, Daly's language and capitalization Be-Speak her Spiraling Voyage beyond the constraints of patriarchal ecclesiastical and academic institutions. In this chapter, I will adopt Daly's capitalization. Like Baldwin, Daly envisions her work as positive and constructive, even if she has become associated with reversals that challenge established conventions and expectations. Daly's use of the phrase "a Prude's Self-centering Lust" in the definition of "Originally Sinful Acts" is analogous to Baldwin's insistence on honoring her own "Inward Urges." In fact, the two phrases mean roughly the same thing. Both Baldwin and Daly joyfully court misunderstanding and disapproval by their vivid and bold use of words in a world where vague language and social conventions have shrouded patriarchal actions and intentions and kept smart women marginalized.

Mary Daly's many carefully negotiated departures, described in painstaking detail in published works that have appeared since the early 1970s, constitute one of her most important contributions. Much of what Daly represents as a feminist teacher and scholar is conveyed in these departure narratives, which return again and again to two central themes: women's protracted, sometimes complicated, extremely personalized process of Be/Leaving, and the challenge of be-ing (participation in Be-ing), for the sake of which all Be/Leaving takes place. Amid all of the developments in Daly's style and subject matter over the past quarter-century, and throughout her evolution from a pioneer Catholic feminist philosopher/theologian in 1968 to a self-proclaimed Postchristian Nag-Gnostic Pirate in 1992, Daly's focus on these two issues has been constant. The dynamic created by the relationship between these two aspects of Daly's life and thought has shaped her Self-consciousness and profoundly affected her approach to Self-disclosure, also called Hagography, in her writings.

Daly's willingness to write about the issues of be-ing and Be/Leaving honestly and concretely with reference to her own life may be among her most abiding legacies. The courageous, often outrageous improvisations/performances that appear most prominently in Daly's works from *Gyn/Ecology* onward may be as important to the future of feminism as the (far more widely acknowledged and appreciated) feminist analysis of patriarchal institutions and language in her first two books: *The Church and the Second Sex* (1968) and *Beyond God the Father* (1973). Each reader can decide to make or to eschew such comparisons. I will not pit the two Dalys (more accurately: the many Dalys) against one another and make them compete for top honors. Instead, I will pay attention, as Daly herself does, to some of the relationships (and internal consistencies) among the many Selves Daly discloses to us in her autobiographical works as well as to the ways in which the terms *be-ing* and *Be/Leaving* provide Daly with the means to name, claim, and take seriously the expanding cast of Mary Dalys who serve as protagonists in her autobiographical writings. I will focus on what Daly has shown us about the fundamental connections between be-ing, Be/Leaving, and Hagography and why that demonstration is so important and sustaining. In so doing, I hope to answer the pundits who continue to ask, from a variety of ideological positions, just what Mary Daly has done for us lately.

In the *Wickedary* (1987), the place where Daly defined and displayed the expanding webs of recovered and recycled words that she had been spinning for almost a decade, she included the following definition of Ontological Courage: "the Courage to Be through and beyond the State of Negation which is patriarchy; participation in the Unfolding of Be-ing—continuing on the Journey always" (Daly and Caputi 1987, 69). This definition, conjured by Daly toward the end of the period in her life that she designates her Third Spiral Galaxy (1975–1987), represents a good place to begin to explore the dynamics of be-ing and Be/Leaving in Daly's life and work. The inclusion of both the negative aspect of Be/Leaving (movement "through and beyond the State of Negation") and its positive aspect ("continuing the Journey always") within Daly's definition of Ontological Courage merely makes explicit what close readers already know: For Daly, be-ing and Be/Leaving are inseparable.

An individual's commitment to and participation in Be-ing necessarily means that she is a Be/Leaver. For to embrace Be-ing wholeheartedly, Daly insists, one must become a Pirate, a Spinster, always on the move, pursuing life as a "Wild-Goose Chase," a "Be-Laughing lark; a fruitful, hopeful, ecstatic Quest" (Daly and Caputi 1987, 180). The joyous and creative process of Spinning and Sparking never ends. There is always another threshold to cross. Daly's frequent recourse to metaphors of movement and travel, as well as her way of describing the feminist vocation as the Call of the Wild, provides important insights into her vision of separatism. In a helpful footnote in *Outercourse,* Daly explains why it is always necessary to discuss separatism within a larger context, why Be/Leaving needs to be understood in relation to be-ing. Separatism, Daly affirms, is "an essential prerequisite" of the "ontological Metamorphosis" that Radical Feminism makes possible. But here she adds a crucial caveat: The name *separatist* is "inadequate" unless it is used "in a context of Lusty words" to connect it with the final cause, "Biophilic communication/participation in Be-ing"

(Daly 1992, 445n15). The term *Biophilia*, first used in *Gyn/Ecology* in 1978, refers to the "Original Lust for Life" (Daly and Caputi 1987, 67) that Daly, the Radical Feminist Pirate, seeks to recover from near-extinction in patriarchy.

The vital connection between Be/Leaving and be-ing shines through clearly in Daly's personal narratives. Since 1975 Daly has incorporated autobiographical narrative into her philosophy along with her growing lexicon of Dis-covered and recycled words. Daly has experimented with a mixed genre that interweaves philosophy/Pyrosophy and autobiography/Hagography because of her conviction that crossing thresholds (Be/Leaving, Original Sinning, asking Nonquestions) is a recurring event, a major component in the lives of those who are "Furiously focused" on the Final Cause, Be-ing (Daly 1985e, xxvii). Personal narratives that capture Moments of Be/Leaving lend shape and substance to Daly's philosophy. Even if Ontological Courage sounds like an abstraction, Daly shows us that there is nothing abstract about *living a life* grounded in Ontological Courage.

By 1975, when she wrote the "Autobiographical Preface" and "Feminist Postchristian Introduction" to the second edition of *The Church and the Second Sex*, Mary Daly knew that if she really wanted to become a philosopher, she would have to become a Hagographer. Three years later, in *Gyn/Ecology*, Daly introduced her New Word, *Hagography*. Like Ontological Courage, Hagography has both negative and positive aspects. Its negative aspect is related to its function as a corrective. It addresses the need to replace the "moldy 'models'" for women featured in christian hagiography, which extols "the masochistic martyrs of sadospiritual religion," with the real lives of Great Hags found in "woman-identified writing" (Daly 1990, 14). Although it is associated with the negative process of removing from circulation plastic patriarchal models of virtuous womanhood, Hagography is primarily a positive, future-oriented enterprise. Daly elaborates: "For women who are on the journey of radical be-ing, the lives of the witches, of the Great Hags of our hidden history are deeply intertwined with our own process. As we write/live our own story, we are uncovering their history, creating Hagography and Hag-ology" (Daly 1990, 15).

Here Daly touches on some of the features of Hagography that make it an effective antidote to christian hagiography. She reclaims a "so-called obsolete" definition of the noun *haggard* found in *Merriam-Webster*. A *haggard* is "an intractable person, especially: a woman reluctant to yield to wooing." This reclaimed meaning becomes the basis for Daly's vision of Hagography: "Haggard writing is by and for haggard women, those who are intractable, willful, wanton, unchaste, and, especially, those who are reluctant to yield to wooing. It belongs to the tradition of those who refuse to assume the woes of wooed women, who cast off these woes as unworthy of Hags, of Harpies" (Daly 1990, 15–16).

Because Daly writes in a very distinctive style that has become her trademark, it is possible to overlook the fact that she situates herself, as a writer and a Radical Feminist Philosopher, within this larger tradition of Hagographic discourse. It is part of the same tradition that Clarissa Pinkola Estés depicts as a "towering column" of women standing on the shoulders of their predecessors (Estés 1995, 19). Daly maintains that a feminist writing her own life is engaged in an improvisation. She becomes a Hagographer, a Spell-Weaver, a "Creative Crone who weaves contexts in which Wonders can happen" (Daly and Caputi 1987, 167). Hagographers do not merely write their lives; they create new contexts, New Space and Time, in which New Selves Weave Spells.

In her three most explicitly Hagographic works, the "Autobiographical Preface," the "Feminist Postchristian Introduction," and her autobiography, *Outercourse*, Daly provides us with glimpses of her girlhood, young womanhood, and formal education. These glimpses constitute carefully prepared and shared Moments situated within their own contexts. Their purpose is to depict Daly's growing Self-consciousness and the process by which she Named herSelf a Radical Feminist, a Hag, a Pirate, and so on. Although these Moments are presented within specific temporal frameworks (within one of her Spiral Galaxies), they do not represent merely a linear series of events. In the Prelude to the Second Spiral Galaxy of *Outercourse*, Daly asserts, almost in passing, "Of course, I had already been a Pirate all my life, accumulating treasures of knowledge that had been hidden from my Tribe." In this same section, Daly refers to Piracy as a Call, an identity, a career (Daly 1992, 129). Piracy represents one way in which Daly participates in Be-ing, pursuing her Final Cause. The Pirate's life is an endless Journey punctuated by Moments of Be/Leaving, in which be-ing is increasingly realized.

When one reflects on the Moments Daly Re-calls in the First Galaxy of *Outercourse*, which cover the years from Daly's birth in 1928 though 1970, it is striking to see how many of them serve to recount and reaffirm Daly's Passion to become a philosopher-theologian, "a woman who could think, write and teach about the most fascinating of questions and earn her living by doing just this" (Daly 1985a, 8). Some of the Moments describe mystical "intuitions of be-ing"; for example, the summer day in early adolescence when Daly, lying on the grass near a favorite swimming hole, had "an encounter" with a clover blossom. For Daly, the Moment had tremendous ontological significance. The blossom "Announced its be-ing" to her

(Daly 1992, 23, 41). These Moments of epiphany continued into woman-hood. There was the Dream of Green that interrupted Daly's study of medieval literature at Catholic University in the early 1950s and reinforced her earlier conviction that she was *meant* to study philosophy (Daly 1992, 48–49). There was the hedge at Saint Mary's, Notre Dame, where she received her first doctorate in religion. When the hedge said "Continued existence" (Daly 1992, 51–52) directly to Daly, it provided her with a whole new set of questions to pursue as a philosopher and reminded her that the philosopher's Quest is personal as well as professional.

Re-calling these Moments sustained Daly's (initially subliminal) Ontological Courage throughout a whole series of disappointments related in the First Galaxy of *Outercourse*. Daly grew frustrated with the Catholic secondary school and college she attended, where women were steered away from science and philosophy and toward literature and the arts. She recoiled at the "enforced narrowness of horizons," and only decades later did she decode the "all-pervasive subliminal message" that had repeated itself in a variety of ways throughout her undergraduate years. The message, disconcertingly clear in her Re-membered Moments, was that "we were not destined for greatness" (Daly 1992, 43).

In a master's program in English literature at Catholic University, Daly disobeyed the unwritten rules and wrote a thesis on literary theory. When a priest who served as a reader for the thesis dismissed her ideas and declaimed her "lack of philosophical *habitus*," Daly's determination to earn a doctorate in philosophy was only strengthened (Daly 1992, 49). For an American Catholic woman in the 1950s, the best way to realize this goal was to study theology first. The pioneering doctoral program for women at Saint Mary's seemed like a godsend, a door in the wall (Mandell 1997, 183–188). But even there, in a program explicitly designed to nurture a new cadre of female Catholic theologians, Daly felt like "a cognitive minority of one."

She welcomed the mental challenge posed by the philosophy of St. Thomas Aquinas (ca. 1225–1274), the centerpiece of the neoscholastic curriculum taught at even the most progressive Catholic institutions in the period before Vatican II. She recalls moments of complete happiness and satisfaction studying Aquinas's theology, moments when she "felt some-thing like pity for people who did not understand the theology of 'the Trinity.'" But there were other painful moments when Daly first articulated some of the Nonquestions raised by the scholastic texts. One day, studying Aquinas's *Summa theologiae* (I, q. 92, a.1 ad 1), she was struck by a passage that depicted women as "defective and misbegotten," the result of a "defect in the active force [male seed] or from some material indisposition, or even from some external influence such as that of a south wind, which is moist." When Daly approached another ("considerably older . . . and somewhat intimidating") woman in her program with her concerns about the passage, she was dismissed with a statement of the Catholic party line: "That's no offense to *your* dignity." Daly could not agree. She "filed away" these moments of isolation, invisibility, and inaudibility in her First Spiral Galaxy. Years later, when she wrote *Outercourse,* she Named them "Moments of Prophecy and Promise" (Daly 1992, 51–53, 6).

Even in the early 1950s, Daly began to appreciate the bittersweet sensation of Be/Leaving, at least subliminally. She learned more about it in the spring of 1954, a few months before she received her doctorate from Saint Mary's. At first her prospects looked promising. She applied to the doctoral program in philosophy at the University of Notre Dame, and Sister Madeleva, president of Saint Mary's, offered her a teaching position that would help pay her tuition. But then Notre Dame denied Daly admission because of her sex, and Sister Madeleva withdrew her offer after Daly joined a student movement to reform her pet project, the theology program for women (Daly 1992, 53).

When Daly left Saint Mary's for five bleak years of teaching at Cardinal Cushing College (and secondary school) in Brookline, Massachusetts, she left a part of herself behind, the naïve self that wanted to believe the promises made to her by the all-female Catholic educational system to which she had been confined by the circumstances of her birth, sex, and background (Daly 1992, 44–45). Daly soon discovered that her doctorate from Saint Mary's opened very few doors, and her final spring at Saint Mary's taught her what Catholic women's colleges did to the outspoken, the marginal, the "uppity" students without funds and family connections (Daly 1992, 53). Daly realized that she would have to seek patrons and opportunities beyond the semi-cloistered world assigned to Catholic women. In seeing this, she caught glimpses of an Other Galaxy that she could reach only by continuing her Journey and learning more.

Daly set her sights on the most prestigious Catholic advanced degree, the doctorate from a pontifical faculty of sacred theology. When Catholic University, which had the only such program in the United States, rejected her because of her sex, Daly found universities in Germany and Switzerland that offered the same degree and accepted applications from women. With financial help from John Wright, bishop of Pittsburgh and a well-known patron of (male) lay theologians, Daly set out in 1959 for the University of Fribourg, where she spent seven years and earned the highest degrees in theology and philosophy available in the Catholic world. Daly thrived at Fribourg and later called her graduate study there "a seven years' ecstatic experience interspersed with brief periods of gloom, . . . a sort of lengthy spiritual-intellectual chess game" (Daly 1985a, 9).

The object of the game was to master the writings of Thomas Aquinas (and his intellectual heirs, the neoscholastics) and apply and interpret them in new ways appropriate to the modern context, all the while remaining within the bounds of orthodoxy. Daly's two dissertations, "The Problem of Speculative Theology" and "Natural Knowledge of God in the Philosophy of Jacques Maritain," attest to her grasp of scholastic and neoscholastic theology and philosophy. She survived the awkwardness of studying with seminarians who avoided sitting next to her and eschewed eye contact. Indeed, some of these same European seminarians broke into applause when Daly passed an especially grueling set of examinations and compared her to the astronaut John Glenn (Daly 1992, 62).

At Fribourg, Daly showed (herself and others) that she could meet the challenges posed by the most demanding Catholic doctoral programs and simultaneously teach American undergraduates studying abroad. Her adventures in Europe, Great Britain, and the Middle East laid the foundations for the pervasive travel metaphors underlying her later Radical Feminist writings. Daly's European sojourn released her from a bondage she had only begun to acknowledge and taught her the meaning as well as the *sensation* of Be/Leaving: "The Stunning thing about my early travels in Europe was the utterly surprising phenomenon of having all the magical images that had populated my imagination since childhood actually materialize and come alive. In Rome, for example, when I first saw the Forum and the Colosseum at night I was transported. I had seen pictures in my Latin textbooks in high school. Now they really existed! So I was Space/Time traveling, participating in the Fourth Dimension" (Daly 1992, 64).

In the same passage in *Outercourse,* Daly captures the sense of liberation, the positive aspects of Be/Leaving, that she Dis-covered in Europe in the early 1960s with a whole array of images already familiar to readers of *Pure Lust:*

> It was as if I had lived imprisoned in a sort of disneyland and was suddenly released into the real world. I was like someone who had known only plastic trees and flowers and who was now let loose in a verdant place—a forest or a jungle. Countless doors and windows in my brain were thrown open and I gulped the fresh exhilarating air. I had been suffocating in a state of sensory deprivation, and that state was behind me. (Daly 1992, 64)

These sensations associated with the Fribourg years survived, and perhaps even catalyzed, Daly's departure from the Catholic church in the late

1960s. For Daly, studying Aquinas and the neoscholastics was not merely a matter of mastering *content;* the neoscholastic curriculum suggested a way of being in the world. Daly calls her forays into Thomistic metaphysics an "exhilarating ride." She was attracted to the "precise and elegant logic" of her professors' commentaries on Aquinas (Daly 1992, 59). She cherished the *way it felt* to be part of the neoscholastic enterprise at Fribourg. As she wrote her second Fribourg dissertation on intuition in the works of the neoscholastic philosopher Jacques Maritain, Daly found herself in a new place: "I learned to trust my own intuitions while demonstrating their implications rigorously, and to articulate my arguments in a way that is inherently clear in itself—which is quite a different matter from being a good 'debater' who argues only to score points but does not seek the truth" (Daly 1992, 75).

Daly was drawn to the study of Catholic neoscholastic theology in part because it promised that truth was available to those who were properly trained in the use of reason and intuition in the pursuit of truth. Historian Philip Gleason suggests that by the middle of this century, neoscholasticism was more than a school of philosophy or theology. It was an ideology that pervaded the entire mental world inhabited by Catholic intellectuals. At the center of this ideology, Gleason maintains, was "the breathtaking assertion" that "human reason alone was sufficient to establish with certainty that God exists, that the divine nature was such that God always spoke the truth and had in fact spoken to humankind, proposing definite truths for their belief" (Gleason 1987, 169).

Daly imported some of this ideology into her Postchristian Radical Feminist Philosophy. One sees this on a superficial level in the many references to neoscholastic terminology (especially such central concepts as Being and the Final Cause) in Daly's works written in all five Spiral Galaxies. In her account of the history of Catholic feminist theology in *New Catholic Women,* Mary Jo Weaver addresses the question of how Daly's neoscholastic education shaped her Radical Feminist Philosophy. Weaver maintains that amid all of the stylistic and substantive changes in Daly's writings over the years, one thing remains constant. In Daly's first article published in *The Thomist* (Daly 1965) and in *Pure Lust,* which appeared nineteen years later, one finds "a consistent search for transcendence or what [pre–Vatican II neoscholastic] theologians called Being" and an emphasis on the need "to strive 'toward a higher level of human existence'" (Weaver 1995, 176).

Weaver asserts that what changes for Daly, the Postchristian feminist, is "the location of the source of transcendence." This crucial change of location is signaled by the new hyphenated spelling of Be-ing. Weaver explains:

In *Beyond God the Father* [Daly] argued that it is impossible to leave God behind and therefore necessary to destroy the "myth of God the Father" in order to be empowered by God the Verb. In *Pure Lust*, feminism, not God, is the Verb, a process that continues and draws us along with it. The Verb has the same function, to encourage belief in the self, community, and a new age; but it is no longer perceived as outside women or alien to their experience. . . . The spirit of transcendence rests within women, yearning for activation. (Weaver 1995, 177)

Daly does not deny the fundamental continuity that Weaver describes, but she revels in the discontinuities and departures. In true Pirate fashion she later Named Thomistic philosophy her Labrys that "[enabled her] to cut through man-made delusions to the core of problems" (Daly 1992, 75). For this reason, she Re-members her "Quest through the mazes of academia" as a "Rite of Passage on my Piratic enterprise of Plundering treasures stolen by phallocratic thieves and Smuggling them back to women within academia itself" (Daly 1992, 78). Still, as Weaver has observed, throughout the Journey, the search for transcendence, which Daly calls participation in Be-ing, remains the dynamic central axis of Daly's Radical Feminist Philosophy. What changed was the context, the way in which she envisioned Be-ing and its place in her expanding cosmos.

This process of Re-calling and Re-vision happened gradually during the final years of the 1960s, and it became Daly's driving Passion by the first half of the 1970s, in her Second Spiraling Galaxy (1971–1974). In the early 1970s, spurred by her recent encounter with phallocracy in the fight for tenure at Boston College, Daly began to explore the possibility of addressing ontological questions outside the church and beyond the Christian tradition. In her second book, *Beyond God the Father*, she argues that women's liberation hinges on women's discovery of a new Space "on the boundary" beyond the Christian realm, a Space where wholeness and participation in Be-ing were possible. Daly Named this new Space the "exodus community" or "Cosmic Covenant" of Sisterhood (Daly 1985b, 132–178), experimental, transitional terminology still informed by her Christian heritage and training. Nonetheless, readers familiar with the conciliatory tone and language of even the most critical sections of *The Church and the Second Sex* could not help but see Daly's second book as a sharp and Self-conscious departure.

Starting with its title, *Beyond God the Father*, and Robin Morgan's quotation on the first page of the Introduction ("I want a women's revolution like a lover. I lust for it."), Daly's second book breathed the spirit of the radical flank of the American women's movement in the 1970s. Her treatment of ontology, arguably the central theme of the entire volume, was also deeply informed by the feminist rhetoric of the early 1970s. She called for the "castrating of language and images that reflect and perpetuate the structures of a sexist world." She did not shrink from asserting that among the candidates for castration are the fatherly God of the Christians and Jews and all traditional religious institutions. Daly explained why castration is not an unduly harsh or violent method of women's liberation: "As aliens in a man's world who are now rising up to name—that is, to create—our own world, women are beginning to recognize that the value system that has been thrust upon us by the various cultural institutions of patriarchy has amounted to a kind of gang rape of minds as well as of bodies" (Daly 1985b, 9).

"Why indeed must 'God' be a noun?" Daly asked in *Beyond God the Father.* "Why not a verb—the most active and dynamic of all?" Drawing on the ideas of other feminist theologians in her own circle of friends, especially Nelle Morton and Janice Raymond, and generalizing from the mutuality and support available to her within that circle, Daly posited that wherever "sororal community-consciousness is present," there, too, is God the Verb, Be-ing. The women's movement participates in the evolution of Be-ing: "The unfolding of woman-consciousness is an intimation of the endless unfolding of God" (Daly 1985b, 33, 36).

Almost twenty years later, in *Outercourse,* Daly acknowledged the "Overwhelming Oversight" in *Beyond God the Father:* her retention of the word *God.* It was not a "simple oversight," Daly explained. "No: it was a complex acrobatic process/problem, . . . engendered by a great desire to save *God.*" Daly vividly Re-called her intense, unquestioned need to keep God in the picture, albeit reconstituted and castrated, the ultimate intransitive Verb, Be-ing (Daly 1992, 161). For all of her newfound Ontological Courage, she could not yet conceive of Be-ing without its connection to the Christian God. Daly's account of the Overwhelming Oversight, which appears in her autobiography, written almost two decades later, preserves for us a Self-portrait of Daly, the Novice Nag, in the midst of a painful Moment of Be/Leaving, still instinctively clinging to a vestigial fragment of her past:

> I was unconsciously afraid of losing my true Self and/or forgetting my intuition of Be-ing, in which I and all Others participate. In traditional language, *God* represented this, although inadequately. The grip of the word *God* was strong: its tentacles were tenacious. After a short time, however, when I did make the "Qualitative Leap" and dispense with "him," I found that Be-ing the Verb was very much alive and well, and so was I. I had lost Nothing. (Daly 1992, 161)

We have already seen that in the early 1970s Daly had begun to make connections between her bent for thinking ontologically and her own evolving woman-consciousness. After the grueling tenure fight with the Jesuits at Boston College in 1968–1969, her public exodus from the church in 1971, and her Dis-covery of her Lesbian identity during this same period, Daly found herSelf on the Other Side, in a new Space/Time. In *Outercourse,* she captured the change in a Re-membered Moment/ Metaphor/intuition: "I Re-Call looking out my office window at trees whose branches met and having an overwhelmingly powerful intuition that expressed itself in the words 'The trees came together.' I would Now call that experience 'an intuition of Elemental integrity'" (Daly 1992, 144). This experience of "Dis-covering . . . an Other dimension of [her] identity" transported Daly into a new mode of be-ing. Suddenly she found herSelf "several woman-light years" away from the author of *The Church and the Second Sex,* on the Other side of a "journey in time/space that . . . could not be described adequately by terrestrial calendars and maps" (Daly 1992, 144; Daly 1985a, 5). Daly would not, and could not, compartmentalize herSelf. She had to honor her intuition of Elemental integrity, which she now recognized as her participation in the cosmic unfolding of Be-ing.

With this in mind, it is illuminating to take a closer look at the spirit in which Daly the Postchristian feminist approached her former Self, the Catholic feminist who had launched *The Church and the Second Sex* in 1968 "with a great sense of pride, anger, and hope" (Daly 1985a, 5). The opportunity for the two Mary Dalys, the Catholic feminist and her more evolved Postchristian Self, to meet in print arose in 1974 when Harper and Row proposed a second edition of *The Church and the Second Sex.* At first, Daly considered both of her options "odious." She could publish a revised edition, knowing that no revisions, however extensive, could make her first book speak for (or from) her current position or she could simply refuse to issue a second edition, silence her former Self, and deprive potential readers of access to a pivotal, if dated, early feminist text.

Almost twenty years later, in her autobiography, Daly explained why she rejected both of these alternatives. She felt compelled to choose between two of the Seven Deadly Sins (assimilation and elimination) as she had renamed (and augmented) them in *Pure Lust.* Then, just in time, Daly discovered "a Transcendent Third Option" that allowed her to avoid "the twin perils of tokenism/assimilation and Self-erasure/elimination" and create "something entirely New." She decided to provide readers with both "the early Daly's book and the radical critique—a tangible record of Intergalactic Travel" (Daly 1992, 186). In the process, Daly showed what Be/Leaving looked like and even, on occasion, what it *felt* like.

Daly was immediately comfortable with her decision in favor of the Transcendent Third Option and made several subsequent decisions based on this precedent. In 1985 she published a second edition of *Beyond God the Father* with an "Original Reintroduction" explaining her relationship to the book and its author. The same year she added the "New Archaic Afterwords" to the third edition of *The Church and the Second Sex*. In 1990, she issued a second edition of *Gyn/Ecology* with a "New Intergalactic Introduction" that bridged the gap between her present and former Selves. For the *Wickedary,* her Radical Feminist lexicon, which appeared in 1987, Daly devised a set of symbols based on the phases of the moon to denote the sites, or Word-Works, where she had first introduced her freshly plundered, recycled words (Daly and Caputi 1987, xv, 59–60, 285n2). In *Outercourse,* Daly incorporated these symbols into her footnotes and provided contextual remarks as well as more recent perspectives on all of the new prefaces and introductions. The dialogue between Daly and her earlier Selves/texts continues in *Quintessence,* published in 1998 (Daly 1998, 13–18).

The process of writing these assessments and explorations of her former Selves and works has prompted Daly to cultivate a deep and rich awareness of the relationships among her multiple Selves, Selves from various stages of her Journey, who coexist in conversations staged in the introductions, forewords, and prefaces of her works. It is significant that she chose not to issue revised versions of her original texts/Selves, nor did she attempt to airbrush the transitions to make them appear smoother. Instead she sought to provide readers with direct access to her own openended unexpurgated conversations with her earlier texts/Selves. She did not want to be complicit in the patriarchal sins of assimilation and elimination. She did not want to isolate herSelf or her readers from earlier Selves and Spiral Galaxies. It would be impossible to write about her central/ontological concern with Be-ing within the kind of two-dimensional linear framework that a conventional revised version of her texts would create. Daly simply could not consign herSelf, even an earlier and very different Self, to what she would later call the foreground past, sealed off from the new sisterhood coming "into be-ing," where women's hearing/healing presence made New Space and Time possible.

Despite everything, and even after all that had transpired to separate them, Daly circa 1975 could still empathize with and show deep affection for Daly circa 1968. ("I felt as if this were the journal of a half-forgotten foremother, whose quaintness should be understood in historical context and treated with appropriate respect.") Granted, she was shocked in 1975 by some of the proposals she had made in 1968. She openly confessed her sense of alarm and disorientation: "Why, I wondered, would anyone want 'equality' in the church? . . . Why did she say 'we' when she meant 'I' and 'they' when she meant 'we'?" (Daly 1985a, 6). After a thorough, chapter-by-chapter critique of her 1968 book and Self, Daly circa 1975 submitted the following measured, but enthusiastic, judgment:

> As critic, what have I managed to say of this work? It has made me alter-
> nately exasperated and joyful. The biographical data accessible to me
> concerning the author indicates that she was not an overly modest per-
> son, so I don't think she would mind my saying that she helped to build
> a tradition in which I now participate. I would be less than just if I failed
> to acknowledge this. I have found the work worth studying at this time,
> and I recommend it to scholars who wish to understand *the process of the
> feminist movement.* (Daly 1985d, 47; italics mine)

It is worthwhile to linger over Daly's use of the word *process* here. *Process* was a buzzword of the 1970s, but in Daly's prose the term always refers back to ontology and ultimately to Thomas Aquinas. While some of Daly's teachers and fellow students at Saint Mary's and Fribourg found in the theology of Aquinas a static textbook description of the ways to describe the perfection of God, the eternal, unchanging, unmoved mover, Daly the Alchemist found in the same texts the raw materials for a radi-cally dynamic theology/philosophy of becoming, an ontology which envi-sions individuals actively striving to amplify the Be-ing that gives Life its very Life. Gradually Daly introduced her own Metaphors of Spiraling and Spinning to convey a sense of the dynamic ontology she had first Dis-cov-ered and embraced within the philosophy/theology of Aquinas.

Thomistic ontology remained Daly's foundation, her touchstone, no matter how many thresholds she crossed. Daly the Be/Leaver took Thomas with her on her Spiraling Journey. Even as recently as 1992, Daly could still state unequivocally that "for decades" the thirteenth century, the century of Aquinas and the scholastics, "has been the century in which I have felt at home" (Daly 1992, 361). She did not have to explain that it was her own reading of the thirteenth century, the one plundered by her Pirate Self, that felt like home. Elsewhere in *Outercourse* she clarifies why she continues to capitalize the terms *Thomist* and *Thomistic* (as well as the name Thomas Aquinas) when the rest of her capitalization has become "capitally irregular," depending on the "ever changing contexts which I created." Daly capitalizes these terms to acknowledge the ways in which her Thomistic training "[pre-pared] the way for the creative work that was to come" (Daly 1992, 60, xxi).

Mary Daly clarifies her debt to Aquinas in a Re-membered Moment in the "Feminist Postchristian Introduction" of *The Church and the Second Sex,* which was written during the summer of 1974. She revisits her treatment of Aquinas in her first book, bringing with her a new set of questions and Nonquestions. She declares the "critique of medieval biology . . . too restrained" (Daly 1985d, 23). (In other words, she should have been far more appalled by Thomas's appropriation of Aristotle's biology and misogyny.) Daly does not need to belabor her point. The single reference to Thomistic biology will do. Then Daly turns to a much more subtle, more revealing kind of exegesis. She treats her 1968 analysis of Aquinas as a palimpsest.

Once again, in this passage, we see Daly herSelf in process. Daly scours the text with a new set of questions, an outgrowth of Be/Leaving and her new/Archaic Radical Feminist context. What interests Daly most at this point in her Journey is what she had *almost* written in her first book, risks she had *almost* taken, hopes she had *almost* expressed. She pores over her old text in search of the faint outlines of the text that she had not yet dared to write but can still perceive within it and between the lines, reading the text from her new vantage point in her Third Spiral Galaxy. She provides a close reading of four pages of the original text of *The Church and The Second Sex* (Daly 1985c, 91–95), paying special attention to ontological questions:

> I think I can detect in Daly's defense of Aquinas's "radically liberating principles" a quality different from her lip service to the single "liberating" Pauline text [Galatians 3:27–28] and even quite different from her general defense of "basic Christian doctrine." In the latter case, . . . she seems to be avoiding the threat of a radical break from Christianity. But in her plea for Aquinas there is, it seems to me, a kind of positive passion. . . . I think it fair to say that she was struggling to find ontological roots for what we know today as feminist philosophy of Be-ing. In the better parts of Aquinas's work she found hints of what a philosophy of being/becoming could begin to say. . . . The ontological process which Daly so ardently sought could only be found in the women's revolution, which had not yet surfaced. Consequently, she took starvation rations from the best of the Christian philosophers. In her time, when sisterhood had not yet emerged, moving too far ahead would have meant venturing into an endless desert, into a state which an uncomprehending world would have called "madness" and treated as such. It is important for our historical sense, I think, that we try to comprehend this situation. (Daly 1985d, 23–24)

I have quoted Daly at length to convey both the seriousness of her tone and the pains she takes to provide a close textual analysis of a portion of the original book that most of her readers were in no position to appreciate without guidance. Daly's attachment to Thomistic philosophy was a part of her Catholic past that remained central to her identity as a radical feminist, a Nag-Gnostic, but neither traditional Catholics nor non-Catholic feminists could understand the way this vestige of her past informed her vision of Radical (Elemental) Feminist identity and integrity. By the time Daly wrote this passage, she was already living a Life of Ontological Courage. She had crossed a threshold to Radical Feminism and was well on her way to a separatist position. She could have simply Moved On with a firm resolve not to look back. Why did she want to Re-member and share the Desire and Need with which she had approached the writings of Aquinas? Why did she want to Re-call her old fears of the desert, of standing on the Boundary, looking/feeling like a cognitive minority of one, maybe even a madwoman?

Daly took the trouble to show her readers (and perhaps remind herSelf) that Be/Leaving is not optional, not tidy, never entirely finished. Even in another Galaxy, Daly continued to participate in the process of Be/Leaving she had begun several woman-light-years before. This partic-ipation provided Daly with a special gift she called the Courage to See: "the Courage to become dis-illusioned, to See through male mysteries, to become a Seer, envisioning an Archaic Future" (Daly and Caputi 1987, 69). This negative aspect of Be/Leaving played a crucial role in developing the Pirate's sight. See-ing *through* disillusionment is the only way to become a Pirate.

Daly's recourse to two contrasting descriptions of Be/Leaving in *Outercourse* parallels her definitions of Ontological Courage and the Courage to See in the *Wickedary.* The contrast between the positive and negative examples suggests the range of emotions and experiences Named by the verb *to Be/Leave.* It also underscores the varying degrees of resist-ance against which and beyond which one chooses to Be/Leave. The first reference to Be/Leaving, quoted at the beginning of this chapter, describes Daly's joyful departure from the world of Catholic liturgy. The second ref-erence, which examines Daly's expanding awareness of the "hidden broken Promise" of academic life, is far more painful to read.

Daly provides the full account of her unsuccessful bid for tenure in 1968–1969, including the student protests and news coverage, in the "Autobiographical Preface" to the second edition of *The Church and the Second Sex.* She relates how, after the students had left for vacation and she for a summer-school post on the West Coast, Boston College's adminis-tration reversed their decision in order to put behind them the negative media attention they had received since the previous spring. Daly received a telegram from the president of Boston College, "informing [her], with-out congratulations, that [she] had been granted promotion and tenure."

Daly's description of her reaction to the news is analogous to her account of leaving during the bingo sermon on Easter Sunday 1968. It is infused with the same undercurrent of anticlimax and finality, and ultimately the same sense of be-ing in a New Place, but it lacks the feelings of lightness and celebration. "It was a strange victory," writes Daly, in an effort to reproduce the complicated feelings with which she responded to the news of her tenure. "Apparently the book which had generated the hostility which led to my firing had generated the support which forced my rehiring. . . . But something had happened to the meaning of 'professor,' to the meaning of 'university,' to the meaning of 'teaching'" (Daly 1985a, 13).

Here Daly's departure narrative shows its kinship with other narratives written by Catholic and post-Catholic women in flight. Crossing boundaries deepens Daly's awareness of the two-sidedness of life. Just as the hymn that had been a taunt in parochial school had turned into her processional out of her last mass in 1968, the book that had closed the door to tenure had miraculously reopened it. In *Outercourse,* Daly explained that it was in response to this ambiguous victory in the tenure process that she first clarified the meaning of be-ing and Be/Leaving and consciously chose life "on the Boundary." "As I came to understand more about academia," Daly maintains, "I still wanted to be in that world, as it were, but not of it—to be there still, but unconstrained. I wanted academia to support my real work in the world." The double sight that accompanied the experience of Crossing Over revealed to Daly a new and better way to be a teacher to a growing population of women outside conventional academic institutions who wanted to learn what she had Dis-covered about the relationship between be-ing and Be/Leaving.

This is where Boundary Living came in. Through her grueling experience with the tenure process (and a similar ordeal when she was denied promotion to full professor in 1975), Daly Dis-covered that "although eventually I could no longer believe in academia/academentia, I could Be/Leave *in* it." Buoyantly, she concluded: "In Other words, I could be a highly qualified Pirate" (Daly 1992, 121). This Moment of Dis-covery informs all of Daly's subsequent strategies as a separatist. Daly understood that be-ing and Be/Leaving did not entail making discrete "either/or" decisions; for example, leave academia or stay and assimilate. She felt the Call of the Wild, a vocation that entailed making Other plans. She sought to build New Space where she and Other women could explore the meaning of their Power of Absence and embrace the Prance of Life, "the large and complex steps required for Macroevolution; the springing, capering, frisking, frolicking, cavorting, romping, gamboling" style of Wild Creatures (Daly and Caputi 1987, 88). Daly chose to adopt this style as a philosopher and a public Presence on the margins of academia. This choice put her in a better position to focus on the Nonquestions at the heart of her philosophy.

Although the first-person accounts in the "Autobiographical Preface" and the "Feminist Postchristian Introduction" might seem, implicitly, to suggest otherwise, Daly did not negotiate her way to boundary-living alone. She made the journey in the company of women—the transtemporal community of Hags and Spinsters that she originally Named the "antichurch" or "cosmic covenant" of sisterhood (Daly 1985b, 132–178) and later conjured by the phrase the "Power of Presence" (Daly and Caputi 1987, 88). The new Postchristian feminist ontology first introduced in *Beyond God the Father* was grounded in Daly's proliferating experiences of Elemental integrity and her expanding woman-consciousness. It grew out of Daly's successful struggle to accept her Life on the Boundary as a positive development, her deepening Realization that she had Nothing to lose. What did it matter if Daly had Plundered her Boundary metaphor from the Harvard theologian Paul Tillich, about whom she was deeply ambivalent (Daly 1992, 148)? Being a Pirate requires a variety of approaches to recycling Smuggled Goods, including the skills of the Prospector and the Alchemist. Daly "sorted out nuggets of partial, i.e., patriarchally distorted, knowledge and placed these in a Metapatriarchal context, so that they could radiate richer meanings." She insisted that "the secret of my Alchemical powers lay in my ability to Dis-cover and create an entirely Other setting for these treasures, that is, Radical Feminist Philosophy" (Daly 1992, 157). Once freed from Stag-nation, Daly's Plundered Metaphors and gems of knowledge become part of an endless process of Re-membering, Re-calling the connections binding Elemental beings (Daly and Caputi 1987, 92–93).

The Other setting that Daly Dis-covered on the Boundary was a separatist vision of community among Hags and Spinsters. In the Third Passage of *Gyn/Ecology,* Daly examines what happens to Spinsters' Selves in the new Space on the Boundary. She contrasts the claim that J. Glenn Gray makes about male friendship ("[It] seeks to expand [the] walls [of self] and keep them intact") with her growing experience of female friendship. Daly explains that sisterhood is about "burning/melting/vaporizing the constricting walls imposed upon the Self." She elaborates: "Female friendship is not concerned with 'expanding walls and keeping them intact,' but with expanding energy, power, vision, psychic and physical space." In Other Words, female friendship/Sparking, which is only fully Realized on the Boundary, is all about be-ing. Separatism, or Life on the Boundary, requires "paring away the layers of false selves from the Self" so that "the Self's original movement" can be set free. These unbound Selves are not clones, they're Crones. Daly insists that "the variety which Crones respect in each other has as its basic precondition and common thread the endurance/fortitude/stamina needed for persevering on the Journey" (Daly 1990, 380–381).

Daly's Words Re-call the spirit, energy, and wisdom of the Third Spiral Galaxy (1975–1987). While Be-ing remains her Final Cause, Be/Leaving, a never-ending process, demands even more endurance/forti- tude/stamina the longer the Journey Spins On. Freeing the Self's/Selves' original movement is not a task that can be completed once and for all. The more Hags See, the more challenging be-ing becomes. Hags' lives are complicated by the Boundary's location on the edge of patriarchy. Not even the most Outrageously Original Sinning, not even the most intense and sustained Be/Leaving can bring about the total eclipse of phallocracy or even one Hag's complete escape from the sado-state. This situation is a given; Spinning Hags work/Spiral around it. Radical Feminism, even sep- aratism, does not mean escapism and the abdication of responsibility. Women's flight has nothing to do with escapism. Nag-Gnostics value and nurture mobility for Other reasons. Commitment to Biophilic Energy entails endless forays into dangerous territory.

The further Daly pursues her Journey, the more Spiral Galaxies she explores, the keener her awareness of phallocratic necrophilia becomes. Pirates can create Separate Spaces, Other Settings for their Plundered gems of knowledge. Crones can crack powerful jokes about the noxious gases of patriarchy. ("When Crones crack their own Jokes, the world splits open.") Still, the noxious gases have not dissipated. Daly's Hagographic writings from the 1980s and 1990s are more insistent than ever that "phal- locracy does not and in fact cannot essentially change. It cannot reverse its destructive mechanisms that massacre women and nature, for these are essential to its necrophilic existence. They are its vital, i.e., lethal functions" (Daly 1985e, xxvi, xv).

It is not surprising, then, to see Daly expand on the timeliness of the Courage to Leave in the 1985 "New Archaic Afterwords" to *The Church and the Second Sex*. Daly herSelf has Named patriarchy and the dangers of patriarchal religion, but she is by no means indifferent to the plight of the women who remain "lost/trapped inside its gynocidal, spirit-deadening maze" (Daly 1985e, xii). She retains a strong sense of empathy for the Self who had written *The Church and the Second Sex* and for others who had yet to encounter its message. It is to this audience that she writes:

> From the perspective of 1985 A. F. [Anno Feminarum] it can be seen clearly, and more clearly than ever, that a tragic error/terror manages to lock women within the prisons of blind/blinded faith. . . .

Acceptance of this error gives rise to terror of Leaving. This terror is itself a major cause of spiritual death. . . . The terror and the belief system to which it is attached are exorcised only when women break through to the Elemental Realization that we owe the church Nothing, since the church has given us precisely Nothing. We then see that we have Nothing to lose by Leaving. Indeed the loss of Nothing posing as Something brings almost inexpressible relief. (Daly 1985e, xii–xiii)

Daly refuses to forget the "terror of Leaving" that kept her in the church and then in a state of limbo, on the verge of Be/Leaving, from the late 1950s through the late 1960s. The fear of "an endless desert" and of being treated as a madwoman (Daly 1985d, 24) stay with her as vivid memories of a still memorable, but no longer frightening, nightmare. In the "New Archaic Afterwords" Daly draws on the power of this nightmare that had almost paralyzed her and still terrorized women of the 1980s. She reassures women that "We have Nothing to lose by Leaving" and that the loss of "Nothing posing as Something" is a genuinely positive experience that opens up new possibilities.

The "New Archaic Afterwords" provides a concrete example of what it means for Daly to be a Pirate. Daly's Journey and her dedication to exorcising the patriarchal demons are endless and boundless. The Spiral Shape of her Journey ensures that Daly is never too far removed from where she has made her latest exit. Her Home on the Boundary, in a subsequent Spiral Galaxy, simply affords her an enhanced perspective from which to speak. The Daly who revisits her 1968 text and Self in 1985 is a very different Daly from the one who took such pains in 1975 to explain the relationship between her commitment to Aquinas's theology and her Radical Feminist ontology. Daly circa 1985 assumes that we understand the roots of her ontology. She brings this Hagography with her to the text, but her chief concern remains the women who are locked within the prisons of blind/blinded faith.

Daly speaks directly to the women of the "dulled-out mid-eighties" who are being "force-fed" media images of Nancy Reagan and Sunny von Bulow and parallel images of Catholic women kneeling at the feet of john paul two (Daly 1985e, xviii, xx). Daly finds New Words befitting the Third Galaxy to describe the connection between be-ing and Be/Leaving: "The timelessness of recession/procession into archetypes which characterizes the mid-eighties a.d. is a pathological mirror image of the Elemental shedding of patriarchal time that is essential to Movement into and creation of an Archaic Future. As women move more and more into Living Archaic Time, our Original Creative Time, we Realize ourSelves and realize that the year of the lord—any year a.d.—is *archetypal deadtime*" (Daly 1985e, xviii).

For all that has changed—the Words, the Setting, Daly herself—the message is familiar: "Original Women, in touch with our Origins, bring forth Original thoughts, words, deeds. Forgetting to remember old creeds, we conjure new and ancient Faith. Ignoring false promises/premises, we hop with Living Hope. Riding the Tides of Present Promise, we bond in the chorus of Be-ing" (Daly 1985e, xxviii). Daly's message here should be read within the framework of her central Metaphor, the Spiraling Journey. Hags partake of Original Time and Space by simultaneously looking backward into archetypal deadtime and Spinning forward into the Archaic Future. Original Movement, by definition, proceeds "from one's Original Self" toward "one's Final Cause," the Good (Daly and Caputi 1987, 152).

Even from the Third Spiral Galaxy Daly can smell the noxious gases of patriarchy smoldering on. She does not embrace an ontology or a separatism that functions as a nosegay, keeping the stench just out of range. Just as Be-ing is not a static destination but a Final Cause, Be/Leaving is not escapism but movement that expands the Space for Biophilic be-ing. *Pure Lust, Outercourse,* and *Quintessence* Be-Speak the truth: The Journey does not get easier, less dangerous, in Spiral Galaxies Three, Four, and Five. The rewards and intuitions of be-ing deepen and expand with each Pirate raid, but the raids themselves Re-call the proximity of normative non-being, phallocracy. Toward the end of the Second Realm of *Pure Lust,* in words that evoke Cixous's images of flight, Daly sketches out the delicate ecology of Life on the Boundary as gleaned from the Third Galaxy:

> It is difficult to avoid the conclusion that when women are most true to our Selves, we are *distemperate,* that is, "out of order, not functioning normally." As supernormally functioning Scolds, Sylphs, Shrews, Wantons, Weirds, and company, Pyromantic women are definitely "out of order." Breaking Out of the male-ordered catalogs of virile virtues is not a tidy affair. Rather, this is achieved through movements that may be compared to tidal waves, and it involves invoking Muses and confronting demons. (Daly 1984, 288)

The Fourth Galaxy of *Outercourse* models for us some of the untidiness of tidal change. In the New Time of the Fourth Galaxy, which cannot be captured by patriarchal calendars, Daly finds herSelf at the Beginning of her Journey as well as at the culmination of the three preceding Galaxies. The Fourth Galaxy sounds Different from its predecessors. Daly speaks more directly, more urgently to her readers and frequently stops to question and challenge herSelf. Sometimes she appears to be answering questions that readers cannot hear. At one point the discussion leads back to a Moment in Cork, Ireland, in 1984, when someone asked Daly why she continued to teach at Boston College. Daly's impromptu answer, "I choose to Stand my Ground," had since become a kind of mantra for her. It Be-spoke to her the deeper meaning of separatism. In her account of the defining Moment in Cork eight years before, Daly explains some of the insights her one-line response had brought to the surface: "I was choosing to Fight/Act (Stand my Ground) at that precise location on the Boundary between Background and foreground where the demonic patriarchal distortions of women's Archaic heritage are most visible and accessible to me, where my Craft can be most effective in the work of Exorcism—reversing the reversals that blunt the potential for Realizing Ecstasy" (Daly 1992, 284).

In the Fourth Galaxy, Daly returns to this pivotal Moment on her Journey with new concerns and an Archaic consciousness. Her spontaneous answer, which had clarified so much for her in Galaxy Three, now poses difficult questions for her in Galaxy Four.

> The important question is: Is my Ground, in the deepest sense, on the Boundaries of patriarchal institutions? The answer is no, not Now.
>
> Oh, yes, I still Fight/Act there, on those Boundaries. But my true Ground, the Ground of that Ground, so to speak, is farther Out, farther Back. Back in the Background.

Daly concedes that she can be distracted by what transpires on the other side of the Boundary, inside patriarchal institutions, but this distraction is weaker in the Fourth Galaxy than in Galaxies One through Three. In Galaxy Four, which she entered in 1987, Daly's life is centered on the "pull of the Verb—the intransitive One." She explains that the pull, or attraction, is "so overwhelming that I fly sometimes, fly into the Unfolding, Enfolding arms" (Daly 1992, 340).

The Daly of the Fourth Galaxy describes herSelf as a commuter to earth who lives with Wild Cat and Catherine the Cow on the Other side of the moon. She senses the Presence of Other Crones in nearby craters and mountain ranges, although she has never actually seen them. "Really, there's been no Time for a conference," she relates. "But everyone is aware of everyone else" (Daly 1992, 347). The final section of *Outercourse* bears the generic label "Concluding-Beginning," but it is entitled "The Great Summoning and the Great Summation." It starts out with Daly, Catherine, and Wild Cat poring over clippings from earth, apocalyptic warnings in real-life news stories about silicone breast implants, depleting ozone, lethal ultraviolet rays. It ends with Daly addressing the multitude, thousands of Cronies and Familiars, sharing the podium (a moon rock) with celebrated Hags of yore, including Granuaile (the sixteenth-century Pirate from Ireland), Hypatia, Harriet Tubman, Susan B. Anthony, and Spider Woman.

This passage, a controversial personal narrative in which Daly shares her soul and her dreams, poses problems for many feminists. Is Daly co-opting the women she mentions, denying the particularities of their lives and words? Is she appropriating their voices and authority for herself in order to promote an essentialized middle-class white Euro-American version of womanhood which fails to understand the power of difference? Or is this visionary passage just another example of what New Time/Space can mean in Daly's Fourth Galaxy? My reading suggests the third alternative. In this fantasy placed near the end of *Outercourse*, Daly constructs the Metaphor of an intergalactic conference of Hags to dramatize what Hagography and the Power of Presence have meant to her and to underscore the vital role community plays in be-ing and Be/Leaving. Daly has maintained that the Spiraling Journeys of Pirates are intertwined with those of the Great Hags of all times, whose life stories have been stolen and hidden from us (Daly 1990, 14–15). In the Great Summation scene, Daly paints a portrait of women's community, what she calls the Power of Presence: the "flow of healing energy experienced by women who are Present to each Other in New Time/Space" (Daly and Caputi 1987, 88).

Daly closes her autobiography with a portion of a speech very similar to the ones she has made all over the world. We see Daly the Nag-Gnostic inspirational speaker in top form. Daly's "Great Summation" is a distillation of her Radical Feminist Philosophy, familiar words, but in an Other Setting. "*Together, Moonstruck Metamorphosing Intergalactic Voyagers can change our world. The Great Summation requires cumulative negation of the nothingness of the state of necrophilia (patriarchy). The Great Summation is following our Final Cause, Realizing our participation in Be-ing. It is cumulative affirmation and celebration of Life*" (Daly 1992, 414–415).

Daly the Radical Feminist Philosopher takes huge risks in *Outercourse*, especially in this final section that takes place in a New Space/Time on the Other side of the moon. The subtitle to the Fourth Spiral Galaxy prepares us to accompany Daly to the "BE-DAZZLING NOW," a Galaxy "Off the Calendar, Off the Clock." An illustration confirms that one Ur-text is indeed the nursery rhyme about the cow jumping over the moon. The Prelude to the Fourth Galaxy, interwoven with Moments of Momentous Re-Membering, is driven by two of Daly's mantras ("Keep going Mary, Go!" and her mother's urgings: "Go do your own work, dear"). It ends with a passage that reminds us that Daly inhabits a world of unceasing motion, Spiraling movements that bring Daly, Catherine, Wild Cat, and us, her readers, that much closer to the Unfolding, Enfolding Arms of Be-ing: "Run right into the Now. There is so much room (no room for gloom). It is so open here, there, everywhere. So full of the sweet, fresh smells of earth and air. Just dare!" (Daly 1992, 331–336).

In *Quintessence*, Daly continues the Journey into the Fifth Spiral Galaxy, "the Expanding Here" (Daly 1998, 27–55), where she finds herSelf in the midst of a postpatriarchal Radical Elemental Feminist Movement called the Anonyma Network. The setting has shifted to the Lost and Found Continent in the year 2048 B.E. (Biophilic Era) but the message comes as no surprise to readers of *Outercourse*. Daly, still commuting between the margins of patriarchy in the 1990s and an Other extraterrestrial environment beyond the influence of the "nectech nasties" (Daly 1998, 220), writes with a growing sense of urgency. She calls *Quintessence* "a Desperate Act performed in a time of ultimate battles between principalities and powers." The apocalyptic imagery accurately reflects Daly's assessment of the stakes of the battle between "Boundary-violating necrotechnologists" and Daly's Cronies, whom she Names "Biophilic Bitches" (Daly 1998, 119).

The battle is about Space, both inner and outer Space. "The space-rapists say they intend to strip-mine the moon," Daly warns. "They are invading and destroying the genetic wilderness and space wilderness." For Biophilic Bitches, "faced with the reality of hideous manipulation and the probability of ultimate extinction, not only of our bodies/minds (ourSelves), but all of nature," Daly maintains that the only option is to explore the Archaic Future. The Archaic Future is the new frontier, accessible by "Time-Space Travel beyond archetypal deadtime and . . . deep in our Memories, our Deep Past" (Daly 1998, 2–3).

In *Quintessence*, Daly uses the word *diaspora* to describe the situation of women in the 1990s. She chose the term because it evokes the "state of dividedness and dispersion of women under patriarchy," both our "external dispersion" and "internalized oppression—the exile, scattering, and enforced migration of consciousness—which cuts us off from deep and focused Realizing of the *Background*" (Daly 1998, 37–38). Daly, proficient at recycling and reversals, suggests that individual women who are Elemental Feminists can each transform their own diaspora into a positive Biophilic Movement. "The workings of Elemental Feminist Genius can almost be invisible at first: One woman Sparks insight in another, and so on. The process, seemingly slow at first, is contagious. Then, apparently all of a sudden, it takes cumulative Quantum Leaps across Time and Space. That's how our Genius works—by Expanding Here" (Daly 1998, 77).

That's what Mary Daly has done for us lately. She has provided New Space for us to think about some of the fundamental questions and challenges that face women and other Biophilic inhabitants of planet earth. Daly started to provide this New Space subliminally and implicitly in her first book, *The Church and the Second Sex*, where she juxtaposed two categories, the unchanging and eternal Catholic church and the demands of feminists of the 1950s and 1960s, encapsulated in Simone de Beauvoir's unforgettable phrase "the second sex." When she experimented with this juxtaposition, Daly Dis-covered an entire range of human discourse: the posing of Nonquestions, which became her life's work. Daly's Non-questions opened up a new frontier analogous to the expanding Galaxies of Outer Space, a frontier that Daly, the Catholic feminist theologian fresh out of graduate school, set out to explore in the late 1960s. This open frontier is what attracted Daly—who had doctorates in both philosophy and theology—to theology; theology seemed to provide more space in which to promote social change and challenge the status quo (Daly 1992, 84).

Daly's first book captured the imaginations of Catholics and feminists of the late 1960s because it opened up vast spaces of the Christian past, present, and future to hopeful and courageous scrutiny. The popularity of the book (as well as its notoriety in conservative Catholic circles) showed Daly still more New Spaces, an expanding universe where she had never thought to look for it: beyond God the Father. In her second book, *Beyond God the Father*, Daly unveiled brave new worlds of feminist philosophical discourse that combined quite naturally with her commitments as an activist for feminist causes. During the early 1970s, when she was writing *Beyond God the Father* and the "Feminist Postchristian Introduction" and "Autobiographical Preface" for the second edition of her first book, Daly Dis-covered still another realm of discourse, in which feminist philosophy and personal narrative/Hagography flow together. Since Daly's personal experience within the confines of academentia had shown her that life and work were *never really separate*, even for phallocrats, Daly was prepared for this new insight, but not for the experience of light and space and bound-arylessness that greeted her in the "newly founded invisible counter-university, the Feminist Universe" (Daly 1985a, 13) that she and her Nonquestions helped to create. Daly was Be-Dazzled. This New Space became and remains Daly's Home.

Starting in 1978 with *Gyn/Ecology*, Daly has envisioned the growth of her Life/Philosophy (her Radical Feminist Metaethics) as an Otherworld Journey, a Spiraling Voyage of Exorcism and Ecstasy. What makes the Journey possible is "the radical be-ing of women" (Daly 1990, 1). The goal of this never-ending Journey is "both discovery and creation of a world other than patriarchy." On the last page of *Gyn/Ecology*, we see what the Spiraling Journey has wrought: Spinsters hearing themSelves and eachOther into be-ing (Daly 1990, 424). In Other words, New Space can produce Otherworldly acoustics with remarkable ontological implications. *Pure Lust,* the *Wickedary, Outercourse,* and *Quintessence* continue the Journeys that Daly embarked upon in *Gyn/Ecology,* and in the Course of these Voyages Daly shows how Metaphor and the Spinning of New Words provide still more expanding Space and Time in which women can Dis-cover themSelves and participate in the Unfolding of Be-ing. As we have seen in the case of the Fourth Galaxy of *Outercourse,* Daly's Metaphors have expanded beyond the Boundaries that the rules of rhetoric have assigned to them. These rules do not apply on the Other side of the moon or the Lost and Found Continent, a place where even the Boundary appears infinitely spacious, far closer to the Enfolding arms of Be-ing than to the sadosociety that sent Daly and her Cronies to the Boundary in the first place.

Since 1968 Mary Daly, the theologian, the Radical Feminist Philosopher, the Nag-Gnostic Pirate, has been Creating, Dis-covering, and Bespeaking the existence of Space for women to pursue their own survival and other Biophilic causes. Much of this Space lies in the Realm of the feminist imagination, but all of it is Real (or can be Realized). Thanks to Daly, women can conceive of the possibility of Be/Leaving; they know that there is Life beyond each threshold and that all Life participates in Be-ing. Thanks to Daly's Hagographies, women can embark with confidence on Journeys through Spiraling Galaxies and find vantage points within the various Galaxies where Hags can realize their past and future Selves. Thanks to Daly, women know about the Boundary, that it is not a two-dimensional line but a four-dimensional Space that expands infinitely toward Be-ing. Finally, thanks to Daly and her courageous, outrageous escapades and experiments, women who challenge constraints placed on Space (Real and imagined) or who refuse to be tidily consigned to their place can approach their own challenges without having to reinvent the wheel. They can muster some confidence from the fact that Daly has been in that place before (and somehow found Space).

Discovering, exploring, and expanding Biophilic Space has been Mary Daly's major achievement for three decades. Daly found the Space necessary for be-ing long before her fellow phallosophers were willing to admit that being could occupy space (or that women could participate in be-ing). Feminists whose Journeys began after Daly's have been beneficiaries of the Space Daly has Dis-covered and Expanded, whether they have been aware of it or not. At the end of a disheartening incident in the Fourth Galaxy of *Outercourse,* Daly, ever resilient, reveals her latest plan: "Blast a hole in the wall between the foreground [patriarchal space and time] and the Background [Biophilic Space and Time]—a hole so big that everyone who is really Alive can get through." Daly adds: "I decided that the way to do that was to just be my Natural Self, who is Extreme" (Daly 1992, 341). Daly, Pirate and Hagographer, shows us the clear and concrete meaning in Leigh Gilmore's enticingly abstract maxim "autobiography provokes fantasies of the real" (Gilmore 1994, 16).

4

A NUN FOREVER

I'm a better nun now than I ever was in the Cloister.

—Armstrong 1995, 280

It was very hot in Charleston. The women in the sewing cooperative in the back room of Covenant House moved slowly around their tables. People came in looking for a cold shower and a little shade. The Ferraros and the Husseys called to tell us that we were loved. It was just another day.

The first day of our entire adult lives as laywomen.

—Ferraro and Hussey 1990, 323

By the 1980s, the turbulence in the Catholic church—the fallout from the reforms of Vatican II and the backlash that had sometimes threatened to negate those reforms—had subsided. The decade and a half between the end of Vatican II in 1965 and the 1980s witnessed a dramatic reversal. In her important study *Women in the Vanishing Cloister* (1993), Helen Rose Fuchs Ebaugh reviews the statistics on convent membership and attrition during that volatile period. The number of sisters in American convents, which had been rising steadily since the Second World War, finally peaked in 1965 with a total of 179,954. This figure was large enough to offset the 1,562 departures from American convents that year. Five years later, in 1970, 4,337 sisters left the religious life: the largest number of recorded departures in a single year in the history of American Catholic women's religious orders. Both departures and new recruits leveled off in the 1970s. In 1980, 126,517 sisters remained in American convents and only 751 women departed (Ebaugh 1993, 47–50). The United States was not unique. Western European convents recorded the same basic pattern of growth through the mid-1960s followed by departures and decline in numbers. Only in developing nations did the number of women religious grow in the decades following Vatican II. In her comprehensive history *Sisters in Arms: Catholic Nuns through Two Millennia* (1996), Jo Ann McNamara includes this ominous observation: "More than one recent American nun-scholar has urged her readers to consider the probability that the sisterhood as it now exists will not survive into a new millennium" (McNamara 1996, 636).

Ebaugh was a graduate student in sociology at Columbia University in 1970–1971 when she collected her data for a dissertation on the increasing number of ex-nuns in America. She discovered that "paradoxically, as religious orders updated and experienced change, the number of 'defectors' who left American convents increased." Then, in the midst of analyzing her data, Ebaugh "became one of [her] own statistics" and left religious life behind (Ebaugh 1988, xv–xvi). While writing her dissertation, Ebaugh experienced what many other Catholic women in a variety of settings and life situations have come to understand: Writing about leaving is a form of departure which leads to other personal and spiritual migrations.

This chapter examines two popular books about convent departure written by former sisters during the late 1970s and 1980s: Karen Armstrong's *Through the Narrow Gate* (originally published in 1981) and *No Turning Back,* by Barbara Ferraro and Patricia Hussey with Jane O'Reilly (1990). These two works depict convent and post-convent experiences that are worlds away from those described by Monica Baldwin four decades earlier. Vatican II and the feminist movement contributed to the profound differences between Baldwin's memoir and these later convent-departure narratives. There are still moments, however, when the parallels between Baldwin's pilgrimage and the spiritual journeys described in the later narratives are palpable.

An important difference between Baldwin and the authors discussed in this chapter stems from the distinction between nuns and sisters. Baldwin literally left a cloister; she had been a female monastic, a nun. Karen Armstrong, Barbara Ferraro, and Patricia Hussey were sisters whose work brought them into contact with the world outside the convent. As late as 1985, Sister Marie Augusta Neal called attention to the still-widespread habit of confusing nuns, who live cloistered lives of prayer in monasteries, with sisters, who embrace an apostolic spirituality and an apostolate appropriate to their lives of service in the world as educators, health care professionals, and providers of other forms of human services, especially among the poor (Neal 1985, 142–143).

Historians of women religious who have rightly insisted on this distinction have fought an uphill battle. Thanks, in part, to the undying reputation of nineteenth-century nativist classics such as Maria Monk's *Awful Disclosures,* the phrase "ex-nun" has resonance, the power to evoke a hidden world that excites the prurient imaginations of non-Catholics in America, Great Britain, and western Europe. "Ex-sisters" has no such power. No wonder those who are interested in sales and in increasing listeners and viewers on radio and television talk shows exploit the power of the phrase "ex-nun" even when they have been told that the author or guest is an ex-sister.

Non-Catholics and anti-Catholics have not been alone in preferring the word "nun" over "sister." In this book, I have succumbed to the conventions of popular—if imprecise—usage and follow the example of the authors whose works are examined. Some writers, ex-sisters included, opt to use the word "nun," even when they know better. Karen Armstrong, a world-renowned authority on religion, refers to nuns for fifty-five pages in her memoir before stopping briefly on page fifty-six to mention that "strictly speaking," the women in the order she joined were "not really nuns at all" (Armstrong 1995, 56).

The period between Vatican II and the mid-1980s was especially eventful, exciting, and stressful for sisters. The new "modern" habits, which startled Catholics in 1965, were signifiers of deeper changes to come. The leaders of women's religious communities, who had been organized since the 1950s to meet new challenges in the field of education, were engaged in reflection and long-range planning that explored every aspect of religious life in their orders and congregations. This process led to a major redeployment of sisters' energies, which ultimately meant proportionately less commitment to middle-class parochial schools and elite private academies and more involvement in parish ministries, the medical and legal professions, social work, and the provision of human services to the poor in developing countries throughout the world. At the same time, between 1966 and 1984, all orders of Catholic sisters throughout the world responded to a papal directive for renewal and the revision of their constitutions. This entailed a thoroughgoing examination of the distinct identity and spirituality of individual congregations and the ways in which their vows, lifestyles, formation (training and probation preceding final vows), and community and governance structures could be adapted to the needs of a rapidly changing post-conciliar church.

When orders and congregations brought their constitutions—the fruits of tireless discussion and revision within communities, committees, and finally general chapters—to the Vatican's Sacred Congregation for Religious and Secular Institutes (SCRIS), the results were mixed. Some constitutions met with immediate approval, while others were rejected or altered, without consultation, by the Vatican bureaucrats at SCRIS. The process could go on for months, even years, and was sometimes derailed when one set of SCRIS theologians contradicted the mandates issued by their predecessors and sisters were left scrambling to satisfy the whims of the small group of SCRIS bureaucrats who currently held their fate in their hands.

In a controversial article on the procedures and underlying attitudes of SCRIS published in the December 21, 1984, issue of *The National Catholic Reporter,* an anonymous author suggested that superiors of women's religious orders and congregations might be called "the battered women of the church." She explained in detail how SCRIS resembled an abusive husband and how the leaders of religious congregations had been put in the position of abused wives. She maintained that SCRIS exhibited the same pattern of unpredictable, irrational abuse of power masked by publicly acknowledged respectability and status found in many wife-batterers and that some leaders of women's religious congregations displayed the qualities (inability to name the problem, self-blame, and fear of recurrence) that we have come to associate with battered wives.

The author, identified elsewhere as "the former superior of a religious women's community" (Gramick 1986, 17), published the article anonymously to avoid reprisals (aimed at her order and herself). She explains the impossibility of her situation in an impassioned aside to the reader: "Those who judge anonymity to be cowardly have to realize that women who are battered have tried the other alternative, they have tried reason, they have gone back over and over, they have tried to make a new beginning, and now finally, they are at the point of desperation." The article was not an invitation to "opt out" but rather an attempt to break the silence "so all in the church can participate in the ministry of justice, reconciliation and conversion" ("Nuns: The Battered Women of the Church?" 25).

In the March 1, 1985, issue of the *National Catholic Reporter*, Gerelyn Hollingsworth, identified as the author of a forthcoming book about the 60,000 women who had left American convents since 1966, posed a whole series of not entirely rhetorical questions:

> What if all the 120,000 sisters remaining in American convents said, "We are grown women, sane and responsible. We won't be pushed around anymore"? What would the men in Rome do? If all the sisters in all the communities revealed their power on the same day, the bang would reverberate down the coming millennium. If American nuns removed themselves from the jurisdiction of men, what would other Catholic women do? Would they feel emboldened to stand with the sisters? How would nuns in other countries react? Would this startling show of solidarity send a message of freedom to girls and women everywhere? (Hollingsworth 1985, 16)

The arresting analogy embraced by the author of "Nuns: Battered Women of the Church?" and Hollingsworth's equally powerful language underscore the highly charged atmosphere in which the narratives discussed in this chapter were written. Read together, *Through the Narrow Gate* and *No Turning Back* illustrate the complexity of the experiences depicted in post–Vatican II convent-departure narratives and touch upon all five themes explored in previous chapters: reversals, border-crossings, diaspora, naming, and recycling. Both works hinge upon the pivotal first step, the "premier pas" immortalized in Mary McCarthy's chapter "C'est le Premier Pas Qui Coûte." For sisters, the first step consists of breaking taboos by shattering the silence that has surrounded convent departures, both within convents and within the church at large.

Karen Armstrong

> Enter by the narrow gate, since the gate that leads to perdition is wide, and the road spacious, and many take it; but it is a narrow gate and a hard road that lead to life, and only a few find it.
>
> —Matthew 7:13–14; epigraph in Armstrong 1995, ix

In the introduction to the second edition of *Through the Narrow Gate*, Karen Armstrong calls the process of writing her convent-departure narrative "a watershed . . . that was, in its way, every bit as important as those crucial years in the convent." During the decade after she left the convent in 1969 and returned immediately to her studies at Oxford, she came to realize that the seven years that she had spent in the religious life were "becoming trivialized." She knew that she was collaborating in this process of trivialization by entertaining her friends with funny stories about convent life while carefully editing out or actively repressing other memories that were "still raw and painful." Finally, with the encouragement of friends, she decided to write a memoir, in part to recover the meaning of her convent experience "before the memories disappeared beyond recall." Twenty-five years after her exodus from the convent, she affirms that writing *Through the Narrow Gate* "redeemed the past" for her in ways she "could not have imagined" (Armstrong 1995, xiii).

Armstrong provides readers with unusually intimate access to the process of writing her memoir and in so doing explains how her decision to write about religious life, rather than simply close the door on it, set her free. The first draft of the book had been "very black and angry" and prompted her literary agent to ask Armstrong to consider including some material explaining why she had stayed in the convent for "seven whole years." The second and third drafts unlocked a different set of memories: a life centered upon the liturgy, "the belief that every single moment of the day had eternal significance," and "the sense of a spiritual quest for meaning that would make [her] life wholly significant" (Armstrong 1995, xii–xiv).

After she had reclaimed these more positive memories of the convent, Armstrong knew instinctively that she had repressed them because she "thought [she] had lost them forever" (Armstrong 1995, xiii–xiv). The act of writing her memoir did not bring Armstrong all the way back to the church that she left after she had departed from the convent in 1969, but it did help her to reclaim the convent years and the part of her that decided in secondary school to enter the religious life. While she does not deny and no longer represses her Catholic girlhood and convent experience, she declines to call herself a "Catholic," a self-definition that no longer fits. She calls herself "a freelance monotheist" and hastens to add that she intends the designation to be "slightly tongue in cheek" (Armstrong 1995, xvi).

Armstrong's title, taken from Matthew 7:13–14, is aptly chosen for her memoir, which explores the many ways in which the road through the narrow gate that leads to life is hard to follow and hard to bear. It turns out that the metaphors of the narrow gate and the hard road apply to the route that leads both to and from the convent. Armstrong knew about the narrow gate from popular literary and film depictions of convent life long before she entered the novitiate in the village of Tripton, Bedfordshire, on September 14, 1962. Although forthcoming with the details of her personal and family life, she discreetly declines to name the order she joined. Armstrong's memoir illustrates how Catholic women's departure narratives (memoirs, novels, and films) have become prototypes, acknowledged and improvised on by the authors of subsequent works within this distinct subgenre.

Karen Armstrong was not alone when, on the eve of her entry into the postulancy, she envisioned her future experiences in the convent through the lenses provided by images in a classic version of the convent-departure story. She pored over the convent sections of Monica Baldwin's *I Leap over the Wall* and imagined herself capable of persevering where Monica Baldwin had admitted defeat. Nor were Karen's parents unique when they took refuge in a version of the convent-departure story that may have provided some comfort to them. Armstrong's family went to see *The Sound of Music* after they bade her farewell at Kings Cross rail station. She left for Tripton feeling as if she were watching a film rather than living through such a strange day in her life; the rest of her family went directly to a matinee (Armstrong 1995, 1–2, 5–6).

The harsh realities of day-to-day life in the convent, which were by no means exaggerated in Baldwin's memoir, only increased Karen's attraction to religious life: "I knew that it was going to be hard; I wanted it to be hard. It wouldn't be worth doing otherwise. What were a few hardships if they led to a close relationship with God? I felt sorry for Monica Baldwin. How could she have given up?" (Armstrong 1995, 2).

The jacket of the first American hardcover edition of *Through the Narrow Gate* promises an account of how the author entered the cloister "as a girl of seventeen—upset with family problems, yearning for the tranquil air of certainty she saw on her teachers' faces." The memoir depicts several aspects of Armstrong's youthful experiences at home and at school that might have led her to consider entering a convent. When she was about 12, her maternal grandmother, whom she resembled and to whom she was close, confided to her that as a 16-year-old student at a convent school in Liverpool she wanted to be a nun. Granny's mother had refused to give permission. "You never know," Granny said, deep in thought, "it might have made all the difference" (Armstrong 1995, 29). What Karen did know was that her grandmother's life had been almost uniformly unhappy: years spent away from home in a tuberculosis sanatorium, a pattern of unfaithfulness to her husband, palpable tension in her relationship with her daughter, and a poorly shrouded alcohol problem. A few years later, in 1960, Karen's father lost his job, which caused gossip and social slights at her convent school. The change had a positive impact on her mother; work in the world made her "alive in a new way." But Karen's mother also visibly worried about her husband, who appeared "snuffed out," depressed and subdued. As she planned for the future, Karen began to wonder about alternatives to marriage and family life: "I thought of my grandmother, still drinking gin in the larder. What kind of a world was this when people shut themselves up with some unhappy secret, unable to communicate it to anybody?" (Armstrong 1995, 33–34).

Karen's mother delivered the kind of injunctions against promiscuous behavior and looking "cheap" that most teenage girls—especially Catholics—had to endure during the 1960s. Karen, whose body seemed to pose problems with her parents and endanger her budding self-confidence, learned that she could always rely upon her mind: Sometimes testing her intellectual talents could be "intoxicating." Her mind was "graceful"; as she explored her talent for writing about literature, she discovered she "could fly" (Armstrong 1995, 33). Karen often felt isolated: at odds with her parents, lacking social confidence, and sometimes marginalized at her convent school, both for her brains and for her status as a scholarship girl.

After a particularly difficult encounter during which her fellow students taunted her about her father's financial problems, she made a visit to the school chapel. She reflected on the hypocrisy of the Birmingham Catholics who had only befriended the family when they had lots of disposable income—they had routinely lived above their means—and showed no loyalty in hard times. She remembered that Jesus had excoriated the hypocrites of his day and demanded that his disciples leave everything and follow him. This moment in the chapel, which took place at some point after her mother went back to work in 1960, had all of the earmarks of "the call," and Karen was ready and willing to respond to it: "Follow me. How much more satisfying to leave all of the emptiness of the world and follow Christ! A nun in the bench in front of me got up, genuflected gracefully in the aisle, and quietly left the church. Her face was serene. It was as though she had tapped some hidden store of strength before plunging into the melee of afternoon school" (Armstrong 1995, 37–38).

Karen recognized the source of the nun's strength and confidence and wanted the same for herself. She realized that "something very important had happened" during this impromptu visit to the chapel. She began to imagine herself a nun: "I wanted to find God so that He would fill my life, and that meant giving my life back to Him. I wanted Him with a desire that was frightening in its urgency." Once she had made her decision that day in the chapel, "the world with all of its confusions seemed to fall into place. Second place" (Armstrong 1995, 38). The call and her commitment to it gave Karen a distinctly new identity and a key that allowed her to interpret even the smallest details of her life as signs confirming and explaining her vocation. They also gave her an alternative to her parents' plans for her to continue her education at a university.

Armstrong's decision to join the order that taught at her secondary school was not unusual. Religious orders and congregations often found new recruits among the older girls in their schools. Nineteenth-century anti-Catholic writers were highly suspicious of this practice and questioned whether the girls entered religious life of their own free will. Armstrong's memoir and works of autobiographical fiction such as Antonia White's *Frost in May,* written by former convent-school girls, illuminate this phenomenon from the perspective of the girls, who were trained to look carefully for signs of a vocation. After a former Lippington student is accepted into the postulancy during a ceremony at the school, White's protagonist Nanda Grey listens to a sermon in which all of the girls are enjoined to be attentive to the possibility of a vocation to the religious life. The priest emphasized "the extreme delicacy of the call. . . . It was the merest whisper easily drowned in the noises of the world." By no means was the call optional: "A vocation followed was the supreme good: a vocation rejected the supreme horror." Moreover, the priest warned, the call seldom came twice. One must embrace it in one's heart, even if one would not be in a position to act on it for years (White 1992a, 54).

In her early nonrebellious years at Lippington, Nanda Grey responded to the sermon and the idea of the call in a manner that probably represented the norm among convent-school girls—even pious, obedient ones—throughout the twentieth century: "Nanda could not decide which alternative was the more frightening, the thought of being in danger of hell or the prospect of having to be a nun. . . . Sometimes she found herself bargaining with God, saying, 'I'll do *anything* else for you. I'll never marry. I'll be poor. I'll go and nurse lepers. Only let me live in the world and be *free.*'" Deep inside, Nanda knew that bargaining was pointless. The "chilly voice inside" spoke compellingly: "The only thing that God wants is the thing you are afraid to offer" (White 1992a, 54–55).

A similar celebration of a new vocation occurred at Armstrong's convent school when she was 12. Mother Katherine, the headmistress, announced at morning assembly that Miss Jackson, who had most recently taught physics to some of the older girls, had decided to enter the order. Later in the day, when Karen and her cohorts were gathered around the bulletin board examining a photograph of Miss Jackson in her postulant's habit, Mother Katherine suddenly appeared to answer questions. When the headmistress asked the girls what seemed to be the most demanding sacrifice that Miss Jackson would have to make, Karen answered: "Never being able to do what you want to do." "'You mean freedom?' Mother Katherine said. She smiled. 'But no one is really free much of the time, Karen. Think of your mother, any mother of a family. She's not really free to do what she wants either.'"

Karen was persuaded by this argument. She was even more convinced when, in response to the girls' objections that nuns weren't free to have fun, Mother Katherine had asked them playfully: "Have you ever seen an unhappy nun?" Armstrong recalls what made her respect and admire Mother Katherine:

> I looked up at Mother Katherine. Her eyes were smiling at me and behind the smile there was a peace and a stability. When she was talking to me, she wasn't like other grownups I knew. Their minds weren't ever with me one hundred percent. The anxious lines around their mouths, the flickering moments of worry in their eyes showed that their minds were teeming with a dozen preoccupations. But Mother Katherine's mind was uncluttered.

Karen pictured Mother Katherine's mind uncluttered, just like her office. It was not empty, but ordered. Karen noticed that when Mother Katherine answered her questions or interacted with the girls in an informal conversation, she "spoke quietly as though she were thinking over something precious and secret." When she thought about it, she realized that "nuns often did that" (Armstrong 1995, 23–24).

At her school, she gained many positive impressions of nuns, both alone at prayer and together as a community. Although she would never share this information with other girls, she began to watch the nuns "walking round the grounds, their hands hidden in their sleeves, their eyes bent on the ground as they glided under the shade of the huge cedar trees on the lawn." The nuns gathered in a circle under those same cedars, sewing and laughing, at midday recreation. Even from a distance, Karen could feel the warmth and community. The nuns represented "a vision of sisterly unity," a contrast to the snobbery and exclusion that Karen experienced within the student body. Karen imagined that they must have "no secrets from one another, living together in such a close, loving community." As she began to envision herself among the nuns, she even imagined their conversations "filled with the joy of seeking God," devoid of the usual human pettiness. She could see that they had "so much in common and so many wonderful discoveries of the mind and spirit to share" (Armstrong 1995, 34).

This was the life Karen envisioned when she approached Mother Katherine at 16 about her desire to join the community. It was an intimate moment with a woman she idolized. Even behind the wimple, Mother Katherine was a beautiful, graceful, charismatic woman with "frightening, passionate" eyes. The girls believed the rumors that she had been an actress before she entered the convent. Mother Katherine listened intently to Karen's reasons for wanting to be a nun. She was heartened when Karen responded with enthusiasm to her warning about the austerities of convent life and commented approvingly on Karen's approach to each new challenge: "The harder something is, the better you like it" (Armstrong 1995, 39–42).

"Becoming a nun is like signing a blank check," Mother Katherine told Karen, providing a metaphor that would become increasingly meaningful in the years ahead. Karen skillfully marshaled her arguments to establish how thoroughly she had thought about the prospect of joining the convent and how mature she was at 16. What went unsaid was how much her respect and love for the sisters at her school had affected her decision. Although she was proud of her mother for entering the workplace in middle age, she did not really identify with her mother. Karen sought to emulate Mother Katherine: "For a long time I had admired her. Everything she did she flung herself into wholeheartedly. Everywhere she looked she found beauty; everything she touched she found significant. She'd given up the world for God and He had given it all back to her a hundredfold" (Armstrong 1995, 42).

With Mother Katherine's help, Karen was able to persuade her reluctant parents to give their permission for her to enter the postulancy at the Provincial House in Tripton in September 1962. Vatican II convened the following month, on October 11th. Only much later did Armstrong understand the significance of being among the very last group of postulants to undergo the "severe Victorian discipline" imposed in the order since its beginnings in England a century before. Sister Karen and her "brothers"—the order's shorthand for the group that entered the postulancy at the same time—would have the same trouble that their predecessors had in adapting to the austerities of convent life and spirituality, but they would have more occasion to blame themselves. Vestiges of the traditional formation process intended to mortify their bodies and erase their individual selves would haunt their consciences and trouble their bodies even as they sought, in the years ahead, to evolve to meet the needs and dictates of the changing church (Armstrong 1995, 57). This only intensified the sense of "*psychomachia,* the struggle within the secret soul itself," that especially troubled Armstrong's cohorts in the convents of Great Britain, the United States, and western Europe in the 1960s and 1970s (McNamara 1996, 598–599).

Mother Katherine's general warnings about austerity did little to prepare Armstrong for the many boundary-crossings that stood between her
and religious life. For years, Armstrong, like Monica Baldwin before her,
had trouble interpreting her physical, emotional, and spiritual discomfort
with convent life. Did it mean that she had not yet met the order's expectations of her or that she lacked a vocation in the first place? From the
start, she reached out to meet each challenge with gusto, a trait that had
won her praise from Mother Katherine and other teachers at her convent
school. She loved being assigned a bare cell: It meant that she had "arrived
where [she] wanted to be." As she changed out of her street clothes and
into her postulant's habit, she welcomed the prospect of "shedding the
whole of [her] past life with its untidy confusions, its degrading fears, its
pettiness." She noted that her new religious clothes—which were voluminous and especially long in the sleeves—were labeled "276." Even this
pleased her. She recalls being aware that 276 was *her* number; she had a
"definite place" among the ranks of her new sisters. In the chapel at the
hooding ceremony her first night, Armstrong weathered a fleeting temptation to run away from it all and then felt suddenly at peace, comforted by
the hymns and the order's prayer, familiar to her from her school. In
moments like this, she saw the community as a "close-knit family, burning
with love for God," a branch of the same family she had watched from a
distance with a growing desire for months, even years (Armstrong 1995,
57, 64–68, 71–72).

From her first night on, Armstrong's body rebelled against the order's
use of food as a means of discipline and mortification. The rules regarding meals—sisters must eat everything and two helpings of something—
were strictly enforced by her superiors throughout her seven years in the
order, with the exception of Mother Bianca, a kind and enlightened superior in London after she took her vows in June 1965. Armstrong internalized these rules and followed them even when she knew that eating certain
foods, especially cooked cheese and some other dairy products, invariably
made her ill. When she was required to work in the kitchen, the smell of
food could leave her nauseated for days. For years, Armstrong's eating
problems were known among the other sisters and her superiors. They
were considered a spiritual malady, like the fainting spells when she was
under stress. Both were interpreted as signs of deep-seated selfishness that
she had been unable to eradicate despite all of her efforts at mortification.
Eventually the stomach disorder was diagnosed as incipient anorexia and
the fainting spells as symptoms of fatigue and anxiety, both impervious
to—perhaps even triggered by—her most intense efforts to erase her individuality and mortify her flesh.

Weekly baths, harsh carbolic soap, the rationing of clean clothing, including fresh underwear: Armstrong recoiled at these traditional privations but quickly assented to them as part of her training. Perhaps the harshest deprivation came with the severe restrictions on communication: no speaking to seculars, only very limited verbal contact with professed sisters, and access only to reading material approved by the sisters in charge of her training. Postulant Mistress Mother Albert explained the rationale behind the silence required of postulants and novices: Even good people in the world are "permeated with selfish values that have nothing at all to do with the self-emptying love of God" (Armstrong 1995, 93). Postulants and novices could jeopardize their spiritual progress by contact with anyone, including a professed sister or a student, who was in contact with the secular world.

For the same reason, postulants were forbidden to select their own reading material. When Armstrong asked if she could take a book of Gerard Manley Hopkins's poems out of the convent library, she was alarmed to hear that "nuns don't waste their time indulging in poetry." Eventually she understood why poetry and, especially, novels were considered a spiritual threat as dangerous to the religious life as worldly friendships, but she could never embrace this perspective as her own. She gradually perceived that she would not be allowed novels or poetry because they were her preference and a luxury associated with her past life in the secular world. Upon later reflection, she acknowledged that she was "like an addict, suffering withdrawal symptoms." Like many convent schoolgirls, she had come to depend on literature "to interpret the world for me." In the convent, when she first realized that she could not have access even to an author as edifying as Hopkins, she was "furious" (Armstrong 1995, 96–97).

There is a sense in which Armstrong's commitment to the religious life was most complete at the very beginning of her postulancy. She began to make small departures almost immediately. She "quailed" at the strict rules about silence: "Hadn't Christ said that we could only approach the love of God through loving one another?" She believed that when the postulant mistress urged them to be "absolutely ruthless in [their] rejection of the world," the advice needed to be more nuanced. Otherwise, it would necessarily "[exclude] the good along with the bad." It took time for Armstrong to accept the goal of the religious life, displacing the self so that one could be full of God (Armstrong 1995, 91–93). Although she could affirm that it was a worthy and beautiful goal in the abstract, she continued to be impaled on the practical applications and implications of this principle when she encountered them in her day-to-day religious training.

Isolation and silence were easier to abide when she could remember that it was all about becoming closer to God and conforming to God's will. Occasionally, she was especially aware of the relationship between doing her small part through prayer and mortification and God's will for the world at large. For example, since the postulants had no contact with outsiders and were not allowed to see newspapers or television, they heard about the Cuban missile crisis, which coincided with the beginning of their postulancy, only in a vague request that they pray for peace and the avoidance of a potential armed conflict between the United States and Russia. She and the other postulants prayed fervently for three weeks, while Armstrong envisioned "fingers poised resolutely over the fatal buttons." At a certain point, Armstrong decided that the apocalyptic world situation might warrant her venturing a question about a secular event. When she asked Mother Albert at recreation whether there was news about Cuba, the postulant mistress looked confused, and then turned to answer Armstrong's question.

> "But that cleared up weeks ago. The Russians moved their ships."
> She looked round the table at our faces, the truth dawning on her.
> "Didn't we tell you?" she asked.
> We shook our heads.
> "Oh!" Mother threw back her head and laughed her characteristic laugh, silent, her shoulders heaving. "We must have forgotten: How terribly funny!"

Armstrong reports that the postulants were not amused (Armstrong 1995, 106–107). They were learning that even professed sisters never reached perfection and that there was a difference between insensitivity and detachment. This was a small early departure. Armstrong could not mortify the part of herself that raised critical questions about the life that she and the others were training to enter, especially as their training appeared increasingly at odds with her strong impressions of life in the order that she had gleaned from her observations of Mother Katherine and the sisters at her school in Birmingham.

It was disconcerting to discover that when Mother Albert visited a sewing session, it was considered "recreation," and still more exasperating to learn that if one postulant asked another to pass the scissors, this was an illicit "personal" communication. Mother Albert patiently explained how such a request was to be handled during recreation, one of the few moments when any conversation was possible for postulants. All conversation was to be addressed to everyone through Mother Albert. The sister in need of a pair of scissors should say, "Mother, I wonder whether I could just ask Sister Karen whether I could borrow her scissors." Armstrong, who had willingly given up the prospects of "intimate conversations" as threatening to her relationship with God, still balked at the prospect of learning this style of communication. She could not help asking herself, "What kind of a life was it if you couldn't even say 'Pass the scissors'?" (Armstrong 1995, 98–99).

These transgressive inner speculations prompted equally fervent repentance. Just as Armstrong began to get depressed about the prospects of living a life that was so contrived and devoid of human contact, she remembered that Mother Albert advised special efforts at perfection when sisters were depressed. Like Monica Baldwin, who had struggled constantly with "turning her outside inward," Armstrong vowed to leave behind her natural habit of self-expression. She willed herself into smiling and resolved to "enter fully into the general spiritual gaiety." She respected Mother Albert and understood the difficulties of her task. The postulant mistress had assured her charges that external observance of the rule would eventually transform their spiritual lives.

> If we acted like nuns, soon we'd really *be* like nuns. I pressed on eagerly. But often the endless suppression of mood and ideas made me long to do something outrageous. Just for once. To smash the silent formality and get it all out of my system. Often when I was feeling like that the rest of the brethren were too. You could sometimes feel the tension crackling in the air waiting to explode. (Armstrong 1995, 99)

When Mother Albert criticized her for her lack of commitment to perfection in all things, especially in domestic tasks and tidiness of dress, Armstrong was only briefly frustrated. She understood that frustration was part of the necessary task of breaking down her will so that God's will could work freely through her. By the time her parents came for their first visit, she believed that she had made genuine progress toward vanquishing her own will, except, perhaps, for the part that wanted above all else to be a perfect nun. Her recollections of the first visit with her family in the convent parlor tell a more complex story. She describes an odd sensation of being pulled apart into two people so that she could somehow—within certain limits—be the good daughter and still pursue her larger goal of perfect obedience and mortification as a nun.

> One part of me knew that I was putting on an act as I had to, behaving as a nun should behave. But it was also true that I couldn't behave differently. It was odd. Like being two people at once. . . .
> All the [family's] questions were just off-center. And my answers were getting more and more remote from the truth. I couldn't tell them

about cheese making me sick, about being miserable and depressed
about the rule, about anything that was really important to me.
(Armstrong 1995, 111–112)

Armstrong understood that she had crossed the threshold Mother
Albert described when she had predicted that, with time, "silence [would]
become easier than talking." She realized that in the wake of months of
silence, "conversation was unnatural" and words no longer communicated
her meaning. Words had become "a screen of misunderstanding and separation." Armstrong was relieved when Mother Albert rescued her so that
she could go to tea with the other postulants. She "felt pulled in two"
between her "natural feelings of sympathy" for her parents and her effort
to cultivate the "pure single-mindedness" of a sister. After the visit was
over, exhausted, she resolved to become a better postulant and find a
"haven of peace" in Christ: reach "a place where I could act simply, calmly,
above this conflicting welter of messy feeling" (Armstrong 1995, 112–114).

Still, Armstrong had recurring intimations that she was headed in the
wrong direction. Mother Katherine assured her that she was a likely candidate for a teaching career, but she spent her days doing the manual labor
required of all postulants, struggling to sew a buttonhole perfectly—and
failing miserably. Meanwhile, the lay sisters, who were permanently
engaged in domestic tasks, lived lives that were visibly and audibly "freer,
less buttoned-up," joyful. As Armstrong grappled with the command to
keep silence and recoiled at learning strategies of indirect noncommuni-
cation with other sisters, she heard "gales of laughter" from the rooms
where lay sisters took their recreation (Armstrong 1995, 101). One part of
her strived for perfection as it had been renamed by professed sisters in
charge of postulants and novices, while the other side—body and soul—
challenged the ideals of spiritual progress and perfection underlying the
traditions of the order.

Nine months after they arrived at Tripton, Armstrong and her cohorts
prepared for another boundary-crossing: the clothing ceremony, which
marked the end of the postulancy and the beginning of the novitiate.
Sisters first appeared in bridal gowns and veils, carrying candles, and
solemnly stated their desire to enter the order. Then they disappeared into
the dormitory for the ceremonial haircut and clothing in the habit. Back in
the chapel, they received a new name; Armstrong had chosen Martha, part
of her attempt to embrace the humility and mundane practical side of life
that had been her crosses to bear during her postulancy. During the ceremony she reflected on the significance of the ritual: "Her old life was dis-

carded now as completely as her hair, which would shortly burn up in the convent incinerator" (Armstrong 1995, 132).

In the novitiate, sisters were isolated so they could learn to live the whole rule of the order beyond the parts explained in the postulancy. Training in humility, poverty, chastity, and obedience converged in an effort to snuff out any remaining manifestations of the "worldly self" so sisters could function as pure channels of God's will. Sister Martha and the other new novices were told that if they "were not finding [the novitiate] unbearably hard then it was a pretty good indication that [they] weren't trying hard enough." When Mother Katherine visited Tripton over Christmas vacation in 1963, Armstrong had her first opportunity to speak without self-censorship since she had entered the order fifteen months before. Her former headmistress comforted her when she said that she could not cross the threshold necessary to kill her individuality. Armstrong confessed: "Often, I keep wanting to shout, 'Hey! This is *me* here, not number 276.'" Mother Katherine empathized. She told Armstrong the unwelcome news that people cannot change themselves as much as they might want to, and that nuns' lives helped them to see that painful fact more clearly than people in secular life ever could. She reminded Armstrong that no matter how hard it was, "It's important to see how awful we are, otherwise we'd want to hang onto ourselves, instead of letting ourselves die. And we'd start talking about self-fulfillment and all that nonsense" (Armstrong 1995, 135–136, 143–144).

Armstrong provides many examples that confirm that the hardest part of her individuality to kill was her mind; her intellectual gifts remained central to her identity. And she clung to that part of her identity for survival, despite the spiritual advice that she received from her superiors. It was difficult enough to agree, as she was required to do, when her superior told her, in the face of all common sense and empirical evidence, that cleaning the stairs with a worn-down pink nylon nail brush was the most effective way to get the job done. At least she could remind herself that the stairs were not the main point in this exercise.

When Armstrong's prescribed gesture of obedience had to do with the content of her faith as well as the dictates of her intellect, the parts of her that had never truly assented to the premises of religious life sounded the usual alarms. In her second year, she was enrolled in a four-year program aimed at a diploma in theology. In one of her exams with Mother Greta, whom she greatly respected, she was asked to "assess the quality of the evidence for the Resurrection." She followed directions to the letter and marshaled the evidence showing why it was reasonable to believe in the resurrection, all the time painfully aware of the contortions necessary to write the essay as she did.

Armstrong was convinced that she had written a persuasive, polished essay, but she was overwhelmed by "a sinking loss of integrity." She knew that the resurrection, which she considered the very heart of Christian faith, was a truth beyond reason, a miracle, and that what she had written was "a sham." When she next met with Mother Greta, she was not surprised to hear that she had done very well on the exam. Still troubled, she asked point blank: "It just isn't true what I've written, is it?" Mother Greta sighed and "rubbed her forehead hard." She answered wearily: "No, it isn't true, but please don't tell the other novices." This incident confirmed a lesson she had internalized her first year: "Leave your brain alone; it can only harm you" (Armstrong 1995, 154–155).

Sister Martha did what her mentor asked; it helped, somehow, to see that Mother Greta was pained to have to give her that advice. Still, a part of Armstrong remained keenly aware of the compromises and contradictions in religious life; that part of her made small departures from the convent even in the postulancy and the novitiate. Put more accurately: That part of Armstrong had never participated in the taming process at the center of the postulant's and novice's training: the extinction of the self and all of its gifts and pleasures. It remained wild and volatile. This wilder part of Armstrong was alive to other voices in the silent novitiate; it was nourished especially by humor, irony, and laughter. When a new, older set of novices joined her cohorts in 1964, the wild side of Armstrong found a partner in crime: a Welsh former art teacher, a convert in her late 20s, who had taken the name Sister David. On a feast day, when talking was allowed, she followed the sound of laughter to the boot room, where Sister David was doubled over before a sign. It was an official notice in Gothic letters above the boot polish providing detailed directions for the prescribed way to polish shoes. It was the final line that had sent Sister David into paroxysms: "Repeat for the other shoe."

Armstrong dimly recalled commenting on the same sign the year before when she had first read it, only to be chastised by Novice Mistress Mother Walter for behavior unbecoming a novice. "'Repeat for the other shoe!' Sister David breathed ecstatically. 'Beautiful! It just sums up the noviceship, doesn't it, Sister? Don't do a thing unless you're told to. Can you imagine! If Mother hadn't had that last sentence printed all the novices would be walking round with one shoe perpetually clean and one dirty!'" (Armstrong 1995, 158).

At first Armstrong hardly knew how to respond. She had been working so hard to be a perfect sister that she had almost forgotten that she had chuckled at the same sign one year before. On the other hand, she knew, as a more advanced novice, that this was a teachable moment. She tried to remind Sister David about the ideal of obedience behind such notices and to ignore how "awfully pompous" she sounded, even to herself. Sister David persisted: "If we don't laugh sometimes, we'll all go mad." She went on to list other "ridiculous" aspects of life in the novitiate that everyone else either ignored or turned into mandatory traditions, occasions for self-mortification. Then she turned serious and confronted Armstrong directly about her use of food as discipline. Even this newcomer knew that Armstrong was ill every time they had cooked cheese on the menu. She would not be persuaded that ignoring sisters' bodies and treating sisters like children could be condoned for the sake of spiritual goals.

To Armstrong's surprise, when Mother Albert joined them, she agreed with Sister David: Sisters *were* supposed to use common sense. Armstrong knew that this advice was counter to all of her training in the order thus far. Rather than reassuring her, the appearance of this new liberal side of Mother Albert's pedagogy exacerbated the internal divisions she had discovered during her first visit with her family. Only years later, when she had examined the historical context, could she understand the novice mistress's about-face. Cardinal Suenens challenged traditional methods of training novices in his groundbreaking book *The Nun in the Modern World*, which appeared in an English edition in 1962. Mother Walter, and others in her position in convents everywhere, had to pay attention to the call for reform in sisters' training, even if it troubled their own consciences, which were products of the traditional methods they were being urged to reconsider.

Armstrong, who had been struggling against the grain for years, realized that she had internalized more of her training than she thought. The occasional encouragement to take some initiative or use common sense now left her conflicted, lacking confidence in her native intelligence, a gift that she had never questioned as a secondary-school student planning to enter the convent:

> Anyway, I told myself, thinking now seems to be the order of the day, so I tried to free my mind from the literal way I had trained it to interpret everything. It was hard; my mind was extremely rusty—I no longer thought easily for myself, nor did I easily take the initiative. A few weeks before, I would have thought that a sign of victory, but now apparently it was a failure. But that was one thing I was learning about this quest for perfection! You'd never finish. You could never tick off a virtue and say, "Done!" and go on to the next one on the agenda. (Armstrong 1995, 158–163)

This was an important breakthrough, an insight with both short-term and long-term value. As Armstrong prepared for her vows on June 25, 1965, and for her return to the world as a student at Oxford and a teacher in the schools run by the order, this expanded definition of perfection would become an important touchstone for her. She no longer believed—perhaps never had believed—in the kind of perfection achieved by a mindless following of orders that contradicted one's inner lights. This kind of perfection was a sham, like the essay she had written for Mother Greta. It was achieved with smoke and mirrors. Still, there had been one constant in Armstrong's spiritual journey. She always returned to the holistic vision of perfection that she associated with following God's will for her, inscribed in the special gifts that she had been given, a definition she had intuited from Mother Katherine's example and advice when she was a secondary-school student in Birmingham.

Armstrong's last two years in the convent, 1965–1967, were spent in the order's scholasticate in London, preparing for the Oxford exams, and then at Oxford University, studying literature. Her physical and emotional symptoms—stomach disorders, weight loss, fatigue, and fainting spells—worsened dramatically. During this intense period of personal and spiritual growth and almost traumatic reexposure to the secular culture of the subways, the university, and the urban parish in the wake of Vatican II, Armstrong observed with interest as her mind functioned in two different ways. In literary studies, she could "start on a train of thought and follow it wherever it led." In her theological studies, she knew she had to "juggle the facts and produce the correct conclusion": "If I let my mind go it would fly away with me and take me away from God, away from true obedience" (Armstrong 1995, 197).

In practice, this kind of self-conscious mental bifurcation eluded Armstrong; she could not stay within the boundaries she had established for herself. She felt compelled to challenge Father Flannigan, a priest in whose parish she taught catechetics to children. As she was explaining to them the prescribed rituals for confession, it became clear to her that the children couldn't grasp what a sin was. She approached Flannigan and asked him whether they could delay the sacrament until the children were ready. The priest's anger and resentment surfaced instantly: "Sister, I don't care what trendy nonsense you're learning these days in your theology. I want those kids *done*. Done, Sister! The sacraments work automatically. We know them by faith! I want them done now, so that we've got it out of the way!" (Armstrong 1995, 199).

The incident—even apart from the confrontation with Flannigan—awakened Armstrong to how she had changed since she had reentered the secular world. She found herself posing a whole new set of questions, the kind that she had been trained to banish from her consciousness:

> What was the church asking me to do? Here I was, pumping these children with the Catholic mechanisms of guilt that would probably haunt them all their lives! Was that what the love of God was all about? I was startled by the violence of my anger. Where had that criticism welled up from? A year ago I couldn't have had an idea like that. Did it mean that I was intellectually proud? Or—and this was a staggering thought—*was I right?* (Armstrong 1995, 198–199)

Armstrong had never stopped asking this kind of question; despite her best efforts, she had found herself entertaining objections to the order's party line even as a postulant. Now she was ready to risk going public with her questions and objections. She discovered that part of her, "the dangerous part that had tackled Father Flannigan," resonated with certain criticisms of the order's policies voiced by her friend Sister Jocasta. This realization constituted a form of consciousness-raising for Armstrong, who had usually entertained such objections alone.

Every now and then, with friends and allies, such as Sister David and Sister Jocasta, Armstrong had the opportunity to express her doubts and reservations about the ideals and policies of the order to another sympathetic soul. In these moments, she understood that her resistance to the practices and spirituality of the order could not be reduced to her own selfishness and spiritual immaturity. She began to see that she had valid objections based on her observations and that they had to be taken seriously. Occasionally Armstrong was shocked at her emerging courage and outspokenness. During the hot summer in London, she cut the long legs off her nineteenth-century underwear, both as a protest and as a practical survival tactic. She then led a movement of younger sisters who finally mustered the courage to ask their superior for briefs (Armstrong 1995, 202, 208–209). This tiny protest movement represents a monumental departure: Sisters were flouting conventions, questioning authorities, and making specific requests for a certain level of bodily comfort in the work they were doing in the secular world. Sisters who took subways in the summer could not afford the affectation of voluminous archaic undergarments.

In 1967, during the short break between London and Oxford, Armstrong spent time at Tripton. There she had a rare opportunity to have a genuine conversation with Mother Katherine about her changing perceptions of the order and her questions about her future in religious life. She finally realized that Mother Katherine and Mother Bianca, her models and mentors in the order, were exceptions, even pariahs—women whose intellectual gifts and holiness provoked jealousies among their sisters and led to ostracism within the order. She referred obliquely to the possibility of leaving the order. Not for the first time, Mother Katherine gave her advice that was both energizing and cryptic. She predicted that Armstrong might "find it difficult" studying at Oxford, but urged her to "hang on." She told Armstrong unequivocally: "Look Sister. Use your brain. God has given it to you. It's a great gift. Use it" (Armstrong 1995, 210–213).

Oxford was a challenge. At least Armstrong had one companion within the order's Oxford community, Sister Rebecca, who was in her final year of reading for a degree in French and Italian. She also had a sympathetic tutor, Miss Jameson, a "lean, glamorous woman with a caustic tongue and a mind like a laser." Jameson was a Catholic laywoman, but she was not at all inclined to curb her irreverence when discussing the church. Her insights on religious life became even more arresting and relevant to Armstrong after she mentioned, in passing, that she "had tried her vocation." Jameson praised the quality of Armstrong's work and confirmed for her that she was still an intelligent woman, however dulled her intellect might feel to her after years of misuse and battering in the convent. She shared inside jokes about the literary family connections of the Oxford superior, Mother Praeterita, and funny stories about the oddities of convents where she had stayed when on the lecture circuit. Perhaps most important, she made Armstrong laugh and urged her to indulge herself with laughter—including laugher about convents—since "convents can be mad places" (Armstrong 1995, 215–216, 233–235).

After her first year at Oxford, Armstrong left for a retreat in Skipton, in the north of England, where Mother Katherine had been appointed superior. The farewell exchanged between Armstrong and the Oxford community was fraught with tension. In the car, as Sister Rebecca drove her to the station, Armstrong's nose bled profusely. Armstrong started to take the box of Kleenex from the car for the train trip, until Sister Rebecca reminded her that the tissues were the property of the Oxford community. Knowing that "there'll be a terrible fuss" if the Kleenex were to disappear from the community's car and granting that "it's stupid, it's unkind, it's wrong," Sister Rebecca offered her own handkerchief. Since that, too, was forbidden—sisters were not allowed to lend each other anything— Armstrong knew that she was being offered "more than a handkerchief. It was an act of love" (Armstrong 1995, 241).

Armstrong felt physically ill on the train, "gripped by a fierce, unreasoning terror." She faced an eight-day retreat: total silence and "the rigorous Spiritual Exercises that scoured out all the places deep within yourself that you couldn't look at." On the eve of the retreat, Armstrong had another one of her episodes; she lost consciousness in an assembly of sisters, aware of a disembodied scream that she only later learned was her own. When she tried to recreate and interpret the incident for herself, she adopted the following shorthand: "Two selves pulled apart. Blackness" (Armstrong 1995, 240–242).

While Armstrong slowly recovered from this episode, a breakdown that no one tried to dismiss or downplay, Mother Katherine approached her and offered to help her leave the order. Her former headmistress also told her more about her own hard times in the order, when she was "considered dangerous and subversive" and was exiled to an unimportant school in Birmingham: "It was difficult. To be in disgrace for fifteen years. Hanging on to what God wants of you and not giving in, just because if you do you'll be patted on the head and called a good girl—and have an easier life." Armstrong seriously questioned whether she had the kind of courage and faith that Mother Katherine had. She could envision herself "carrying on, willing to be in disgrace" but could not discount the possibility that she could become "a damaged person, maiming people around [her]." She saw the most recent fit and the piercing scream that she could not control—initially, could not even claim as her own—as a sign, a "moment of truth" (Armstrong 1995, 247–248).

Back at Oxford, Armstrong tried to pray, though all she could achieve was a physical attendance to prayer and the sacraments in the midst of a "dark numbness." The study of eighteenth-century literature—"cool, severe, and healing"—fortified her; she could feel her mind growing stronger and more focused. The order had never treated her with more flexibility and kindness. She still cherished the "ideal of perfect self-giving and close union with God" (Armstrong 1995, 253, 248). Meanwhile, the secular world, as she encountered it in the public spaces at Oxford, filled her with anxiety and caused her to examine her own life and conscience. She prepared herself to make a decision.

Armstrong first explained her plans to Mother Frances, who had been her superior at the scholasticate in London. Her former superior knew of her decision before she spoke the words. It was complicated: Armstrong feared staying in the religious life out of "cowardice" and she feared facing the world alone for the first time since she was 17. "I'll be on my own. Up till now wherever I've gone outside I've been a representative. Not just me. Me in my own right, standing for myself. I've stood for God—just by my clothes—for all of you. Now I don't stand for anything. I've got to be myself. And I don't know who I am" (Armstrong 1995, 255–256).

Mother Frances reassured her that "there is still a lot of what you were still there." Only a short time before, those words would have been the ultimate reproach, but Armstrong had crossed a threshold and reached a place where the words had new meaning. She discovered that in this new place Mother Frances could comfort her in ways that had been unavailable to her before. She told Armstrong that she "would have to build [herself] up again, bit by bit," but she was strong enough to start a new life in the world. Then she explained the steps that needed to be followed: a conversation with Mother Provincial and a letter to the bishop requesting a dispensation, which he must forward to the Sacred Congregation in Rome. In this new relationship, Mother Frances felt liberated to coach Armstrong on the proper strategy for approaching the bishop. She urged her not to mention her recurring illnesses or any regret or uncertainty about her decision to leave: "Tell him that you've decided that your Christian vocation lies in the world" (Armstrong 1995, 256–257). Seen from the new vantage point available to her during the departure process, Armstrong watched as the dysfunctional aspects of religious life receded before her eyes and the sisters again began to resemble the ones who had made her want to join the order in the first place.

On Thursday, January 27, 1969, Armstrong heard from a smiling young sister in the kitchen of the London scholasticate that the necessary paperwork had arrived from Tripton. She remembered the moment in detail. The sisters were bustling about doing their chores; Mother Constantia, who supervised kitchen work, was "bemoaning the custard" as usual, and Armstrong, who had been in limbo, awaiting her official release from her vows, already felt invisible, as if she was watching the scene from across an invisible but palpable boundary: "Everything was the same, and it would be the same after I had gone, the waters of the religious life closing over me without a ripple" (Armstrong 1995, 260–261).

We know from elsewhere in Armstrong's narrative that she sometimes saw her own experiences running parallel to those of Sister Luke, as played by Audrey Hepburn in the film version of *The Nun's Story*. When, as a novice, she had occasionally done penance in the refectory by kissing the feet of the sisters as they dined, she had thought explicitly of the scene in the film when Hepburn had done the same thing (Armstrong 1995, 153). We can surmise that when she met for the last time with Mother Frances, Armstrong kept in mind Hepburn's performance in the departure scene at the end of the film. Both women used the prescribed formula, a businesslike ritual of departure "with no room for personality." Mother Frances informed Armstrong that once she took the papers releasing her from her vows in her hand, there was no going back. She would no longer be a nun. Mother Frances asked Armstrong if she wished to accept the papers, and Armstrong answered in the affirmative. She received Mother

Frances's blessing and took off her rosary and profession ring. She put them on the desk. She reports matter-of-factly: "My life as a nun was over" (Armstrong 1995, 261).

The final pages of *Through the Narrow Gate* describe Armstrong's return to Oxford to begin the next term as a laywoman, the recipient of a prize for literature that won her the respect of her peers and £100. Still, it was as if her body, the same one that had rebelled against the constraints of convent life, could not find a comfortable niche in the secular world. Even alone in her own room in the residence hall, she was incapable of relaxing:

> It didn't matter how firmly I told myself that I was now a free agent and no longer vowed to poverty and the renunciation of comfort and luxury; I couldn't do it. . . . Instinctively I went toward the desk and pulled out the leather cushioned chair. Then I stopped. *No,* I told myself firmly. *You've got to start somewhere.* Gingerly but determinedly I sat in the armchair. It felt very odd. There had been no armchairs in the convents. . . . I tried to lean back in the chair, but it was impossible. Again, there was that strong sense of something forbidden. I reclined stiffly and awkwardly for a moment and then gave up the struggle, resuming my accustomed upright posture. (Armstrong 1995, 262)

Like Monica Baldwin in the months and years after her departure from the cloister, Armstrong discovered that reentry into the world required an endless series of halting little steps. Sometimes she found that even tiny thresholds were beyond her capabilities; she had to admit that she "was a person who could no longer sprawl in a chair" (Armstrong 1995, 263). One lesson that she had learned in the convent which could be recycled in the secular world was the power of her will. In almost the same spirit of disciplined resignation in which she had submitted to the alien regimen of the postulancy, she reached out for help from two Catholic students, Rose and Bridget. When they heard that she was no longer a nun, they promised to look after her. Immediately they knew what needed to be done. The final scenes of Armstrong's memoir begin with a last-minute shopping spree at a department store, Marks and Spencer's, just before closing time. The scene is another clothing ritual that is every bit as powerful as those she had participated in at pivotal moments in the postulancy and novitiate.

What gives this final clothing ritual its power is precisely the way in which it provides Armstrong access to what she has surrendered during the religious life. Unlike the carefully orchestrated convent rituals, which took place after a period of preparation, this secular ritual of reversal happens spontaneously because Rose and Bridget know instinctively that it will be more natural and less painful that way. Rose and Bridget take Armstrong in hand like secular novice mistresses. They set the process in motion, making the major decisions about what to buy. They offer Armstrong limited options—the cardigan must be blue or pink, not gray, which is too close to black—because they know that what she needs is practice making decisions that affect her life and the confidence that comes with the experience of making such decisions. Later that night, when Rose is cutting her hair, Armstrong begins to realize that she has embarked on yet one more formation process and that the gate to the secular life is narrow, too, at times.

Gradually Armstrong began to see the convent clothing rituals and the more recent shopping trip to Marks and Spencer's as part of the same journey. She had entered the religious life in search of the integrity and wholeness that she had seen in her mentor, Mother Katherine. In the noisy collegiality of a college room, while Rose cut her hair, it all came together for Armstrong:

> I remembered the day I had arrived at Tripton, throwing my clothes away joyfully, thinking I was discarding an old life. I knew better than that now. You couldn't exchange one life for another simply by a change of clothes. Clothes were only a symbol of something far deeper. And this time too I wasn't joyful about the change. I was doing something necessary and inescapable, not rushing forward confidently to meet the future. (Armstrong 1995, 273)

When Rose finished, Armstrong looked at her new haircut in a mirror—another everyday gesture that it would take many small steps to get accustomed to—and saw a stranger. But she recognized herself in the stranger, just as she acknowledged that she still was, in many ways, a nun. She asked herself: "How long would it be before we joined up—the nun that I really was and that girl in the mirror?" (Armstrong 1995, 274). Because the memoir starts with a flashback, we know the complex answer that only gradually became comfortable for Armstrong to acknowledge: She would always be a nun, just as she would always be that girl in the mirror, only she was a better nun and a better woman for her departure.

Barbara Ferraro and Patricia Hussey

In the late summer and fall of 1984, a group of ninety-seven concerned Catholics, including two priests, two religious brothers, and twenty-six nuns from fourteen communities, signed an advertisement that would appear in the *New York Times* on Sunday, October 7. The headline read: "A Diversity of Opinions Regarding Abortion Exists Among Committed Catholics." The ad was sparked by public attacks on vice-presidential candidate Geraldine Ferraro's pro-choice position launched by New York's Archbishop John O'Connor and other prominent clerics. Sisters of Notre Dame de Namur (SND) Barbara Ferraro and Patricia Hussey first heard about the *Times* ad in mid-September 1984 from Marjorie Tuite, a Dominican sister on the faculty of the Chicago Jesuit School of Theology's Urban Training Center and a dear friend and mentor from their graduate-school days in Chicago in the late 1970s. They signed the statement without hesitation because they wanted to "stand in sisterhood with Geraldine Ferraro." They also believed that they were calling for an intramural Catholic dialogue on abortion, something parallel to the protracted, and ultimately productive, conversations that had produced "The Challenge of Peace," the American bishops' 1983 pastoral letter on nuclear war. In their memoir *No Turning Back,* published in 1990, Ferraro and Hussey reflected on their decision to sign the document with characteristic candor and self-deprecating irony: "It didn't seem to be a very big deal at the time" (Ferraro and Hussey 1990, 219–220, 204).

When they signed the ad, Ferraro and Hussey had no way of knowing that they were becoming embroiled in a controversy that would precipitate a painful departure from the Sisters of Notre Dame or that the many steps that led to their departures from religious life would be of interest to other Catholic women. By the time they signed the letter, they considered themselves to be professional activists with a vocation to speak out for those who had not been given a voice (or a hearing) by those in power. Since 1981, they had been directors of Covenant House, an ecumenical center that served the poor, elderly, unemployed, and homeless in Charleston, West Virginia, and sought ways to implement long-term social change. Tuite planned a stopover in Charleston on one of her many trips from Chicago to Central America, fact-finding missions sponsored by the citizen's-action wing of the New York–based ecumenical group Church Women United.

Ferraro and Hussey were part of a women's group convened by Tuite at the Jesuit School of Theology in Chicago (JSTC). Tuite challenged the members of the group to think about what it would mean if they could spend their lives "[turning] the patriarchal triangle into the sacred and human circle" wherever and whenever they could. She encouraged them to make the larger connections between their academic study, their spirituality, their personal lives, their church, and world events (Ferraro and Hussey 1990, 148–149). Ferraro and Hussey asked Tuite to stop in

Charleston to help them and the local community reflect on a recent confrontation with Bishop Hodges of the Wheeling-Charleston diocese. They had participated in a protest against spending millions of dollars on a new pastoral center in an upscale Charleston suburb while the number of poor and unemployed in that part of Appalachia rose steadily.

> It was a nice old-fashioned protest. About twenty of us stood along the highway, looking much more bedraggled than we felt, handing out pamphlets and a press release. We tied helium balloons snappily printed with "Human Needs, Not Buildings," onto the bulldozer. After a prayer and a song, we all went home, a day's work in the cause of justice well done. (Ferraro and Hussey 1990, 208)

After this small-scale peaceful protest, Ferraro and Hussey were dismayed to hear that Bishop Hodges had asked two Jesuits who had participated in the event to leave the diocese. They also discovered that Hodges had complained about Ferraro's dissenting activities to one of the SND's leadership group in Rome. (Even before they challenged the plan for the new pastoral center, they had spoken against the Parental Notification Bill which came before the state legislature in 1982 and 1983.)

In September 1984, Tuite met with Ferraro, Hussey, and several female colleagues who were prominent in various Catholic ministries in West Virginia and helped them to sort out their divergent reactions to the protest and its outcome. She worked her magic and left the group "healed and happier than [they had felt] in months." Later, at a celebratory dinner at the Firehouse Restaurant in Charleston, conversation turned to the political scene, especially the behavior of Archbishop O'Connor. Along with Bernard Law of Boston, O'Connor had been openly campaigning against Democratic vice-presidential candidate Geraldine Ferraro. O'Connor had even convened a television news conference prior to the Democratic convention declaring that he did not believe that a Catholic could "in good conscience" vote for someone who favored abortion. Tuite speculated that since Geraldine Ferraro was not, strictly speaking, pro-abortion but was pro-choice—like Ted Kennedy and Mario Cuomo, both of whom had escaped O'Connor's criticism—perhaps O'Connor had not clearly stated his objections to Ferraro's candidacy. When Tuite shared her suspicions that "this has more to do with the fact that [Ferraro] is a woman and a feminist than it has to do with abortion," Barbara Ferraro (no relation to Geraldine) and Patricia Hussey were strongly inclined to agree (Ferraro and Hussey 1990, 216–217).

Gradually, during the intense years between 1984 and the publication of their joint memoir in 1990, Ferraro and Hussey grew to understand that the *New York Times* ad and the furor that followed it were part of a whole series of turning points that Ferraro had named "full-fledged feminist moment[s] of truth," "those 'Aha!' moments that change your life" (Ferraro and Hussey 1990, 141). Their friendship had been built and solidified in these moments of truth. The two women met in September 1978, when they roomed together in a residence for graduate students at JSTC. Ferraro, then 35 years old, already had a master's degree in pastoral studies and was starting a doctorate in ministry at McCormick Presbyterian Seminary in Chicago. Her experience working on pastoral teams in Auburndale, Massachusetts, and Tucson, Arizona, had taught her about the pressing need for female counselors in Catholic parishes. Ferraro began the new program with the premise that "to begin to be considered equal to the clergy, [she] needed to work 150 percent harder than they did" and "become so well-qualified, so over-credentialed, that they would *have* to accept [her]" (Ferraro and Hussey 1990, 128). Later, she realized that even this was an overly optimistic strategy.

Hussey had arrived in Chicago just in time for her third and final year in the master of divinity program at JSTC, straight from the general chapter meeting of the SND in Rome. The meeting was the fifth in a series that had convened every three years since Vatican II to work on a new constitution and long-range plans for the future of the order. Hussey, 29, was one of only two young American sisters at the meeting who had not yet taken final vows. In Rome, she saw glimmerings of the institutional side of Notre Dame life that would become much more apparent to her in the years ahead. For example, she discovered that even in a long-range planning meeting composed of busy delegates who had cleared their schedules to meet daily for six weeks and up to twelve hours a day, old patterns of convent behavior prevailed. Potentially fruitful disagreements were defused with polite dodges that could not be effectively circumvented. Those who wished to dismiss a potential challenge could dispose of it by reminding the adversary: "Patricia, dear. We do not express our disagreements on the chapter floor." Nonetheless, Hussey saw real progress being made. She took hope from a mission statement in which sisters made a commitment "to use conscientization (the process of raising consciences; learning to perceive social, political and economic contradictions and to take action against the oppressive elements of reality) as a process of education, especially directed to our mission among oppressed people, and ... as a means of education ... for our own membership" (Ferraro and Hussey 1990, 137–138).

Hussey also witnessed the beginnings of the papal conclave that elected the short-lived Pope John Paul I in 1978. She instinctively avoided

the group of SND who left the motherhouse on a bus at six in the morning in the hopes of finding seats toward the front at the nine o'clock mass
that marked the opening of the conclave. She arrived alone and wandered
into the basilica without the "separate but special" status that she might
have claimed as a member of the "church's ladies' auxiliary." Hussey's
description of her gut reaction to the historic mass mirrors Mary Daly's
impressions of the final session of Vatican II, included in the "Autobiographical Preface" to the 1975 edition of *The Church and the Second Sex*
(Daly 1985a, 10). Hussey reconstructs why the opening mass of the conclave became an unexpected turning point, a moment of departure.

She watched "rows and rows of old white men in lace dresses" with
their eyes on the cardinals processing into the sanctuary. She had spent
enough time in Rome to know something of the political maneuvers and
intrigue, the "nearly audible rustle of plot and counterplot," as "the pews
whispered with the anxiety of factions." Hussey noticed her own alienation
and impatience with all of the pomp and circumstance: "The Mass started
with the singing of the Kyrie Eleison, and I suddenly felt I had to get out of
there. I couldn't stand the pageantry. I never had liked pageantry, and this
particular spectacle seemed especially devoid of reverence or even dignity."

Almost unconsciously, Hussey found herself moving out of the sanctuary as fast as she could, "trying to get to a place where I would feel the
presence of God." She wandered through the crowd until she found herself
in the crypt beneath St. Peter's Basilica, standing opposite the tomb of
Pope John XXIII. She prayed, "out loud, and very sternly," without any self-
consciousness, at least until the woman next to her smiled: "John, if there
really is a Holy Spirit, please inspire that gathering of men up there,
because it truly looks overwhelming and hopeless to me." Then she walked
out of the crypt silently with two other women, one of whom was old and
lame and needed the strong arms of the other two. Even at the time, she
thought: "This is what the church really is. It is people, not pomp and
pageantry and make-believe piety" (Ferraro and Hussey 1990, 138–140).

Hussey came by her impatience with pomp and make-believe piety
honestly. From 1973 to 1976, she had served as a "cottage parent" at Long
Lane, a state institution for juvenile delinquents in Connecticut. At Long
Lane she had learned two important lessons that she later recognized as
her first steps away from the SND. First, she stumbled on the "obvious but
painful truth that it was not necessary to be a nun to be committed to
humanity." Second, she realized that her mentors at Long Lane—"old and
young; single and married; black, Puerto Rican, and white; Jewish,
Protestant, Catholic, and atheist; born of both the poor and the middle
classes"—knew more about building a tolerant, loving, functional

community than her so-called "primary community" back at St. Justin's Convent in Hartford (Ferraro and Hussey 1990, 85, 80–81).

Ferraro had never worked outside the church, but she, too, had learned to be suspicious of Catholic institutional structures. Her own "feminist moments of truth" in Arizona and Massachusetts had taught her that the post–Vatican II church provided as many opportunities for parish priests to abuse their authority as the pre–Vatican II church had. There were other, more positive, moments of sudden clarity among fellow Catholics enrolled in summer-school sessions at Loyola University in Chicago in the early 1970s. She had the opportunity to discuss Catholic theology and ethics with nuns, priests, and laypeople and to discover that many shared her concerns and hopes for the church. Her questions about the possibility of women's ordination, the prohibition of birth control, and the limits of male God-language "turned out to be everyone's questions." She read the works of Rosemary Radford Ruether, Elisabeth Schüssler Fiorenza, Daniel Maguire, and Charles Curran. She found a community of like-minded Catholics, "a new and larger community of people whose lives were committed to realizing justice and love" (Ferraro and Hussey 1990, 106).

That first summer at Loyola, Ferraro also fell in love with a priest named Dan, whose terse parting words at the end of the summer session were, "This only happens here." It ended sadly, but Ferraro had crossed an important threshold. At 28, she had found an opportunity to revel in experiences that she might have had at 18 had she not been a postulant, carefully sheltered inside the SND novitiate in Ipswich. After parting with Dan, she "sobbed [her] way across the Midwest" on the return trip to Lawrence, Massachusetts, but she also felt "awakened." She was certain that having fallen in love would ultimately "strengthen [her] as a nun":

Even if it was only holding hands and hugging, now I knew what I had given up when I took a vow of chastity. I had given up a unique source of connection, solace, and joy, *and* all the authentic emotions from creative to despairing, that that connection can inspire. I hoped I would never again respond to people's most intimate problems with the ignorant certainties of a cardboard saint. (Ferraro and Hussey 1990, 108)

Ferraro realized that from this point on she "would have to choose, over and over again, to remain a nun." From what she had seen of love in that brief summer, she suspected, for the first time, that she could be happy as a wife and mother, and yet she still felt confident electing to remain a sister. In the exciting world that she had discovered at Loyola,

Ferraro saw many reasons to remain in religious life. She was "sure the role of women in the church was going to broaden, and that [she] would not have to leave the convent in order to live out God's plan for [her]" (Ferraro and Hussey 1990, 108–109). In a sense, she was right. Her life as a nun had changed dramatically since she had entered in August 1962, and more prospects for change appeared all the time. Ever since her first year at Loyola summer school, Ferraro had known what it meant to be part of a network of Catholic feminists, and gradually this network became her real community.

Before they met at the beginning of the fall semester in 1978, no one could have predicted that Barbara Ferraro and Patricia Hussey would become close friends and collaborators. Although they were only six years apart in age, they came from different generations within the Sisters of Notre Dame. Ferraro had entered the convent in 1962, the same year as Karen Armstrong. Like Armstrong, she had endured the traditional formation process intended to mortify the body and remove traces of individual identity. She was assigned the number 878. She had worn the old habit; her body had "rebelled" against the habit and the life by ceasing menstruation for months and breaking out in boils all over, except for her face, neck, and hands. When the boils healed, she got stomach cramps, the beginnings of ulcers. After six months in the postulancy, Ferraro surrendered her given name—part of the identity-eradication process—and became Sister Charles Marie (Ferraro and Hussey 1990, 29–35).

By the time she took her vows and moved beyond the novitiate on January 27, 1965, Ferraro knew there were changes afoot in the order and the church. One symptom of change intruded into the novitiate itself: Only thirty-five of the sixty-two postulants who had entered with her remained to receive the black veil that signified that they were professed sisters. In 1966, when Ferraro graduated from Emmanuel College, which was run by her order, her superiors decided where she should teach. From 1966 until 1973, she worked in parochial schools in Salem, New Hampshire, and Lawrence, Massachusetts. Even this traditional "sisters' lifestyle" had been transformed by the spirit of renewal that accompanied the end of Vatican II. Ferraro might have felt naked the first time she walked across the schoolyard in her new short veil and modest skirts and blouses, but she was relieved to see glimpses of her old self returning (Ferraro and Hussey 1990, 92). She still taught parochial school and lived in a convent, but she also looked accessible enough for the mother of one of her students in Lawrence to confide to her that she had had an abortion.

Ferraro's instinctive response to the mother's pained admission— "tell me about it"—opened up a new world for her and a new vision of sisters and laywomen bridging the chasm that had separated them over the centuries (Ferraro and Hussey 1990, 99). She imagined herself doing pastoral work with women and families, having conversations that parishioners could not have with priests. She may have looked like a typical nun teaching in a parochial school, but she was already planning her next moves. When she heard about the possibility of taking summer-school courses in pastoral studies at Loyola in Chicago, Ferraro and three other sisters from her convent applied for grants and scholarships. They began retooling themselves for the work they hoped to do, educating themselves to become the "new nuns" that they, and almost everybody else in the American Catholic church in the early 1970s, were talking about, with various overtones ranging from heartfelt desire to deep anxiety.

Patricia Hussey brought very different baggage to the partnership of Ferraro and Hussey that they formed almost immediately after their meeting in September 1978. Hussey joined the SND on September 8, 1967. This was only five years after Ferraro had entered, but those five years made a monumental difference in her early experiences of religious life. Unlike Ferraro, who arrived at the convent equipped with a "binder" to flatten her breasts and a whole array of specialty items acquired at Doherty's, a nuns' clothing and accessories store in Boston, Hussey brought "regular clothes—skirts and blouses in dull tones and baggy shapes." Hussey, unlike Ferraro, never had to wear the traditional habit. During Hussey's postulancy, she became aware of adjustments to traditional convent life that her generation would never have to make, boundaries that they would never have to cross. One memorable moment that helped her to understand the distance separating her cohorts from the sisters who had entered only a few years before them occurred during her first winter in the convent when she was doing her assigned chores, taking garbage to a basement incinerator room: "I walked in with my bag of trash and there, before the roaring, crackling flames, stood the mistress of novices, Sister Patricia Agnes. In full habit, her black skirts whirling in the heat, she was dropping into the incinerator, one by one, an armload of what were quite obviously whips. We stood there, me burning the trash, Sister Patricia Agnes burning whips." The fact that Hussey calls the novice mistresses' trash "whips" rather than using the conventional term "disciplines" testifies to the great divide between her generation and their pre–Vatican II sisters.

Because of the renewal underway in religious orders across the world in the late 1960s, Hussey was allowed to ask questions where only five years before Ferraro could not. Moreover, Hussey's questions brought answers that were very different from the ones Ferraro had been given as part of her training in the early 1960s. For example, concerning the practice of kissing the ground as a form of penance, Ferraro had been told that it was an act of mortification to kiss the "sinful earth," which constituted a stumbling block to spiritual growth. When Hussey was in the postulancy, she learned that kissing the floor was a way to express "reverence for the earth."

Due to the accidents of history, Ferraro had much more traditional training to undo, but that meant that she also had an opportunity to see more dramatic changes take place within the order than Hussey did and reason to hope for more of the same. In the early 1970s, Ferraro had to reclaim her individuality and the right to feel and express her own emotions. This made her voice and her inner convictions all the more sacred to her and her rage against the erasure of women's voices all the more powerful. As Hussey put it, "Thanks to Pope John XXIII, my wings, unlike Barbara's, were never clipped. Plucked, perhaps, with a loss of some of the downy underlayer, but the primaries remained intact" (Ferraro and Hussey 1990, 18, 50–51).

As it turned out, Ferraro and Hussey complemented each other perfectly. Both of them had been at the historic first meeting of the Women's Ordination Conference in Detroit over Thanksgiving weekend 1975, but when they met three years later, they discovered that they had responded to it in disparate ways. For Ferraro, seeing more than 1,000 nuns and laywomen gathered in Detroit that weekend gave her "exhilarating hope" that women's ordination might be a reality during her lifetime. Hussey, who later identified the Detroit meeting as the moment she began thinking as a feminist, had found less to be exuberant about. She knew, suddenly, but with certainty, that "if she were to be ordained, it would not be in order to follow the role model of most of the priests she had ever met." Still, Hussey was unprepared for the depth of her own cynicism and depression three years later at the papal conclave. Ferraro helped her make the transition between an intellectual feminism—which could still build a protective wall around one's most vulnerable self—and "[feeling] the truth of your ideas." In their first long conversation at the Mellow Yellow Café in Chicago shortly after they met, Barbara Ferraro recalled the words of a song by Carol Etzler that captured the complexity of emotions that accompanied a "full-fledged feminist moment of truth": "Sometimes I wish my eyes had never been opened." Ferraro resonated with Etzler's lyric and supplied the implicit feminist conclusion: "But there is no turning back" (Ferraro and Hussey 1990, 122–123, 141).

When Ferraro and Hussey attended the second Women's Ordination Conference held in Baltimore in 1978, Ferraro realized that she shared Hussey's reservations about joining the "present clerical caste structure of the church." Back in Chicago, she was happy that her talent and instincts for ministry were apparent to her Protestant fellow students at McCormick, who urged her to switch denominations and be ordained, but she was not even tempted to leave the Catholic church. At times, she admitted feeling "way out of [her] depth" in theological conversations at McCormick. It was Hussey's turn to facilitate Ferraro's transition into the world of theological jargon, familiar territory to her after two years at JSTC. Hussey also got Ferraro involved in the local Catholic women's group led by Marjorie Tuite, whom Ferraro calls "the mentor and goad and inspiration to our entire generation of progressive nuns" (Ferraro and Hussey 1990, 143, 145, 147).

From Tuite, both Ferraro and Hussey learned important lessons about the practical aspects and implications of feminist activism. Once, at an informal social gathering over pizza at a local hangout, Ferraro backed down instead of challenging a male friend who preferred complicity with injustice in the church to the discomfort of risking his own status and position. She discovered that Tuite's mentorship extended to this kind of social event. Later, Tuite urged her to reflect on how she had handled the situation. Ferraro recalls: "[Margie Tuite's] idea of 'reflecting' was to shout, 'How could you do that Barbara? I saw you trying to justify your actions and sweet-talk John because you didn't want him to feel bad. The personal is political. You don't have to hate them, but you can't support them'" (Ferraro and Hussey 1990, 149–151).

When Hussey got her master of divinity degree in 1979, she went to work as a stringer and racker in a jewelry factory, the High Point Metal Company, in Providence, Rhode Island. At first, she did not disclose that she was a nun to her co-workers; she hoped to gain the kind of insights into the lives of working people that came only from laboring alongside them. The more Hussey learned about the details of her Catholic female co-workers' lives, the more she understood why growing numbers of working-class Catholics were staying away from Sunday mass and not seeking advice from their pastors. She wrote Ferraro, sharing her frustration with traditional parish priests who sided with husbands threatened by their wives' efforts to educate themselves and improve the lives of their children. Ferraro consulted with Tuite, who offered to introduce Ferraro and Hussey to some Chicago worker-priests she knew. The priests had been inspired by French clergy who allied themselves with the working classes after World War II and liberation theologians who worked alongside the poor and oppressed in Latin America. They rejected the vision of the priesthood as a privileged caste that stood apart from the people.

Meeting the worker-priests provided Ferraro and Hussey with a concrete example of the kind of joint ministry they might pursue together.

When Ferraro and Hussey suggested that one way to avoid the temptations of status and power would be to leave the priesthood, the worker-priests explained what they hoped to gain by staying. They sought to discover and teach their orders a new model of priesthood. One of the priests predicted that given the views of the new pope, John Paul II, who was "deaf to women," sisters, too, would soon have to "decide between [their] principles and the commands of the Vatican." Afterward, Tuite pointedly asked Ferraro and Hussey for their reactions: "Is that the kind of work you have in mind?" While the idea of "doing instead of just preaching" strongly appealed to both women, they had trouble with the prospect of keeping their identity as nuns a permanent secret from the people around them, and they still cherished their close connections to the Sisters of Notre Dame (Ferraro and Hussey 1990, 176–177).

Ferraro finished her doctorate at McCormick and brainstormed with Hussey about their plans for the future. Together Ferraro and Hussey clarified their goals; they even committed them to writing. They wanted to "identify and work with working-class people," promote social and economic justice, and live an appropriately simple lifestyle. They would meet regularly with other nuns in social-justice ministries and with members of other groups with whom they collaborated. Through their expanding network of sisters in social ministries, they heard about the Charleston Interdenominational Council on Social Concerns (CICSC) in West Virginia and its plan to launch Covenant House, a still partly undefined ministry to "people who fall between the cracks." In February 1981, Ferraro and Hussey were interviewed by CICSC, and the following August they moved to Charleston to begin work. Although there were five other SND in West Virginia, the closest ones were an hour away. The move to Charleston placed Ferraro and Hussey in an unfamiliar situation, where Catholics represented a minority, 5 percent of the state population. Ferraro and Hussey embraced the fresh new environment in which they found themselves. They had successfully sloughed off the privileges sisters enjoyed as part of a large Catholic bloc in New England and Chicago; they had found their way to the margin, the frontier. Ferraro explained: "It was wonderful to be away from the nunny culture of New England. Nobody gave us any special treatment. No deference and no discounts. No free tickets to the movies, no free parts for the furnace just because we were nuns" (Ferraro and Hussey 1990, 179–180, 188).

Working through CICSC, Ferraro and Hussey were instrumental in nurturing the beginnings of a sanctuary for Central American refugees in the Unitarian Universalist Fellowship in Charleston in 1983. The following year, they joined three women friends from Charleston and traveled to

Nicaragua, a trip sponsored by AMNLAE, an organization commemorating Luisa Amanda Espinosa, the first woman killed in the Nicaraguan revolution. They stayed with Sandinistas, including many women who had lost husbands and children in the fighting, and insisted that Christ would be on their side. They celebrated International Women's Day in an extinct volcano in Nicaragua. Ferraro and Hussey shared what they had learned about Nicaragua with local groups in West Virginia. They became increasingly aware of the parallels between the plight of poor women in Nicaragua and the situation of many Appalachian women who found their way to Covenant House.

> The poor people live on [the] land [owned by giant corporations], wherever they can find a nook or a hollow where they are allowed to live, have inadequate schools, no health clinics, and no opportunity. When they organize, they are accused of being subversives. And yet, we have met women living in those remote hollows who have borne a number of children by the time they are twenty, who carry water from their wells, and survive the winter eating squirrels they have caught, and vegetables and fruit they have grown and canned. And yet, they still plant flowers. Like their sisters in Nicaragua and El Salvador and all over the world, they are noble and brave.

As Ferraro put it: "We just agreed, without needing to speak, that we would do all we could, however we could, to help those women claim the dignity they deserve" (Ferraro and Hussey 1990, 203).

Back in Charleston, as Ferraro and Hussey sought to live out what they had learned in Nicaragua, they found a new clarity. They had reached still another feminist moment of truth and confirmed their abstract commitment to justice by direct experience. As had Hussey at the papal conclave, they had "felt the truth of their ideas." Their heightened awareness of the connection between the poor women in Nicaragua and their counterparts in Charleston sharpened their judgment and illuminated their priorities. It was almost like renewing their vows. Patricia Hussey had publicly affirmed the final vows that she had written for herself in a ceremony on September 13, 1980. She had embraced the "call to create a world more justly loving" and dedicated her life to "the cause of the poor and the powerless" (Ferraro and Hussey 1990, 162–164). Although Ferraro had taken a more traditional set of vows ten years before Hussey, since their meeting in 1978, she had joined Hussey in this commitment.

The involvement of Ferraro and Hussey in the heated four-year controversy over the *New York Times* ad (1984–1988) needs to be understood in the context of the pilgrimage that brought them to Charleston and

Nicaragua in the early 1980s. Ferraro and Hussey did not have to deliberate over whether to sign the document when Marjorie Tuite first showed it to them because they had already come to see women as their primary community. As Hussey put it in their joint memoir: "We had finally realized that we, too, are *women*" (Ferraro and Hussey 1990, 204). Accepting their primary commitment to women had required crossing many smaller thresholds along the way. Ferraro's formation in the order prior to the reforms of the late 1960s and early 1970s had sought to eradicate sisters' attachment to their women's bodies, their instinctive emotional responses, and their connections with other women. Even Hussey's training in the postulancy and novitiate after Vatican II had presupposed the separate roles and status of sisters and laywomen.

One of the painful lessons Ferraro and Hussey had to learn during the negotiations and intramural Catholic wrangling that resulted from the Vatican's response to the *New York Times* ad was that not all sisters were in the same place regarding their solidarity with laywomen. This startled and dismayed them. The interdenominational work they were doing at Covenant House, with the blessing of their superiors in the Sisters of Notre Dame in Connecticut and Massachusetts, had given them hope that it was possible to promote justice and love without the structures that separated people into castes and categories. The whole point of their ministry was to dissolve the boundaries separating people according to class, race, sex, or religion and to concentrate on larger issues of healing and social change. This is why they were so disconcerted—if only temporarily—to discover that a local Catholic pastor in Charleston wanted "housenuns" who would teach catechism classes rather than "nontraditional" nuns who sought to address local poverty directly (Ferraro and Hussey 1990, 189).

When the first call came from Sister Catherine Hughes, the general superior of the SND in Rome in December 1984, a little over two months after the ad had appeared in the *New York Times,* Ferraro and Hussey were too busy with the usual emergencies at Covenant House to give it their full attention. The washing machine was broken; a woman fleeing an abusive husband had had a heart attack in the sunroom, leaving two mentally retarded children to be cared for; there were violent altercations over personal possessions simmering in the laundry room. Hughes explained that she had received a harsh letter from the Vatican bureaucrats at SCRIS presenting an ultimatum: Ferraro and Hussey should retract their statement or be dismissed from their religious communities. This was alarming, but less urgent than defusing violence, calling an ambulance, and fixing the washing machine. Ferraro and Hussey were not surprised to hear that SCRIS had sent the letter to their superiors instead of directly to them. The same thing had happened when their bishop had been displeased with their public stand against the West Virginia Parental Notification Bill. In a sense, the familiar pattern of indirect communication mitigated their concern. The bishops' complaints to Ferraro's superiors over parental notification and the protest over the diocesan pastoral center had seemed to disappear. Maybe this, too, would pass.

A few days after Hughes called, Ferraro and Hussey received the duplicate copy of the letter from SCRIS that she had promised to send them. The letter, signed by Archbishops Jean Jerome Hamer and Vincenzo Fagiolo, accused the signers of the *New York Times* ad of making "misleading and erroneous statements" and failing to show the appropriate "religious submission of mind and will" to the teaching authority of the church (Ferraro and Hussey 1990, 226–227). Reading her copy of the letter from SCRIS to Hughes transported Ferraro back to the novitiate, where her own voice and self had been drowned out by the admonitions of her superiors: "'We don't ask questions, Barbara, dear. . . . You must mortify your curiosity.' . . . 'Sister Mary Kevin, may I ask forgiveness for speaking on the stairs?' . . . 'It is not possible for you to major in mathematics, Barbara, dear.'"

She realized that the letter made her feel like a "pre–Vatican II novice"; that was its intent. Self-consciously, she reminded herself that the Vatican's ploy could work only if she let it. On the other hand, she could use it as a reminder of how far she had come and the strength it had taken to get there. She told herself: "I am not a novice. . . . I am forty-one years old. I have spent all the years of my adult life trying to discern God's will for me and to act on it. That is why I signed the ad." Ferraro knew that if she focused on who she was and who she had worked to become, she could use the Vatican's tactics against them and gain strength from them. She also knew that was easier said than done.

As usual, Hussey's response perfectly complemented Ferraro's. When asked how she felt when she read the letter, she replied: "You mean how do I feel about reading a letter that dismisses my conscience and my intelligence as 'lack of submission'? How do I feel about knowing that a man in Rome can threaten to take away my work and my vocation and my community without even having the common decency to write to me personally?" When pressed by Ferraro, Hussey moved beyond irony to a one-word answer that strengthened both women in their stand and made their proper response to the SCRIS missive crystal-clear: "I feel insulted" (Ferraro and Hussey 1990, 228–229).

After the Vatican expressed its displeasure and issued its ultimatums to the signers of the ad who were members of religious communities, some found ways to distance themselves from the statement they had signed. The two priests and two brothers were no longer identified with the ad and the protest it represented. The sixty-seven laypeople did not receive letters asking for recantations because the Vatican did not have the same leverage against them; they were not under the authority of SCRIS. Reprisals against lay signers were more subtle and took place behind the scenes. Lecture invitations were canceled and job prospects suddenly disappeared. Meanwhile, two of the twenty-six nuns who had signed the ad were removed from the list for different reasons. One was never identified by name. The other was a missionary whose order was not under SCRIS's authority; her case was handled separately. The public showdown between the Vatican and the signers of the ad polarized into two opposing bodies: SCRIS and the group of sisters that became known as the Vatican 24.

Both nuns and laywomen who had signed the ad met in Washington, D.C., on December 18, 1984. Ferraro reports a conversation she had with Hussey that morning before they left Charleston for Washington. It was a moment of recognition, a Thelma-and-Louise moment. Ferraro and Hussey had crossed over. They knew for certain what they would do, and what they could never do, not even to defuse the crisis that loomed ahead. That morning Ferraro and Hussey made a threefold agreement and never wavered from it, even as the crisis escalated over the next four years. First, they would not sign anything that might be misinterpreted or misused by the Vatican. Second, they would not recant: The ad had called for dialogue, and they still wanted dialogue. Third, they accepted the possibility that as a result of the controversy over the ad, they "might no longer be nuns" (Ferraro and Hussey 1990, 230).

Eighteen of the Vatican 24 were present that morning in Washington: prominent activists and academics whose names were already familiar to those who had attended Women's Ordination Conference and Woman-church meetings. Nobody argued in favor of recanting, but there were different visions of how not to recant. Should they use their knowledge of Vatican politics to avoid the recantation SCRIS's letter requested? Should they resist by ignoring the Vatican's demands altogether? The Vatican's response to the *New York Times* ad confirmed the suspicions of many in the room that for the Vatican 24, the controversy over their right to dissent on abortion could not be separated from another question: Could Pope John Paul II succeed in reversing the progress that sisters had made in redefining their vocations since the close of Vatican II? A document entitled "Essential Elements in the Church's Teaching on Religious Life" that had been issued by SCRIS the previous year indicated that John Paul II and SCRIS intended to try.

Ferraro and Hussey left the meeting with mixed feelings. What worried them the most was Marjorie Tuite's visible anxiety. Tuite had stated that she found clarity more difficult this time because for the first time in her forty-four years as a Dominican, everything was threatened, including job security, her home, her retirement, and her status as a nun. Ferraro and Hussey had learned so much in the meetings of Tuite's women's group in Chicago that they could not help hearing her voice providing an alternate message, urging them to stand together and risk everything. This was the message they had to take away from the meeting, especially since the other option was to "submit—and deny the truth of everything we had learned and experienced in the last twenty years" (Ferraro and Hussey 1990, 235).

Another source of concern was the way in which the sisters' leadership groups had resorted to traditional hierarchical models of the religious life. They had chosen the "patriarchal triangle" over the "sacred and human circle" (Ferraro and Hussey 1990, 149). Representatives of the leadership groups of the orders to which signers belonged had met separately and reported back to the signers. They would inform SCRIS that they had received their letter and postpone further joint action and discussion until January 1985. Given the timing of the controversy, in the midst of efforts within several orders to gain approval of their new constitutions from SCRIS, the superiors' decisions to move slowly were understandable. Still, their strategies for keeping the controversy contained were unacceptable to Ferraro and Hussey. Some superiors had even advised sisters not to attend the meeting with the lay signers scheduled for December 19th. Ferraro and Hussey had signed the ad in the first place out of solidarity with other women; separation of women into different camps only bolstered the efforts of SCRIS and the Vatican to turn back the clock (Ferraro and Hussey 1990, 230–240).

For the next three years, Ferraro and Hussey attended meetings of the gradually dwindling ranks of the Vatican 24 and wrote letters to their superiors in Boston and Connecticut. They appeared on *The Phil Donahue Show* with Marjorie Tuite in January 1985 and received outpourings of support from Catholic women across the country who agreed with them about the need for dialogue on abortion within the church and about Catholic women's right to explore questions raised by abortion and contraception. They resolved to study the history of the church's position on abortion and examine the effects of Vatican policies on Catholic women and their families. By March 1986, their studies, discussions, and prayers had paid off; they had reached clarity. "We were no longer calling for dialogue. We were publicly, urgently, demanding recognition of women's right to choose" (Ferraro and Hussey 1990, 250). On March 9, 1986, they spoke in favor of choice at the March for Women's Lives in Washington, D.C. They were also involved in the publication of a second *New York Times* ad, with the headline "A Declaration of Solidarity," that was published on March 2, 1986. They were later told that their participation in these two events placed them in "a different category" than other remaining members of the Vatican 24 (Ferraro and Hussey 1990, 277). SCRIS would consider their case in isolation.

It is exhausting to read Ferraro and Hussey's account of the pivotal year between February 1985 and March 1986: endless meetings with governing teams, leadership groups, and entire provincial communities of Sisters of Notre Dame; the composition of four letters explaining their actions and beliefs to their superiors and members of their communities; communications with others in the Vatican 24; in-depth study of the evolution of the Catholic church's teachings on abortion; and finally, their more-than-full-time ministry to the poor at Covenant House. In retrospect, they realized that they might never have fit the exhaustive discussions, soul-searching, extra reading, and study into their busy schedules had SCRIS not challenged their right to make the modest request for dialogue contained in the *New York Times* ad. Ultimately, they were grateful for the crisis, which helped them to cross boundaries and name the problem they faced: "The Vatican considers us less than men. Therefore, they can deny our experience, our connection to God, and our sacred dignity as human beings." The controversy was not merely about abortion; it was about women's position in the Catholic church. Acceptance of this fact brought pain, but it also liberated Ferraro and Hussey "to join the great circle of women determined to define ourselves as whole in God's eyes" (Ferraro and Hussey 1990, 251–252).

On Saturday, March 22, 1986, Ferraro and Hussey met with a delegation from the Vatican in the parlor of the convent at Trinity College, which was run by the SND in Washington, D.C. It was the last in a series of meetings between members of the Vatican 24 and SCRIS. Ferraro and Hussey entered the meeting knowing that through various means, all of the other signers of the original *New York Times* ad had settled their cases with Rome. For Ferraro, it was time for another flashback, prompted by the smells and the ambiance: "wax, boiled vegetables, incense . . . and secrets." She was "little Barbara Ferraro again, dressed in [her] Sunday best," visiting the sisters at Emmanuel College in Boston. Then she was a novice, "trying to walk like a nun, thumping instead of gliding silently and piously." The ghosts of her convent past were relentless: "Every polished inch of corridor we passed seemed to murmur in disapproval. 'Barbara, dear, where is your humility? Where is your submission? Barbara, dear, who do you think you are? Barbara, Barbara, what are we going to do about you? Barbara, *dear,* it is not possible to say no to the pope'" (Ferraro and Hussey 1990, 291–292).

Finally she caught her breath and remembered that she was now an adult, one who owed a great debt to the SND for helping her to find her mission and for teaching her "to keep faith with the people of God" (Ferraro and Hussey 1990, 292). Inside the parlor were representatives of Ferraro's leadership team in Boston and their counterparts from Hussey's province in Connecticut. Ferraro and Hussey arranged the furniture in a circle to symbolize the equality they envisioned in the church rather than the hierarchy they had been protesting. Mary Linscott from SCRIS, the highest-ranking woman at the Vatican, appeared, followed by Archbishop Fagiolo from SCRIS—"one of the men who can decide the very existence of women's religious communities"—and finally, Archbishop Pio Laghi, the Vatican's ambassador to the United States. Laghi said a prayer and then explained that the meeting was to be a "dialogue," a "pastoral meeting," rather than "an inquisition." He quickly added that by the end of the meeting, Ferraro and Hussey would have to commit to writing a statement of submission to official Catholic teaching on abortion.

Ferraro and Hussey spoke politely but refused to defer to the archbishops. After a while, Laghi left and Fagiolo addressed the group. He gave a brief report on Catholic policy on abortion, beginning with the assertion that "No member of the church, especially priests and sisters, can legitimately dissent from the official teaching on abortion because it has been a consistent teaching since the first century" (Ferraro and Hussey 1990, 297). Toward the end of his remarks he urged Ferraro and Hussey to assent to church doctrine for the sake of their parents. Linscott's diplomatic translation did not quite capture the tone and tenor of Fagiolo's Italian, which Ferraro caught. What Fagiolo really said was "What would your mommies and daddies think if you were no longer nuns?" With great restraint, Ferraro and Hussey told him that both sets of parents had been supportive, even when they did not agree with the particulars of their daughters' positions on abortion.

The discussion was not going well. Fagiolo was not accustomed to sisters sitting face to face with him, presenting their own counterarguments on the church's teaching authority, on Aquinas's attitudes toward women, and on the possibility of more than one position on Catholic moral teachings. Every now and then, Fagiolo stopped to ask if they would state their acceptance of the church's teaching on abortion. Each time, Ferraro and Hussey expressed their belief in their right to dissent. Fagiolo's affectionate overtures—arm-stroking, cheek-pinching, and suggestions that Ferraro and Hussey resembled members of his family—only made the interview more uncomfortable. Fagiolo gave Ferraro and Hussey until April 4th to submit a statement acceptable to SCRIS or accept the consequences. On April 4th, they brought the following statement to representatives from their leadership groups gathered in Boston: "We stand with those in the church who believe in all women's rights to make moral choices; who value integrity and do not compromise it; who respect conscience and do not undermine it; and who seek the truth and do not fear it" (Ferraro and Hussey 1990, 298–303).

Some members of the leadership teams expressed hopes that Ferraro and Hussey might insert a reference to the sanctity of human life, something that could be construed as implicit acceptance of the church's teachings on abortion. Ferraro and Hussey were unmoved. They had clarified their views; there was nothing more to say. In late June, they received a three-page, single-spaced press release from the SND government group in Rome, intended for the International Catholic News Service and all members of the Notre Dame order. It reprimanded Ferraro and Hussey for the public methods they had chosen to express dissent and for the contents of their dissenting statements. It accused them of resisting dialogue within the order. It called for a process of "clarification of their full position and examination of their stance in the light of the Church's teaching and of our congregational statement of mission" (Ferraro and Hussey 1990, 308). The government group had also enclosed a set of questions about the position that Ferraro and Hussey had taken on choice and abortion that they wanted answered in writing by August 1st.

As Ferraro and Hussey reflected on how and whether to enter into the next stage of clarification with the members of their order, which, they understood, could possibly lead to reprisals, Ferraro prepared a speech on the abortion controversy for the annual assembly of the Boston province of the Sisters of Notre Dame. As she wrote, she realized how little common understanding of women's experience with abortion and of the broader implications of the abortion controversy she could presuppose within her audience. She put all that she had learned about the need for solidarity among women and the need to challenge official Catholic teachings on women into this one speech to the group that she had been taught to consider her primary community. There was warm applause when she finished but no evidence that anyone had heard anything worthy of further discussion or response. The assembly moved immediately to their next agenda item: the need to support Father Charles Curran (a Catholic moral theologian reprimanded by the Vatican in 1986 for his position on contraception). Ferraro was stunned by her community's failure to "make the connections" between her presentation and the case of Charles Curran (Ferraro and Hussey 1990, 313–315).

Communications between Ferraro and Hussey and the various leadership structures of the church and their order degenerated between 1986 and 1988. Ferraro and Hussey continued to speak publicly about the right to choose and the abuses of power within the institutional church. They received warnings of possible dismissal from their order in January 1988 and February 1988 and then a formal reprieve in June 1988. They were grateful to the Sisters of Notre Dame for not succumbing to Vatican pressure to make an example of them. They held a press conference on June 9th in Washington, where they announced that they had not been ejected from their order for their views and proclaimed: "You can be publicly pro-choice and still be a nun" (Ferraro and Hussey 1990, 320).

In their memoir they explain that their order's decision not to dismiss them "freed us to leave." They read the fine print in their letter of reprieve and fastened on the phrase that said that they would not be dismissed "*at this point.*" They could envision years of "debilitating internal argument with other women" in their order and with the other nun-signers of the *New York Times* ad who had begun to criticize them publicly for their refusal to engage in dialogue with their order and for their willingness to speak publicly about their criticism of the church. In a high-profile article in the December 7, 1988, issue of *The Christian Century,* Jeannine Gramick, S.S.N.D., who was engaged in a pioneering ministry for lesbian and gay Catholics, used Carol Gilligan's *In a Different Voice* to frame her feminist critique of the direction that Ferraro and Hussey's dissent had taken. Gramick maintained that Gilligan's work suggested that "as far as possible, the dissenter should communicate and dialogue with those who will be most seriously and immediately affected by the dissent." Dissenters within an institution must remain in dialogue with the institution's leaders and representatives because they are immediately affected by the dissenters' actions (Gramick 1988, 1124–1125).

Ferraro and Hussey were no longer interested in protracted dialogue with the leadership of the church and their order. They had reached clarity: Their disagreement was not with the Sisters of Notre Dame but with patriarchy both inside and outside of the church. At Covenant House, they had found a place where they could pursue "a life-giving mission." At long last, they had to admit what they had learned between September 1984 and June 1988: "Nundom . . . seemed to be dying." They saw the SND's new constitution, which contained a loyalty oath to the pope, as a symptom of bad things to come and a negative legacy of their conflict with SCRIS. Finally, Ferraro and Hussey decided to cast their fate with laywomen; that was how and where they had entered the controversy over the *New York Times* ad in the first place: "Who had supported us since we signed that fateful ad? Laywomen. Who were the women who were actually *doing* what they preached? Laywomen. Who were the least privileged, most powerless, most despised people in the Catholic church? Laywomen" (Ferraro and Hussey 1990, 321–322).

On July 13, 1988, Ferraro and Hussey sent letters of resignation to their communities in Boston and Connecticut. They explained the reasons for their resignation in their memoir: "To truly stand with people who are struggling, one must be in a relationship of equality with them. Thus, for us to stand with women, we need to renounce the differences, limitations, and even privileges that are part of membership in a religious community in a patriarchal church" (Ferraro and Hussey 1990, 323).

Read in the context of their narrative, the reasons that Ferraro and Hussey resigned from the SND sound strangely like vows taken when crossing a threshold to the next stage in the religious life. They contain the same powerful combination of renunciation and affirmation. Given their combined experience of forty-seven years as sisters, Ferraro and Hussey could hardly avoid making this connection. Their lives since first entering the convent had been a process of refining their vows, even augmenting them, by taking on new responsibilities and rejecting any power and privilege they had inadvertently obtained by belonging to an institution within another powerful institution. In a passage in *No Turning Back* in which Hussey reflects on the final vows she affirmed in September 1980, she writes: "Nearly ten years have passed since that day. I am still trying to live out my vows just as I wrote them. Only one thing changed. It turned out that the only way to keep my promise to God was to stop being a nun" (Ferraro and Hussey 1990, 166).

5

COMING HOME

The pull of the Church is very strong. It is like one's native language and, though one may have become denationalized, one cannot help reverting to it, and even thinking in its terms.

—Antonia White, November 10, 1940 (White 1992b, 1)

Those sacred spaces were very formative, and irreplaceable. I began to understand that the habit of mind that was generated by those sacred spaces was very important to who I am, and that if I didn't honor my hunger for that, I would be less than truthful about who I really am.

. . . I needed to be in the psychic space that only church ritual and the ethical framework that is expressed in ritual could give me. Nothing else would substitute for that.

—Mary Gordon on her return to the church (Mudge 2002, 198)

I wasn't fallen away anymore; now, magically, the Church had fallen away. What remained of its colossal architecture was a frail structure of wonder, long forgotten.

—Patricia Hampl on her return (Hampl 1992b, 16)

To those outside the fold, or rather, those without benefit of Catholic girl-hoods, Catholic women's departure narratives are much easier to understand and empathize with than accounts of their return. To secular feminists who, quite logically, consider voluntary affinity groups more satisfactory than ties to organized religions, the return of self-proclaimed feminists to the church is mystifying, exasperating. It is difficult for feminists who do not come from a Catholic background to understand how a woman who has managed to place herself beyond the constraints of the Catholic church would willingly return to such a blatantly patriarchal institution.

Most Catholic women who return to the church from self-imposed exile and diaspora admit that their decision does not appear rational. For such a decision is not primarily rational or necessarily logical; emotions and gut instincts play the major role. Those who set out to explain their reentry into the fold do not really expect outsiders to understand. Otherwise articulate feminists who cannot find the words to make their non-Catholic friends understand why they want to give the church a second chance frequently feel isolated, stuck between two communities they once called home. And yet for some women who took great pains to distance themselves from the church in girlhood or adolescence, their return at midlife has a note of continuity. It is almost an extension of the spirit of transgression that propelled them out of the church years ago and brings some of the same sense of isolation and displacement with it. Such women reserve the right to be complex and inconsistent, to defy the conventions associated with the liberated woman just as they rejected the role of good Catholic daughter.

In response to inquiries, they tend to highlight the contradictions inherent in what they have done. They resort to irony and paradox to provide outsiders access to the adult Catholic woman's experience of returning to the church. Sofia, a twice-married grandmother in her late 40s who had reconnected with the church ten years before, told interviewer Jeanne Pieper: "I can truthfully say that every day I quit the Church maybe once or twice. But I'm still here. I wouldn't have it otherwise" (Pieper 1993, 195). Sofia calls herself a radical feminist and openly disagrees with many church policies but still finds in the Catholic church a spiritual home.

Many who left in adolescence when they could no longer ignore the moral and intellectual shortcomings of the church return at midlife with their misgivings about the institutional church and its policies intact. At a certain point, after much self-scrutiny, these women return because they have come to recognize how deeply the church has impressed itself on their morality, personal identity, or artistic imagination. They return not out of choice but out of a necessity that they have trouble explaining to those who have not shared their spiritual pilgrimage. The narratives of Antonia White, Mary Gordon, and Patricia Hampl (1946–) illuminate the variety, complexity, and, especially, the unfinished quality of Catholic women's homecomings. Adult Catholic women do not return like sheep or lemmings to the church of their fathers; they find ways to rebuild—or at least remodel—the church of their girlhood so that it is fit for habitation. In the process, they discover that coming home can feel like leaving, for it can require still more departures, ones they had postponed long after they had left the church behind.

Antonia White

According to her diary, Antonia White left the Catholic church in 1926 or 1927. This departure, which she had every reason to consider an act of closure, a decision to nurture a more "natural," less guilt-ridden version of herself, was never as complete and definitive as she thought it was at the time. Even the lives of Mary McCarthy and Mary Daly, whose separation from the church became a central component in their adult identities, suggest that it may be impossible for a woman who has been a Catholic to leave it all behind. Vestiges of prior Catholic belief and sensibilities linger on. They become the parchment upon which women who "were Catholic" write the subsequent installments of their life stories. Antonia White is unusual because she provides such honest, sustained, meticulously detailed documentation of the contours of one woman's love-hate relationship with the church and of her protracted struggle to find a way to be Catholic that would not erase her identity as a writer or a woman.

The account of Antonia White's unsuccessful attempt to make a clean break from Catholicism is found primarily in her diary, which she kept from 1926 until late 1979, a few months before her death, and in a series of letters later published as *The Hound and the Falcon* (1965). The subtitle of the *Hound and the Falcon*—*The Story of a Reconversion to the Catholic Faith*—makes White's return to the church sound simpler, more fundamental yet less profound, than it really was. We have already seen in the case of Mary Daly how untidy and incomplete Catholic women's departures can be. It comes as no surprise, then, when Antonia White shows us that the process of returning, a reversal that constitutes yet another kind of spiritual departure, can also be unfinished, never quite as satisfying as one would have hoped.

Chapter 2 explored the many small departures made by White as a schoolgirl at Roehampton. These subtle, sometimes imaginary, experiments in resistance and flight faithfully preserved in *Frost in May* taught White that she could survive, however tentatively and uncomfortably, on the margins of the institutional church. White's chronicle of Nanda Grey's painful realization that she could never fit into Lippington's mandatory version of Catholic girlhood and womanhood has familiar resonance. Like Mary Daly, who in the 1950s stopped short of leaving the church because the place beyond it was "a desert" that "an uncomprehending world would have called 'madness'" (Daly 1985d, 24), Nanda Grey could never quite envision life beyond the Catholic church. She spent her early adolescence at Lippington improvising her faith in an expanding borderland that she created in her imagination. This life on the boundary constituted her own chosen form of rebellion against the genteel Catholic totalitarianism fostered by schools such as Lippington, where Nanda "could not eat or sleep or read or play without relating every action to her secret life as a Christian and a Catholic." Nanda "rejoiced in [convent-school life] and rebelled against it," but she conceded that Lippington had done its work. "She could never, she knew, break away without a sense of mutilation." Imagining life outside of the church was "as impossible as imagining death or madness or blindness" (White 1992a, 136–137).

White's daughter, Lyndall Hopkinson, writes that her mother "vaunted her Catholicism" when she first left her convent school at 15 to become a day student at St. Paul's, a non-Catholic institution. White "festoon[ed] herself with medals and scapulars" and wrote the feast days of the church on her essays in lieu of the date. Soon, however, as she began to feel accepted in her new non-Catholic environment, "the medals disappeared inside her clothes" (Hopkinson 1988, 33–34). From this point on, her major transgressions were against her father, not the church. She rejected his vision of her as a serious scholar en route to Cambridge. After graduation from St. Paul's, she tried her hand at acting and then found true success in the field of advertising. Both of her career choices were as distasteful to her father as her adolescent novel had been, and he showed his displeasure. White and her father remained trapped in their old conflict, but suddenly she was a free agent, calling the shots.

In her mid-20s, a little over a decade after she had left Roehampton, White risked the free-fall into the uncharted territory beyond the church. When she resumed work on *Frost in May* in the early 1930s, she had been "a lapsed Catholic" for at least half a decade. That five-year period was eventful, even turbulent. White was employed at Crawford's advertising agency and briefly in Harrod's advertising department, where she did work she found demoralizing but too lucrative to give up for freelance writing. She pursued a long-distance affair with Silas Glossop, a mining engineer whose work took him to Canada and Mexico while White gave birth to his daughter (Susan) in England in 1929. The same year, her father died of a brain hemorrhage. White divorced her second husband Eric Earnshaw Smith and, in 1930, married Tom Hopkinson, a writer she had met while working at Crawford's. A second daughter, Lyndall, was born in 1931. White lived through all of these changes convinced that she had left the church for good. She turned her vivid memories of Roehampton and the unfinished business she had with that school and with her father into *Frost in May*, published in 1933. Temporarily, she might have found what her biographer Jane Dunn sensed in the "cool, precise language" and "sense of absolute truth" in this first novel: "a kind of absolution" (Dunn 1998, 5).

White was socially and sexually active during the "lapsed" years (ca. 1926–1940). She entertained a "lively, artistic gossipy set of friends centered on Chelsea, a raffish and less serious pole to Bloomsbury, but with members like Desmond MacCarthy, Logan Pearsall Smith and various artists who navigated between both" (Dunn 1998, 110). One component that defined White's distance from the church during these years was her attitude toward her second and third marriages, both of which were open. With Earnshaw Smith, who was gay, there was a tacit arrangement; they would find sexual intimacy elsewhere. The lines of communication were less clear between White and Hopkinson, and they were repeatedly unfaithful to each other, in keeping with the mores of their social group. When White sought to reconnect with the church, she closed the door on her promiscuous years. Like Graham Greene's female protagonist Sarah Miles in *The End of the Affair* (1951), a novel with which she was certainly familiar, White equated returning to the church with embracing chastity.

In 1954, White maintained that she had had "no sexual life at all" since 1940, the year she was reconciled to the church (Chitty 1992, 274). This statement overlooks a brief passionate affair with another woman, Benedicta de Bezier, in 1947 (Dunn 1998, 286–289) and the final throes of a long-term relationship with Ian Henderson, which ended the summer after she returned to the church. White allowed herself these two exceptions and could still maintain that she had left sexual activity behind to reconcile with the church. She could tolerate complexity and contradiction in her new relationship with Catholicism. White knew practicing Catholics who were chaste and faithful to their spouses and those who were not, but she was reassured by her ability to break off her relationship with Henderson. The sacrifice signified the authenticity of her return to the church (White 1992b, 39; Chitty 1993, 100).

A second and related component of White's distance from the church during the late 1920s and 1930s was her strenuous effort to locate and cultivate her "natural self," which she believed she had almost eradicated in her girlhood efforts to please her father and the nuns. White's attempt to focus on her natural self was encouraged by her friendship with a new circle of women intellectuals and activists that included Emily Coleman, Peggy Guggenheim, Djuna Barnes, and Phyllis Jones, a group with whom she spent intense weeks of writing and socializing in various rented country houses starting in 1933. The poet Dylan Thomas, whom she met through Guggenheim in 1936, compared White to a domesticated wild animal living in a suburban zoo who briefly "escaped into liberty" only to find it "far more terrifying" than captivity (cited in Dunn 1998, 211–212). "Why is it I can't be 'natural.' And what *is* 'natural' to me?" White wrote in her diary in April 1939. "The silly thing is I am always even now trying to be 'good' . . . whatever I mean by that" (Chitty 1992, 163–164).

Between 1926 and 1940, White worked hard at living the wild unrestrained life of a "natural woman," which she associated with that of the (non-Catholic) female writer and intellectual. It was not a life that felt all that natural to her. The whole time she grappled with the recurring depression that plagued her throughout her adult life. A diary entry dated August 21, 1937, is fairly typical and makes the connection between her Roehampton experience and her inability to envision herself as a mature natural woman. In it, White declared herself "a terrible failure" both as a woman and as an artist, and asserted: "I cannot bear being an intelligent schoolgirl forever for I am nothing else but that it seems" (Chitty 1992, 103).

There were reasons for White to feel especially burdened by her memories of her father and Roehampton—to be stuck in her identity as a schoolgirl—during the second half of the 1930s. From 1935 to 1938 she confronted her depression and feelings of worthlessness head on with the help of a young Freudian analyst, Dr. Dennis Carroll, whom she saw four times a week. Early in 1935 she complained in her diary about the "high priest attitude of the psychoanalysts" who insisted that they were the only mediators, the only route to truth. This exclusive claim to be the one true mediator ("I am the way and the truth and the life") had made her relationship with her father and the institutional church untenable, and now it resurfaced in the psychoanalysts with whom she sought to address the damages sustained by trying so hard to be good during her Catholic girlhood (Chitty 1992, 34).

There was no suppressing White's Catholic side, however. The period of analysis with Dr. Carroll gave White the courage to confront her two ghosts: her father and the church. She experimented with alternatives, such as Eric Earnshaw Smith's secular spirituality based on the writings of

Santayana and the quiet, reasonable, socially responsible faith espoused by her Quaker friends. White tried, but could not join, Earnshaw Smith when he embraced Santayana's view of "religion as *poetic* truth." She was equally uncomfortable with the "joylessness" and "complacency" she found in Quaker meetings (Dunn 1998, 99, 186). Neither of these two spiritual frameworks provided White with the strength to face the depression brought on by the breakdown of her third marriage. A diary entry dated August 31, 1936, recorded a major milestone: "I have given Tom back himself. I must somehow learn to take *myself* back" (Chitty 1992, 77). When her ex-husband remarried, White bridled under the strain of renouncing her former ties with him and became acutely aware of a "great many blank spaces" in her life. In July 1939 she wrote that she felt "like someone with a lot of spare capital to invest and not knowing the best place to invest it" (Chitty 1992, 165).

Despite sporadic efforts to explore faiths and philosophies that she considered more modern and rational, during her thirteen years outside the church White remained a lapsed Catholic rather than a generic atheist. Two distinctly Catholic presences remained central to her consciousness even as her faith in the church and its teachings receded. First, White held on to her belief in the Virgin Mary, "an odd, isolated fact which nothing could destroy" (White 1954, 41). Second, she remained attached to Thomas Aquinas, for whom she had had special devotion since age 11. She had been drawn to his prayers in the missal because "they asked so simply and directly for things one sincerely wanted to have." She especially recalled one of Thomas's prayers, which began, "O God to whom belong [*sic*] all things," which was so beloved and habitual that there was a "black thumb mark" next to it in her prayer book. She later confessed that she "often found [herself] saying it unconsciously during [her] thirteen years out of the Church" (White 1954, 45).

The Second World War turned White's life upside down, placed her at a distance from her two daughters, and required her to live for over a year in other people's homes, doing work for the BBC that she called her "hairshirt" (White 1992b, 82). Her mother died in 1939, and that same year, at age 40, White had a second abortion. Then, in December 1940, she unexpectedly found her way back to the church. She had set out that Christmas to attend mass at the Carmelite Church in London where she had gone as a child. She insists that she went "not from real devotion or as an act of submission to the Church," but for "sentimental reasons": "I have always loved Christmas and going to Mass and hearing the first *Adeste fideles* is part of it and is too much stamped on my mind, or feelings, not to feel Christmas day very empty and meaningless without it" (White 1992b, 32).

White went to the church the Monday before Christmas to find out what time Christmas mass would be, since midnight mass, which she usually attended, was precluded by air-raid policies. On "a sudden impulse— one of those automatic ones over which one seems to have no control and which later appear to have been either foolish or extremely relevant," she stood in line for confession. Eighteen months before when she had gone to confession, the priest had informed her that she had been excommunicated (automatically) in 1930 for marrying in an Anglican church. He told her that in order to be reconciled to the church, she would need to sign a series of articles of submission, an abjection which she could not bring herself to do. This time, after checking with his vicar-general, the Carmelite priest reassured White that since everyone was in danger of death during wartime, the process of returning to the church had been simplified. He heard her confession and gave her absolution (White 1992b, 32–33, 1).

White "came away in a queer state: happy, apprehensive, bewildered and amused at [herself]." She received communion on Christmas day 1940 in the church of her girlhood, "a very blind, doubting Communion" that reproached her with recollections of what the sacrament had once meant to her. Her old memories and new questions "came up together like two photos on the same film." Still, "there was . . . a sense of peace and relief and 'home again'" (White 1954, 43). After all she had been through, White had no intention of adopting a childish faith, one that precluded questions and criticism of the church. Returning to the church was a form of reclaiming herself; she could not return to the church if it meant turning her back on the progress she had made toward understanding and valuing herself. In a diary entry written in August 1938, she expressed the need for a religion to help her "behave as an ordinarily decent human being" and a God to rely on so that she did not have to be so dependent on other finite human beings. Still, she wondered whether she could "ever again accept the restrictions and superstitions of an organized religion." Finally, she concluded: "I feel the Catholic religion to be the only possible one for me but I can only accept it in a new way" (Chitty 1992, 147–148).

This was an important threshold for White. She realized that reclaiming her life meant confronting Catholicism, but she also understood that the process of recycling the most important elements in her past life hinged on choices she must make. Starting in 1940, she adopted her own version of what post–Vatican II Catholics would later call cafeteria-style Catholicism. White had been accepted into the church with her convert parents when she was 7. She had been a precocious child, both intellectually and spiritually. She had observed Catholics closely over the years, both from within the church and from the margins. She knew that there were distinctly different kinds of Catholics. "Question the most devout Catholics," she wrote in 1943, "and you will find very different opinions combined with deep loyalty" (Chitty 1992, 181).

She was acutely aware of this variety among Catholics late in 1940 and was heartened by it. She had just begun a flurry of correspondence with a married former Jesuit seminarian, Joseph P. Thorp, who had read *Frost in May* and written to White inquiring about her current attitude toward Catholicism. White needed an audience for her evolving thoughts on Catholicism, and Thorp provided it. In the course of a little less than a year, while she worked full-time for the BBC during the blitz in London, she wrote 80,000 words to Thorp. She then used some of her letters to Thorp in an article about her return to the church entitled "Smoking Flax," published in the August 1950 issue of *The Month*. The article piqued the interest of literary friends at a dinner party in 1964, including John Guest of Longmans, Green, and Company. The result, *The Hound and the Falcon*, which appeared in print the following year, was White's most controversial and popular book since *Frost in May* three decades before.

Thorp's side of the correspondence did not survive, but we know by the tone and content of her published letters to him that he espoused a different vision of Catholicism than White did. White's old friend the Irish Catholic novelist Kate O'Brien praised *The Hound and the Falcon* profusely for its "intelligence, vision, modesty, tolerance and human warmth" and noted that these characteristics were patently lacking in White's "unheard correspondent" (Dunn 1998, 263). The opportunity to disagree publicly with an articulate, seminary-educated, male Catholic of her father's generation on questions related to the church was therapeutic for White. She had never had conversations of this sort with her father.

The Hound and the Falcon gave White a public podium from which to declare which elements of the Catholic religion and its institutional trappings she reserved the right to reject. She "[detested] most of the saints" for their "morbid preoccupation with sin and guilt," their "smug intimacy with what they call God," and their "anxious, niggling concern with their own salvation." She preferred "a God who was indifferent to [her] and destroyed [her]" to one who "was jealous and revengeful and 'suffered' if [she] did not love him" (White 1992b, 8). She refused to countenance "any sort of coercion, even the kindest and gentlest," from the church or those acting on its behalf: it "always makes me feel like an animal in a trap and I'll bite my own paws off to get out" (White 1992b, 9–10). In the letter in which she told Thorp about her return to the sacraments on Christmas day 1940, she insisted that "there is only one thing for me and that is to be drawn by love and not driven by fear." She speculated that her "rebellious" response to the church in the past had represented "an amateurish way of getting rid of fear" (White 1992b, 35).

The path back to the church had not been a smooth one. In *The Hound and the Falcon,* White reveals that she had first sought to return to the church eighteen months before Christmas 1940 (White 1992b, 33, 66–67). The war, the failure of her third marriage, loneliness, and her abortion gave her many possible reasons for seeking spiritual support in the church that remained so central to her identity, even after she had made strenuous attempts to sever her ties to it. Still, she was inclined to keep her distance and dictate the terms of her envisioned aloof, post-Catholic relationship with the church. "I thought, after years of puzzling and tormenting myself, I'd reached a position of neutrality. I could even go to Mass occasionally in the spirit one might revisit a house one had known and loved when a child but never intended to live in again" (White 1950, 115).

On a whim she visited the Brompton Oratory and stopped to say a prayer before the statue of St. Joseph. She developed a sudden flash of empathy for the figure of Joseph, who had to spend his whole life "content with being second" to Mary and Jesus, a totally unexceptional man in a family of exceptions. She saw that "he must sometimes have been tempted to be envious and jealous and self-pitying and assertive . . . just like me." This quiet discovery in the presence of St. Joseph, a saint she had never really noticed before, gave White intimations of the resources she still might find in the church. With the help of St. Joseph, she suddenly understood that she did not have to be "first and best in everything." It was ludicrous for a grown woman of 40 to be seeking the adult equivalents of green ribbons and praise from her father and the nuns. Somehow, like Joseph, who "was a very good carpenter," she must be content with doing her best work and not focus on status and recognition conferred by the public or the church. This moment of epiphany was broken when White approached a priest whom she belatedly discovered was a "spiritual fascist." He told her that she had been excommunicated for marrying outside of the church and then accused her of seeking "an emotional kick out of religion." He perfunctorily prescribed "one of the worst fifth-rate 'apologist' works, written condescendingly and exceedingly illogically." The reading assignment, along with the priest's tone, temporarily stifled White's desire to find her way back to the church (White 1992b, 66–67).

When she did return on Christmas day 1940, White resolved to adopt a new approach to her old faith—a softer touch, a calmer, less desperate tone: "I feel one shouldn't feverishly clutch one's faith but simply, quietly immerse oneself in it and not mind if the sea closes over one's head" (White 1992b, 98).

White tried very hard to see Catholicism as "a life to be lived, not a theory to be debated about" (White 1992b, 99). At the same time, she knew that her theology was changing. She could not believe in a judgmental God, a God who is "hurt" by our sins. All at once she realized that God the Father was her "great stumbling block" (White 1992b, 102). She had no such problems with the Virgin Mary, as long as Mary could be extricated from the traditional teachings concerning women's submissiveness and self-abnegation. The central fact of Mary retained its power and poetry for White, who asserted that "no rationalizing can be as beautiful as the Virgin pregnant with God" (White 1992b, 83).

White's perspectives on Mary and Thomas Aquinas evolved after her return to the church in 1940. She discovered a Dominican priest named Victor White who was incorporating Jungian psychology into his lectures on the *Summa*. She also attended lectures on scripture by Father Richard Kehoe. She perceived a new spirit at work in the church: "What had appeared so rigid and exclusive and opaque gradually appeared as living and growing, extending backwards and forwards in time and including everything from the homeliest to the highest" (White 1954, 45). White realized that it was possible to be a Catholic focused on the Incarnation and the Eucharist and still assert that "a little might be left to individual conscience" in the areas of extramarital sex and birth control (White 1992b, 85).

All of these opinions, contained in White's letters written in 1941–1942, still sounded fresh, even controversial, when the letters were published in book form in 1965. *The Hound and the Falcon* prompted a wide range of reactions. At a meeting of the Children of Mary, a sodality associated with the Society of the Sacred Heart, White was confronted by a nun who accused her of having written "a very 'bad' book that was full of 'wrong opinions.'" White told the nun, who quickly added that she had not read the book herself, about many prominent Catholics, including priests and sisters, who had praised it publicly. This incident confirmed what White already knew: The Lippington pedagogy had no statute of limitations. *The Hound and the Falcon* might have made her a spiritual advisor to a widening circle of readers who wrote to her for counsel, but she would "always be suspect to the Sacred Heart nuns" (Chitty 1993, 147, 144).

White paid close attention to the new currents in the church during and immediately after Vatican II. In 1964, partly in response to discussions underway in Rome, the Society of the Sacred Heart joined the other orders that had abolished the hierarchical distinction between choir sisters and lay sisters (Williams 1978, 281–282). White had a long conversation with an elderly lay sister for whom the change only brought anxiety and social awkwardness. White, who understood the pain that sometimes accompanied attempts to belong to the exclusive community of the Sacred Heart, empathized deeply and added that she "could have talked to [the old nun] for hours" (Chitty 1993, 138). In 1965, White was the kind of Catholic who could declare John A. T. Robinson's *Honest to God* "*full* of light" and express thanks that the controversial book brought "a certain relief" (Chitty 1993, 120–121). She was buoyed by Rosemary Haughton's letter to *The Guardian,* published December 22, 1966, which reminded Catholic readers: "Whatever happens, we are part of what is happening, the guilt as well as the suffering." Haughton's honest confidence and her comfort with the idea of a church composed of the remnant appealed to the kind of Catholic Antonia White had become by the end of Vatican II (Chitty 1993, 166–167).

Even in the final decades of her life Antonia White did not call herself a feminist, but starting in the late 1930s she began to pose questions that we now associate with the Catholic feminism of the 1960s and beyond. Some of these questions were related to her efforts to find her "natural" self and to dissolve artificial boundaries separating the natural, the self, and the sacred. As early as 1935 she wrote to Tom Hopkinson: "Somewhere in everyone there must be a love which gave one independent life, not father, mother, lover or friend, but oneself . . . one's own spark that persists in spite of every loss of beauty, money, good opinion, human affection. I have known mine to go right out in madness, lost all sense of personal identity. . . . and yet, it is there. Call it life, call it nature, call it God" (cited in Dunn 1998, 6).

Throughout her life, White continued to believe in something unifying, powerful, inalienable at the core of life, something to which the Catholic church gave her access, but only because of the particularities of her personal history. Sometimes she lamented that she had been brought into the Catholic religion without being mature enough to make an adult choice for herself. Still, even long after her parents' death, she could not leave the fold for good. In 1971, at age 72, she compared her connection to Catholicism to other ailments that could not be cured. She wrote, "I can no more escape from [Catholicism] than I can restore the lenses to my eyes or straighten my broken finger" (Chitty 1993, 224).

White's return to the church did little to mitigate her struggles with doubt and depression, which plagued her to the end, but that little made a decisive difference. "Only being a Catholic stops me from taking an overdose," she wrote late in December 1952 (Chitty 1992, 256). White developed a sense of irony that helped her to share the dark humor in the stories of other Catholic women. In a diary entry dated October 11, 1966, she recounted how a friend, Barbara Wall, had recently confessed to a priest that she had been "lacking in faith, hope and charity," only to be interrupted by the impatient cleric. "I don't want this airy-fairy stuff," the priest had interjected. "Have you eaten meat on Friday?" (Chitty 1993, 159). Gradually, in her later years, White even learned to laugh at herself. After rereading her diaries and notebooks, she wrote on September 1, 1965, "at least God must be *amused* by me," and added, "I feel as if I'd have made NO progress in all these 25 years since my return" (Chitty 1993, 129). As early as the summer of 1941, when composing a diatribe against "Catholic writings," she struck upon a metaphor that would capture her complex and contradictory relationship with the church to the end: "The Church sticks in my throat: I can neither swallow it nor reject it" (Chitty 1992, 177).

At times, however, White found moments of peace and equanimity within her new understanding of the church. This began to happen long before Vatican II. In 1954 she wrote:

> The older I grow, the less I look for external "accommodations" or worry about the differences in individual Catholics who may be profoundly shocked by each other's ways of apprehending their religion. The communion between them at the deeper level where we are nourished by the same sacraments and united in the same Mystical Body is too profound to be broken by differences of temperament and approach. How profound that communion is, how rich the source of life—that life which Christ came that we should have more abundantly, not merely in eternity but here and now—is something no one can realise more literally than a person who for many years cut themselves off from it. (White 1954, 47)

Mary Gordon

It did not take long to decide that Mary Gordon belongs in the chapter on girlhood and adolescent departure narratives. Her absence from that chapter would be unthinkable. Gordon has earned her reputation as mouthpiece for the obedient Catholic daughters throughout America who suddenly and definitively transgressed—or came into their own—at that apocalyptic moment just after mid-century when the meaning of being a Catholic and a daughter and an American all came up for debate at the same time. Her characters Isabel Moore and Felicitas Taylor (*The Company of Women*, 1980) represent a whole generation of Catholic good girls who had to negotiate their own safe passage between the sanctuary of the pre–Vatican II church—including the bastion of the Catholic family—and a rapidly changing America, caught in the cultural roller-coaster ride of the Kennedy and Johnson years, with all of the elation, turmoil, and loss those years engendered. Gordon gives voice to the generation of American Catholic women who faced adolescence and Vatican II simultaneously, just as they would later experience college and the feminist movement simultaneously: two inseparable dramas, the smaller inside the larger, two refrains in their own responsorial psalm.

But including Gordon in this section on homecomings initially required thought and deliberation, even a small flurry of research in an effort to pin down Gordon's precise location vis-à-vis the Catholic church at the opening of the twenty-first century. It was tempting to place Gordon alongside Mary McCarthy, whose departure from the fold at adolescence was never recanted or even reconsidered but who, nevertheless, felt a deep and abiding responsibility to enlighten people—clergy included—about the Catholic church. In some sense, Gordon modeled herself after McCarthy, whom she claimed as her "ideal literary mother" when she was a young aspiring writer. Gordon admired McCarthy's honesty, style, rigor, and clarity. *Memories of a Catholic Girlhood* had a profound effect on Gordon's identity and on her own writing. Most of all, perhaps, McCarthy, the author and the icon, provided Gordon and others of her generation with a way of being in the world that Gordon's own father, David Gordon; her fictional creation, Professor Moore; and most other Catholic fathers of the 1950s and 1960s never acknowledged. As Gordon explained in a 1991 public-radio interview with Tom Smith:

> [McCarthy] was Catholic and a bad girl and had left it. And that was extremely encouraging to somebody like me. Because to be Catholic in Protestant America was to feel that you didn't own the country. And you certainly didn't own the language. And your stories were not going to be of any interest to anybody. So she was a very, very important model in that she was a bad Catholic girl. She was very, very encouraging. (Smith 2002, 77–78)

McCarthy was Gordon's model, but Gordon improvised on the model. This was in the spirit of the model itself. One inescapable subtext of Mary McCarthy's life and writings is that the Catholic bad girl must strike out on her own. Ultimately, she cannot rely on the comfort, support, or understanding of others, even other Catholic bad girls. From her traditional convent-school beginnings, McCarthy transformed herself into a female post-Catholic version of James Dean. She spoke in many voices, was a rebel with many causes. Her life and writings together proclaim unequivocally that each bad girl must set out on her own and see where it leads. This does not mean that Gordon and McCarthy have not covered some of the same territory or that Gordon did not learn about the lay of the land from McCarthy. Gordon's reflections on the way in which Catholic spirituality is inscribed on the deeply embodied sensual details of her earliest childhood memories (Gordon 1992, 161) evoke McCarthy's earlier meditations on the reasons why she "isn't sorry to have been a Catholic" (McCarthy 1985, 24–27). The "real test" defined by McCarthy, featuring the trapped baby and the burning tenement house (McCarthy 1970, 273–274), touches the same chords as Mary Gordon's explanation of what keeps her in the church:

> I am grieved every time I enter a parish church and hear an unlovely liturgy, and I often have to leave for my own protection. I'm in a queer position: the Church of my childhood, which was so important for my formation as an artist, is now gone. As Gertrude Stein said of Oakland, "There is no there there."
>
> But there *is* something there, something that formed me and that touches me still: the example of the nuns killed in El Salvador, of liberation theologians standing up to the Pope, of the nuns—the "Vatican 24"—who signed the statement asserting that it was possible for Catholics to have different positions on abortion and still be Catholics. (Gordon 1992, 175)

This is, nevertheless, a far cry from Mary McCarthy's final pronouncement on the subject of her relationship with the church and God at the end of her prefatory remarks in *Memories of a Catholic Girlhood*, where she leaves no room for a future return or reconsideration. Perhaps because she has just said some positive, affectionate things about her memories of the church in girlhood, which could mislead her readers, McCarthy clearly repeats her decision to remain a lapsed Catholic. She invokes Pascal's wager only to reject it as cowardly and dishonest. She considers the wager unworthy of a Catholic bad girl and asserts: "For myself, I prefer not to play it so safe, and I shall never send for a priest or recite an Act of Contrition in my last moments. I do not mind if I lose my soul for all eternity. If the kind of God exists Who would damn me for not working out a deal with Him, then that is unfortunate. I should not care to spend eternity in the company of such a person" (McCarthy 1985, 27).

Gordon has moved beyond her literary mother in many ways, and prominent among them is her willingness, in middle age, to leave her relationship with the church open-ended, a work in progress, where McCarthy, at the same stage of life, apparently needed to shut the door publicly once and for all. As McCarthy taught Gordon through her writings and her example, part of being a Catholic bad girl is finding your own voice and not being afraid to use it. Gordon told interviewer Sandy Asirvatham that she had worked hard to lose the "idolatry of rigor and formal perfection" that had kept McCarthy from growing after her early books, *The Company She Keeps* and *Memories of a Catholic Girlhood*. Gordon is referring to literary style, but she may be hinting at something more. McCarthy's remarks on Pascal's wager exemplify another kind of rigor or perfectionism with deep Catholic roots that hounded her to the end. McCarthy sought a closure, confidence and clarity in her dealings with the church and God that Gordon and her generation of Catholic feminists knew was impossible.

With the later McCarthy's counterexample in mind, Gordon has self-consciously curbed her attraction to formal perfection and rigor and allowed her writing style to become "less severe and less formal" (Asirvatham 2002, 166). The effort of Gordon the writer and stylist to relax and worry less about control was eventually accompanied by a willingness on the part of Gordon the Catholic woman to let her complex bond to the church develop naturally. Where for McCarthy, writing had been a way to build a fortress of words and images that kept experience pinned down and classified, orderly and manageable, Gordon's more open and intuitive approach to writing has made it a venue for self-exploration, the source of inner voices from which she has learned a great deal.

Gordon negotiated many small departures from the church between her pivotal confession to Father W. at age 12 and her strategic retreat at 17 to Barnard College, worlds away from the intellectual, cultural, and aesthetic limitations of the Catholic world in which she had come of age. In *Seeing through Places* (2000), Gordon underscores the distance she traveled in the company of two good friends between her Catholic girls' high school in Queens and Barnard College on the Upper West Side of New York City in the fall of 1967:

> In six months, we went from processions where we crowned a statue of the Virgin with a wreath of flowers to linking hands with strangers, learning what to do in case of tear gas or cops run amok. The same girls who in the spring had been singing "O Mary we crown thee with blossoms today / Queen of the Angels, Queen of the May," were chanting the following autumn "Hey, hey LBJ, how many kids did you kill today?"

And when the Columbia riots started the following semester, Gordon and her friends rose to the occasion. She recalls: "A year earlier I had been presiding over student council meetings where we had to decide on an appropriate punishment for girls who'd been caught getting into a car with a boy while still in uniform; now I was sitting in on teach-ins on the lawn in front of Butler Library where we contemplated 'burning the whole fucking place down'" (Gordon 2000, 243).

At least for a while, total immersion in Columbia University and Barnard during the apocalyptic years preceding her graduation in 1971 made new departures seem natural. Gordon found a world beyond the church, a world of student radicals, homosexuals, drug dealers, non-Catholic classmates from Missouri and North Dakota, drugs, sex, and marches on the Pentagon. Meanwhile, her teachers, "well-born women with hair hanging down their backs or in coiled blond knots at their napes," and "elegant men in houndstooth jackets who smoked pipes," took her seriously, made her work hard, and told her that she was gifted (Gordon 2000, 243–245). Her college years led to other departures, marriage outside the Catholic compound, divorce, remarriage, and children. Finally, in 1988, she joined the faculty at Barnard; two years later she was awarded a named chair.

For Gordon, who maintains that Catholic language and metaphor are a part of her, "in [her] bones," her "framework of language" (Bannon 2002, 18), Barnard represents a second home and a loving family in which she could finish growing up outside the compound where she had been asked to sacrifice her girlhood (or, in the Catholic lexicon of the period, to "offer it up"). On the final page of *Seeing through Places,* Gordon expresses her profound gratitude to her alma mater, which gave her back her girlhood and, more recently, literally, gave her a home. She calls Barnard (and Columbia): "The here that was always the here for me. The here that allowed me for the first time to have the kind of youth that others of my age were having, so that when I left I was younger than I was when, four years earlier, I arrived" (Gordon 2000, 254).

In a sense, her close personal identification with Barnard confirms Gordon's successful departure from the working-class Catholic compound of her youth, where "they were against any intellectual achievement at all" (Occhiogrosso 1987, 69). Yet there is another sense in which Gordon's bond with Barnard made it possible for her to find her way back to a new understanding of the church, the Catholic world that she originally left for Barnard, and, especially, her father, who would never have approved of her choice of college. "I believe that if my father had lived, I wouldn't have rebelled against him," Gordon writes in 1996. Ensconced in Columbia's Butler Library, doing research on her father's life and writings for *The Shadow Man,* she was keenly aware of the contradictions inherent in her situation: "I am here in this place of marble, silence, high windows, chandeliers, this place where I am happy, where I have always been happy, where I always think I will be learning something of great value that will bring enlightenment and joy. A place my father would have kept me from, and yet a place he enabled me, by his love, to inhabit" (Gordon 1996b, 53).

Like Antonia White, Gordon made a momentous journey from her father's Catholic world to her own chosen world beyond the church and then back, to a different church that her father would not have recognized. She took upon herself the arduous task of learning the truth about her beloved father, even when the half-truths she inadvertently discovered threatened to shatter her love for him, her cherished memories of childhood, and her own identity. She could have chosen other routes. She explored some of them a decade before, in her essay "Coming to Terms with Mary," published in *Commonweal* in January 1982. This essay might be seen as an end run around her father and childhood memories, back in the general direction of the Catholic tradition. Her first child, Anna, named after her mother, had been born in 1980 and her second, David, named for her father, would be born in 1983. Gordon was not exactly reconciled to the church, but she stayed on the margins, in part, for her daughter's sake. Five years later, when interviewer Ann Lally Milhaven asked her, "Where are you in relation to the church?" she responded:

> The institutional church is not at the center of my life. I come in and go out of the institutional church as I have more or less patience for it. I have periods where the whole thing makes me so impatient that I lose hope. I feel so alienated. I feel like these bishops and the pope have nothing in common with me; they have nothing to give me and I leave. It's not a great cost to me to be in or out of the church.

Still, Gordon does not consider her answer to Milhaven's question finished until she adds a word about her respect for the sisters who have "taken very courageous stands" (Milhaven 2002, 42–43), almost certainly a reference to the Vatican 24.

It is against this backdrop that we should read Gordon's 1982 *Commonweal* article venturing a Catholic feminist interpretation of Mary. When she wrote it, Gordon was a Catholic feminist in diaspora, the mother of a toddler, struggling with how to relate to the Catholic tradition that was so deeply inscribed in her own memories of childhood. After beginning her article with juicy stories about high school, the "Mary-like" prom dresses that the good girls were encouraged to wear, and her oft-quoted one-liner—"in my day, Mary was a stick to beat smart girls with"—Gordon tackles the topic of how she, as a feminist, approaches Mary in the 1980s.

It is not as if Gordon has set herself a goal, that is, returning to the church, and now has a checklist of pitfalls, including Mary, to eliminate.

Rather, as a feminist brought up Catholic, Gordon recognizes in Mary "a potent female image," the object of "universal, ancient" devotion who has been "rejected" by some Catholic feminists of the late 1960s and 1970s "in favor of her son." Gordon, speaking for a more evolved, more nuanced— even more radical—version of Catholic feminism, sees the challenge to the centrality of Mary as premature and nervous, actually a capitulation to the patriarchal value system. Gordon recommends a timely attempt to "salvage the valuable things that the past ascribed to females." She acknowledges the problems inherent in this mission, chief among them the insurmountable fact that what we know about Mary has been mediated and transmitted by a misogynist tradition. Gordon hopes to formulate a spirit of devotion appropriate to Catholic mothers and aging Catholic women, a Mary purged of "sexual hatred and sexual fear." Her suggested method evokes images reminiscent of Mary Daly, the Radical Feminist Pirate:

> One must sift though the nonsense and hostility that has characterized thought and writing about Mary, to find some images, shards, and fragments, glittering in the rubble. One must find isolated words, isolated images; one must travel the road of metaphor, of icon, to come back to that figure who, throughout a corrupt history, has moved the hearts of men and women, has triumphed over the hatred of women and the fear of her, and abides shining, worthy of our love, compelling it. (Gordon 1982, 11–12)

This passage describes an intellectually responsible way for Catholic feminists of the 1980s to confront Mary, a central component of the Catholic tradition that became a stumbling block for so many Catholic women of Gordon's generation. One could adopt this approach to recycling problematic aspects of the Catholic tradition and still bypass potentially painful personal baggage. After all, the church to which Mary Gordon and Antonia White returned was a different one than the church of their girlhoods. Not everyone was called to be Mary McCarthy or Flannery O'Connor, whose atheism and orthodoxy had the same all-or-nothing quality (Smith 2002, 78–79). Feminism is about making choices, and at least some versions of feminism are all about constructing space where none appeared to exist before. The salvage operation, the reclamation of a Virgin Mary unburdened of patriarchy's accretions, could conceivably be one means of creating a habitable space within the church for post–Vatican II Catholic feminists.

Yet even in this early essay, there are hints that Gordon might not be satisfied with this relatively safe intellectual salvage operation, which could be performed without disturbing the ghosts she might have thought that she had exorcized during her undergraduate years at Barnard. Gordon moves beyond an intellectual and spiritual agenda, sifting through the shards and rubble—that could be taken on as a group project for Catholic feminists as a community. Instead she stakes out a project—actually a posture—that can only be embraced alone. Again, we see images of the solitary figure, a bad girl striking out on her own, Cixous's woman in flight:

> For a woman to come to terms with this woman who endures beloved despite a history of hatred, she must move lightly and discard freely, she must take upon herself the ancient labor of women: she must become a gatherer, a hoarder. She must put out for those around her scattered treasure, isolates without a pattern whose accumulated meaning comes from the relations of proximity. (Gordon 1982, 12)

It was as a lone figure, a hoarder, a gatherer that Gordon first set out in the early 1970s to search for her father. She was familiar with Mary McCarthy's *Memories of a Catholic Girlhood* and with McCarthy's painstaking efforts to separate potentially unreliable personal recollections from the facts she presents in her memoir (McCarthy 1985, 4–5). Gordon proceeded methodically; she tracked down her father's publications, from his pre-Catholic "men's magazine" phase through his post-conversion reactionary Catholic phase and read them as objectively as she could. She placed his works in context and analyzed the style. She willingly subjected herself to more departures, more painful goodbyes: "I lost another father; the father of the brilliant sentence, the brilliantly shaped phrase" (Gordon 1996b, xxi). Then she consulted public records and interviewed friends, relatives, and historical experts, frustrated by the lack of reliable information available to her. Even worse, she discovered that "his life had been made up of lies, some tragic, some pathetic, all of them leaving me with the feeling that I'd been stolen from. I had lost him as the figure in history I thought he was; I had lost my place in America" (Gordon 1996b, xxii).

To find her father and become reconciled to him, Gordon discovered, she needed to follow him in the flight from his family and his past that had originally led him to convert to Catholicism. She needed to follow the tracks he tried so diligently to obscure. When she came upon his self-hatred as a Jew and his lingering anti-Semitism, which was laced with bitterness and shame; when she read his political observations on the Nazis and the Fascists and on twentieth-century secular art and culture, she felt the shame and bitterness splashing back on her, the daughter and the reader. An occasional piece, such as the poem entitled "A Prayer for My Mother," briefly redeemed and purified David Gordon in his daughter's sight and gave her the strength to go on with her project, which at times resembled Isabel Moore's grueling, self-imposed penances in *Final Payments*. Finally, at least for a brief moment, she decided to judge him only by his personal letters to her, the letters of a loving father who hoped for nothing short of sainthood for his daughter. As soon as the decision was uttered, however, she knew that she could not allow herself this kind of insulation from her father and her evolving sense of herself as his daughter: "The waters of his contradictions rise around my head and I am drowning in the seas that surround me. The sea of the impossible love of a child for her father, the sea of oblivion, the sea of a daughter's shame" (Gordon 1996b, 105).

After all of her reading and detailed conversations with family members, local historians, Mormon genealogists, and specialists on early twentieth-century soft porn, Gordon almost lost her way. She concluded the first three sections of *The Shadow Man* by describing her research process with the words: "I no longer remember why I was looking or what I thought I'd find" (Gordon 1996b, 164). Then she took a monumental risk in the hope that even without all of the facts, she might find a way to join her father in his flight from his immigrant Jewish background into the Catholic church. Perhaps that way she could begin to understand the parts of his life that filled her with shame and revulsion. To complete the picture of her father and his pilgrimage, and thereby reassemble the pieces of her own identity torn asunder by her internal and external investigations, she decided to impersonate her father, to become him, and see what she could learn: "I will become a filament, an X-ray, the negative of a photograph, the chalk outline on the sidewalk after the dead body has been removed" (Gordon 1996b, 170).

She follows her father, "a child who is terrified," from his birthplace in Vilna (Lithuania, Kingdom of Russia) before the turn of the century—a date and birthplace he has hidden from her—to Lorain, Ohio, where the first lesson he learns from his father and all the semiotics of his adopted home become encapsulated in the phrase "Everything you are is wrong." He learns how to camouflage the wrongness: "Walk quickly, keep your eyes ahead, miss nothing, learn the jokes, take a drink. Read books. Remember what is in them. Forget nothing. Keep moving." The local public library becomes his sanctuary, where he keeps a vigil and discovers a Christian Europe that becomes his new home. He is no longer a Jewish immigrant living in "packed rooms above the store . . . crowding one another with reproaches, disappointments." In the reading room, with its high ceiling and marble pillars, he partakes of "the open spaces of Rome, the dappled woods of the Middle Ages, the majestic palaces of the Renaissance." Here he plans a solitary escape: "My mother and my father and my sisters will always be Jews. I can see by their faces that there is nothing they can do about it. But things are not so fixed with me. In dreams I plan, over and over, my escape. One day to awake to a rich, saturating silence. One day to awake without reproach" (Gordon 1996b, 172–177).

At this point, Mary Gordon discovers that there are limits in her ability to impersonate her father, so she shifts gears. She becomes a witness to her father's anxious and fearful confrontation with America. There are two Americas on David Gordon's horizon: One is full of promise, the other full of endless reproach and closed doors. David Gordon, Jewish immigrant, does not believe that the promises apply to him, but he discovers a way to claim them. In a fantasized marble building, perhaps his sanctuary, the public library, the room with the marble pillars, he reads "words that do not accuse but absorb accusation": "*Assisi, Provence, Langedoc, Toscana, Chartres.*" The scene changes suddenly. Now Mary Gordon is facing a police lineup, composed of Bernard Berenson, H. L. Mencken, Ezra Pound, and Henry Roth, whose influential and seductive voices, she suspects, poisoned her father's mind and made him the self-hating Jew, the bigoted Catholic reactionary, of whom she is ashamed. She hears the testimony of the four men (speaking in chorus): "Everything beautiful was Christian. . . . All that was flawless and pure and bold and courtly and chivalric was goyish. . . . Jews lack the qualities that mark the civilized man. . . . The kike . . . the kike . . . the kike" (Gordon 1996b, 181, 184–185).

Finally, in a dream, Mary Gordon confronts her father, a man she cannot recognize, "a disagreeable old Jew with an accent," but she does most of the speaking. She remembers the accusations of her Christian relatives: Her impurity and her intelligence represented "the Jew in [her]." She will not deny her intelligence, "a Jewish place" where she could be with her father forever, nor will she deny that her father's conversion to Catholicism was also intended to provide her a safe place with him. She finally understands that with his conversion, he achieved his "boyhood dream," for himself and his daughter. "The Catholic Church is the one place a Jew can go, not hide his Jewishness, and at the same time be free of it." Her investigation is complete. As she files away the evidence, she discovers "something . . . left over," some "residue" that is "neither pathetic nor repellent," which she must understand and articulate to complete the grueling process (penance?) she has begun. Speaking to her father, she attempts to locate the residue and name it:

> I believe that in the midst of the tumult, the vilification and self-hatred,
> the immigrant's terror, the weak son's dread, the Eastern Jew's American
> abashment—or perhaps because of and including all of it—there was
> something else. You didn't get it from your accusers; it was neither

pitiable nor the stuff of shame. Perhaps it was the voice of God. The God of singleness and silence. The font of pure, accepting love. (Gordon 1996b, 188–192)

Mary Gordon's search for her father is exhausting, even for the reader. Like Mary Daly, she throws herself as far as she can go into a search for her Jewish Catholic father that she, and we, know cannot end neatly, without pain and loss. Still, Gordon does what she can. She arrives at an understanding, something far beyond denial or détente, with her dead father, "a Catholic who saw the face of God [she] cannot fathom and only partially [believes] in" (Gordon 1996b, 194). Her own path back to the church, or the discovery of a closer and more intimate form of diaspora, is tightly bound up with her encounter with her father in *The Shadow Man*.

Gordon's memoir ends with a chapter in which she describes the exhuming and reburial of her father in 1995, thirty-eight years after his original burial. Gordon needs to move her father from his anonymous resting place under a stone marked Gagliano (her mother's family name), where he is buried "among people who at best tolerated or patronized him, at worst despised him." When he died, she was only 7, and too sick with chicken pox to be fully present at his burial. Her trauma at the time was so great that she blotted out the memory of seeing him in his coffin and can speak of "a gate closed . . . between the girl who saw her father and the person who did not." She reports: "when my uncle carried me out of the funeral home the film snapped" (Gordon 1996b, 245, 249–250). Gordon, whose childhood memories—especially memories connected with her father—are usually so meticulously detailed, could not replay the film or review the memories of saying good-bye to her father's body.

Because of the complex process of searching for, reclaiming, and confronting her father that preceded it, the reburial in 1995 takes place when Gordon's ties to the church are closer than they have been in the three preceding decades. Gordon has found a priest she trusts and who clearly trusts her. She calls him by his first name; they work on the service together in his rooms. The priest wears running shorts and a T-shirt as they sit with two texts, the old Latin ritual and the new English version, the *Modern Order of Ritual,* open before them. He recites the Latin words "*In paradisum deducant te angeli.*" They are the beginning of a blessing that translates: "May the angels take you into paradise. May the martyrs come to welcome you on your way and lead you into the Holy City, Jerusalem. May the choirs of angels welcome you, and with Lazarus, who was once poor, . . . may you have eternal rest."

"This," Gordon proclaims, "is the best of the Church." She is profoundly moved by the texts they choose, which combine the best from the old and new orders of service. She is confident that her father would approve of their choices. Facing death often paves the way for a spiritual homecoming; this freely chosen confrontation with death is even more self-consciously a gesture of return. Gordon does not deceive herself; she knows that the ritual is not merely a matter of therapy or aesthetics:

> There is no way that the words I have chosen can be of use without the structure or the semblance of belief.
>
> I don't know what I believe about the fate of the life these bones represent. But the form of belief seems deeply precious, irreplaceable. The form can contain more than most forms and it is therefore conducive to more beauty, more truthfulness.

Then, possibly in response to the unheard voice of Mary McCarthy, she continues:

> Is this hateful, a cowardly hedging of the bets?
>
> Whatever it is, I will not give up these forms, these words. (Gordon 1996b, 268–269)

Here Gordon brings us close to the experience of coming home as she has encountered it, not once for all, but over and over again. Sometimes, when she is alienated by the impoverished liturgies or abuses of power in the church, she reminds herself that "if the Church is about anything, it is about engagement" (Gordon 1992, 237). At other moments, such as the reburial, when she seeks to make peace between herself and her father and form a bond between her father and her two children, she rediscovers the meaning of ritual. For Mary Gordon, as for so many American Catholic women of her generation, part of the complexity of leaving and returning stems from the burden of perfection that she has grappled with throughout her journey—even in diaspora—a burden that keeps reappearing no matter how many times one attempts to leave it behind. Gordon thought she had left it in the church the day of her confession to Father W. and in her mother's house when she left for Barnard. She thought that she could stash it wherever she kept her father's unrealized ambitions for her, but it remained a part of her baggage, more taxing than ever, because, as a grown woman, she knew that it did not go with her experienced feminist body and soul.

In an interview with Tom Smith in 1991, Gordon addresses questions about how she situates herself in relation to the American Catholic female literary icon Flannery O'Connor. She focuses on the sticky question of perfectionism. Gordon relates a dream in which she was a mess, with dirty hair, bedraggled clothes, and disorganized lecture notes, and O'Connor appeared in a great dress with a flawless hairdo. "You're a mess," O'Connor said to her. "Your problem is that you don't believe in perfection." Gordon answered, "No, I do believe in perfection, but we have a different idea of perfection. You think perfection is flawlessness. And I think perfection is completeness" (Smith 2002, 78).

Mary Gordon's homecoming to the Catholic church is best understood in the context of this dream and her revised definition of perfection. The notion of perfection as flawlessness, which Gordon's dream links to the spirituality implicit in Flannery O'Connor's writing, haunts Catholic women long after they have managed to place some distance between themselves and the church. Gordon's redefinition recognizes the limits in the conventional notion of perfection inflicted on Catholic girls of her generation, who were enjoined to model themselves after Jesus' perfect virgin mother. Like Gordon's self-conscious choice of a writing style that transcends the constraints of excessive formalism, her definition of perfection is organic, expanding, always incomplete. As her memoir *The Shadow Man* shows us, completeness is itself a relative term; what passes for completeness one moment is surpassed in the next.

Mary Gordon's definition of perfection applies to rough drafts as well as published works; it pertains to life as well as art. It even includes dead ends and false starts that eventually lead somewhere where they will complete themselves. Finally, perfection defined as completeness implies the existence of a perspective that transcends human limitations. It implies a viewer who can see, as humans cannot, around the next corner, and the next. Gordon's act of redefinition—a kind of renaming—is itself a leap of faith.

Patricia Hampl

Patricia Hampl is known for her two highly acclaimed memoirs, *A Romantic Education* (1981) and *Virgin Time* (1992), and for an important recent collection of essays, *I Could Tell You Stories* (1999), subtitled *Sojourns in the Land of Memory*. Because Hampl is Catholic, and only three years older than Mary Gordon, the content—and even some of the details—of her memories overlap with Gordon's. Because Hampl went to a convent school run by a French order of nuns, she also has much in common with Antonia White, who had the same kind of education fifty years before her. These commonalities are important to us; they delineate the contours of the neglected tradition of Catholic women's narratives of departure and return. Hampl's personal narratives are also important for their unique touches: her Czech heritage, her identity and special vocation as memoirist, and the bonds connecting her to the writings of Czeslaw Milosz, Walt Whitman, and others.

Like Antonia White and Mary Gordon, Hampl writes about her departures and return to the church with remarkable candor; irony and humor are important components of her repertoire and are among the traits that she most admires in others. At one point in *Virgin Time,* she speculates that faith may be "the smart little laugh that holds the world up" (Hampl 1993, 7). Like White and Gordon, Hampl does not express any doubts about whether she is welcome in the church that she has left or whether she has a right to criticize aspects of the Catholic church that made it an unacceptable spiritual home for her during an important stage in her life when she first came of age as a writer and a woman. Like White and Gordon, she provides readers with carefully crafted narratives of both her departure and her return that focus on specific moments in which boundary-crossings, renamings, and the recycling of girlhood experiences in the church can be closely observed. Hampl, like White and Gordon, revels in the complexities and contradictions, as well as the ultimate simplicity, of her ties to the church. The church becomes what it once was, her home. What has changed is both the self who is being housed and the worlds in which the rebuilt home is situated.

Patricia Hampl endorses Milosz's assertion that memoir is not only, even primarily, about the individual self; rather, "inner experience, as it is preserved in the memory, will . . . be evaluated in the perspective of the changes one's milieu has undergone." The story is always bigger than the individual self: implicitly or explicitly, it reflects upon the surrounding community, Hampl's generation, her hometown of St. Paul, and the Roman Catholic church in which she was raised. According to Hampl, "true memoir is written, like all literature, in an attempt to find not only a self but a world" (Hampl 1999, 85–86, 35). Hampl's earliest memories of "what it was like to be a child, talking with other children" in her native city in the early 1950s are associated with a social ritual centered on a repeated question: "What are you?" Children at St. Luke's School knew the proper answer: Irish, Norwegian, or German. ("I'm American" was "frowned upon and considered an affectation.") For the inevitable follow-up question was "What are you *really*?" Hampl recalls her answer, complete with accompanying gestures: "'I'm half Irish,' I said, sweeping my hand like a cleaver exactly across my midriff, 'and half Czech'" (Hampl 1992, 27–28).

It was in this world of postwar midwestern Catholic children, "ashamed of the actual presence of . . . non-Irish American qualities" but "enthralled" by their own blood connections to the Old World that Hampl grew up (Hampl 1992, 27–29). In 1952, at age 6, she stayed awake, albeit briefly, on summer nights in the little screen house behind her grandmother's home, worrying about "*Communists* who lurked in the dark." This fear was "literally in the air," she explains. It didn't come from her parents, who faithfully voted the "straight Democratic ticket and a yes vote on all bond issues." It entered through the living room, in the "hushed, bluish" light around the television, along with *I Love Lucy*. Hampl does a wonderful job of explaining the mystique that surrounded television viewing for young Catholic baby boomers in the 1950s: a "silent religiosity" bolstered by the frequency of refreshments served afterward, which reinforced parallels between mass and television (Hampl 1992, 37–38).

Hampl's was a Catholic girlhood, but a Catholic girlhood divided between the dominant Irish Catholicism that prevailed at St. Luke's and elsewhere in the diocese and the nation and her Czech Catholic heritage first gleaned from her grandmother's picture album of Prague, from whence she had emigrated alone at 16 in 1896. The division deepened when her dying Czech grandfather, "a gentleman" with a "dry sense of humor," refused the ministrations of a priest—"priests were crooks"—so the family had to content itself with saying the rosary at a funeral home in lieu of a funeral mass. Her Irish Catholic mother, "her loyalties badly at odds," kept reassuring Patricia of her paternal grandfather's place in heaven (Hampl 1992, 57). This departure from Catholic protocol made Hampl aware early of the possibility of finding one's own way to heaven, an important lesson in her protracted spiritual pilgrimage.

Hampl also remembers being intrigued by the cathedral in St. Paul where her parents were married in 1940. "*The cathedral will never be finished*": Hampl recalls her parents saying this repeatedly in her younger days when they happened to pass the building. The future memoirist also registered their tone: "It was said with pride." The metaphor stuck with her, and the cathedral became a spiritual touchstone: "The eternal was the progress of the fragment, of what was inevitably incomplete, unfinished. Its essence was longing and movement, not permanence and wholeness at all" (Hampl 1992, 60).

Hampl's recollections blend together details that could have come from Antonia White or Mary Gordon, always seen through the filter of her Czech heritage, her St. Paul beginnings, and the popular culture of the 1950s and 1960s. Hampl's rendering of the St. Blaise's Day blessing, one of the reasons why Mary McCarthy was not sorry to have been a Catholic, contains the baby boomer's skepticism that the television generation brought to this homely ritual: The priest held "oversized beeswax candles in an X around our necks, to ward off death by choking on fishbones, a problem nobody thought of the rest of the year" (Hampl 1993, 48). In almost a direct paraphrase of Antonia White's precocious protagonist

Nanda Grey, Hampl asserts that in the church of her girlhood, "Nothing was just itself." For example, tulips and hyacinths were not just spring flowers; they were oblations. Hampl and her friends "[lugged] bouquets almost as big as [themselves] to their true owner, the Queen of the May." These, they knew, were qualitatively different from the little "nosegays" that public-school students brought to their teachers, and not just because of their size. Raised in a competitive atmosphere, where public- and parochial-school children were always sizing each other up, Hampl could say without Nanda Grey's impatience and weariness that hers was "a Catholic girlhood spent gorging on metaphor—Mystical Body, transubstantiation, dark night of the soul, the little martyrdom of everyday life." Hampl's own chosen metaphors depicting her impressions of Catholic life in her girlhood partake of this spirit of competition. Catholics were propelled by "the Cadillac language of Catholic spirituality, looking on with pity as the Protestants pedaled their stripped-down bicycles" (Hampl 1993, 6–7).

For Hampl, unlike White and her protagonist, the steady diet of specifically Catholic metaphor did nothing to stand in the way of her adolescent strivings as a writer. She fondly remembers her convent school with its close connections to F. Scott Fitzgerald, the most famous local writer and one that the Catholic community proudly claimed as their own. Fitzgerald's mother had gone there, and his daughter had been baptized there. One of the older nuns who taught English regaled the girls with her memory of dancing with Fitzgerald at the cotillion (Hampl 1992, 62). Literature was valued at Hampl's convent school. It was "the only stable bridge from the fading colonial life of the finishing school to the mainland of modern careerism, where, largely unwittingly, we were all being transported into the future" (Hampl 1993, 57). Perhaps this is why her chemistry teacher Sister Celestine, aware that Hampl was writing poetry behind her textbook, only occasionally interrupted her to make sure that she had written down the equations on the blackboard.

Even students without Hampl's literary gifts were taught to respect literature as a practical art. Class discussions of Jane Eyre and Dorothea Brooke taught "the meticulous art of character assessment"; the figures of Macbeth and Hamlet became case studies where male behavior was scrutinized and the moral for the girls was clear. They must exercise "constant vigilance" and not be a "ninny" like Ophelia. Still, there were no easy answers. Patricia Hampl was not the first or the last convent-school girl to learn that being good was not good enough. "The upshot of literature seemed to be that while evil didn't pay, goodness was notoriously dumb, a lack rather than a radiance. There was no future in being good or in being bad. What was left?" (Hampl 1993, 61–62).

The students were given a more lofty and pointed goal; they were to model themselves after the Virgin Mary, as interpreted by the nuns: Mary, the contemplative who "saw all these things, and returned to Nazareth, where she pondered them in her heart" (Hampl 1993, 62). The art of pondering was the real lesson at Hampl's school, "the highest vocation, as if sainthood were a matter of who kept the best notes." Hampl's homeroom teacher Sister Marie Helene encapsulated this supreme lesson in a metaphor drawn from American popular culture. She asked the students: "Who sees the parade better," the baton twirler at the center of attention or a viewer unseen in a balcony? The answer, of course, was the viewer in the balcony, who could see the entire scene, other viewers included, and ponder its meaning. Later in life, Hampl made an explicit connection between Sister Marie Helene's story and the work of the cloistered choir nuns in her school, who sang the Divine Office daily out of sight but within earshot of the girls. "I doubt if I was the only one, pausing in study hall over the memorization of irregular French verbs, who heard that music and took the bait, going deep with the beauty of it, seeking whatever lagoon a creature dives for with the lure still bright in the imagination, though the hook had already imbedded itself and any chance of escape is lost" (Hampl 1993, 62–63).

This contemplative aura and the attendant conviction that "we were not the point"—the girls were, in fact, baton twirlers—lent an air of detachment to the entire enterprise. "The light *was* different there." It was "not church light" but "the light of the mind, rendered right before us, substantiated." In this atmosphere, "ordinary things carried a sacred charge." Not that any of this was articulated; that would have broken the spell. "It was pure aura and it acted, as a powerful atmosphere always does, as an influence more indelible than the lessons we were taught, far stronger even than the 'Catholic values' we were meant to have writ deep in our personalities" (Hampl 1993, 65–67).

The actual lessons at the convent school were of mixed quality, sometimes bred of Catholic "provincial snobbery," which, Hampl reminds us, is "the only snobbery that has real staying power." She gives an example, a most memorable lesson imparted on January 20, 1961, the day of John F. Kennedy's inauguration. After the school watched the ceremony on television in the assembly hall, Sister Dolorosa brought some of the school linen, silver, and china into Hampl's history class and took the class step by step through the arcana of the state dinner, culminating in the after-dinner toasts. The lesson gave the girls and their teacher a way to participate even more directly in the Catholic celebration of having arrived and achieving recognition among the leadership caste of American society. The nun even taught the girls how to toast, sounding a bit like a wimpled Miss Jean Brodie: "One does not *clink* glasses when toasting. But it is perfectly correct to call out 'Hear, hear!'" And they practiced with empty champagne flutes, commemorating the "bright future" they and the new Catholic president were to share (Hampl 1993, 68–70).

The nether side of Catholic tribal celebration also showed itself on the inauguration afternoon. In what at first seemed to be merely a pop quiz on clothing etiquette, Sister Dolorosa made a point of asking the girls to compare the coats Mrs. Kennedy and Mrs. Johnson wore to the ceremony. Mrs. Johnson's choice of a mink coat became an object lesson. "Never, never wear a mink before five," the nun intoned. "Mrs. Kennedy no doubt has several mink coats in her closet. . . . But she knows, as Mrs. Johnson obviously does not, that a lady does not wear a mink coat in the middle of the day" (Hampl 1993, 69). Coming in the wake of the televised inauguration ritual, this discussion of mink coats in the afternoon provided a rare opportunity to combine class superiority and Catholic triumphalism, a moment to suggest how, in the hands of the Catholic elite, even wealth and worldliness became a kind of spirituality beyond the reach of the most powerful and hard-working Protestant Americans.

For Hampl, and so many American Catholics of her generation, the early 1960s, the Kennedy years, constitute a unique moment of Catholic status and confidence. Hampl grew into womanhood learning to ponder, following the example of the nuns and Our Lady, writing poetry in her notebook while well-born, detached nuns looked on approvingly. She recognized the first glimmerings of her vocation to write personal narrative at about 12, even before she attended her convent secondary school. There was a moment in spring in the closing years of the 1950s when she and her classmates at St. Luke's School were lined up in the corridor waiting for the sister to give them their marching orders. Lilacs in Mason jars and coffee cans arranged at the feet of plaster Virgins on classroom altars situate the moment in May.

> We are talking, of course, but in low murmurs, and Sister doesn't mind. She is smiling. Nothing is happening, nothing at all. We are just waiting for the next ordinary moment to blossom forth.
>
> Out of this vacancy, I am struck by a blow. *I must commemorate all this.* I know it is just my mind, but it doesn't feel like a thought. It is a command. (Hampl 1999, 218)

Because this seems as if it could be any writer's beginnings, Hampl underscores the specifically Catholic aspect of the experience. In a passage reminiscent of Garry Wills's famous essay "Memories of a Catholic Boyhood," Hampl recalls how Catholics of the 1950s "commemorated" without ceasing. Everything signified. "The year was crosshatched with significance—saints' feast days, holy days, Lent with its Friday fasts and 'Stations of the Cross.'" This repeated, habitual commemoration gave each moment meaning and the days and weeks a unity that was missing outside the Catholic framework. Hampl received "the call," which Catholic children her age had already been prepared to listen for; only in her case, it was a "secular" call to commemorate what she saw and show how and why even the smallest details matter (Hampl 1999, 219).

Here the intersection with Antonia White's and Mary Gordon's departure narratives comes into play. There comes a point in Hampl's life when she needs to depart from the atmosphere of the parish and the convent school to learn about the world. This self-conscious departure mirrors White's attempt to discover her natural self and Gordon's flight from the burdens of her mother's home to the relatively carefree life she hoped was waiting for her at Barnard. Still, there is a difference between Hampl's narratives and those written by White and Gordon. For White and Gordon, departure is a major theme in their early writings; Hampl's memoirs are primarily about spiritual pilgrimage and return. Hampl's departure in her early 20s is a relatively minor event, overshadowed by accounts of her many varied attempts to come home.

The first opportunity for public departure from the Catholic compound came, as Mary Gordon's had, with Hampl's college plans. With gusto, Hampl turned down a scholarship from a Catholic women's college where she was told she would get more "individual attention." Individual attention was not on the agenda. "I wanted to be left alone to lose my soul," she confesses over three decades later, after many strenuous efforts to find a way back to the church that did not mean compromising her adult feminist self and values (Hampl 1999, 201). Writing in 1992, she could still recall "the hard face" and the words of one nun who had heard of her decision to attend the University of Minnesota in Minneapolis. The nun accused her of "[turning] against [her] friends" and predicted that she would lose her faith. Hampl's inner response shows her suddenly heightened awareness of life's two-sidedness, a prominent theme in Catholic women's departure narratives. In this solemn moment, facing the nun's disappointment and dire prediction, Hampl discovered her own "ecstatic face lurking all these years under the head I had been canny enough to bow submissively before her" (Hampl 1993, 111).

During her years at the university, "self-expression" became Hampl's "true faith" and Walt Whitman her spiritual advisor (Hampl 1993, 17). Like so many American Catholics in colleges and universities in the second half of the 1960s, Hampl was much more engaged in news of the Vietnam War than in media coverage of Vatican II and its aftermath. Whitman's dictum, "dismiss whatever insults your soul" (Hampl 1999, 52), which seemed to be speaking directly to some of the draft resisters she knew, also had powerful resonance for Hampl. Hampl engaged in the same arguments over marijuana, Vietnam, and long-haired boyfriends that became the locus of powerful generation-based comedy on the television program *All in the Family,* but hers were "ornamented in our baroque Catholic way where hierarchy was the whole point" (Hampl 1999, 48). Finally, on a Sunday morning in 1968, while her father changes a light bulb in a fixture above the dining-room table, he casually asks her what mass she plans to attend. She drops the bombshell and informs him that she isn't going to mass anymore. She tells herself "I can't believe I've said it, this thing that has gnawed at me for months, years." Her father responds in two uninflected words: "Your choice." A week later in the kitchen, her mother, "the voice of the marriage," tells her "You broke your father's heart." Again, the response from a distant place, like Mary McCarthy watching her water wings drift away: "*Good.* That rotten killer instinct of the young which also happens to be the life instinct. The strange thing was, my heart was broken, too. But I was glad it was broken. I was expressing myself" (Hampl 1993, 16–17).

Hampl, whose literary pursuits had been encouraged by the nuns, who had begun to find her voice and vocation as a writer at a relatively early age, still needed to explore new ways of self-expression. The subliminal training in following the ways of Mary and pondering complexities in her heart left her far short of where her activist instincts and her womanly instincts sent her. In an essay entitled "The *Mayflower* Moment: Reading Whitman during the Vietnam War," Hampl describes her 1968 visit to the gynecologist in search of reliable contraception. She had rehearsed the visit with her girlfriends down to the tiniest detail. They had warned each other against Catholic doctors and discussed the pros and cons of pretending to be engaged. Hampl decided not to lie; freedom of expression was at the heart of what she sought. As it turned out, the doctor, whose toupee somehow reassured her, handed over the pills cheerfully and routinely.

Across the street at Brother's Delicatessen in Minneapolis, Hampl took the first pill with a celebration meal: a Reuben sandwich, chocolate cake, a pot of tea, and a glass of water. She compares the pill she first took at Brothers to a communion wafer. She sat contemplating "the lozenge of personal revolution" at the "modern altar" that she had finally reached "after long tarrying in the vestibule of Catholic girlhood." With this carefully planned transgression, she crossed the boundary to womanhood and left the Catholic world of her family and the nuns behind. The pill "instantly became metaphorical" signifying "not only freedom but safety" (Hampl 1999, 38–42).

By 1973, she had made further departures. She had stopped reading Whitman, whose writings virtually begged her to move on and strike out on her own; she no longer believed in the pill as a panacea. Her mother got breast cancer and recovered. Just to be safe, she switched to the diaphragm. Neither her body nor her sexual relationships were as simple to regulate as she had thought in 1968. In some ways, saying goodbye to Whitman had been the hardest departure of all. For he had given her a spiritual home and a sense of belonging when she had moved beyond church and family and nation and could only claim the semisecure niche of belonging in a specific generation with its own history and its own truths (Hampl 1999, 48–49).

In her 30s, Hampl started on a pilgrimage of return to her family and its roots that took her twice to Prague and produced her first memoir *A Romantic Education*. She did not make this transition alone, exactly, for she was in the company of her cohorts. Once again Hampl's sense of her own generation as her community, which was often more welcoming than church and family, comes into play. Hampl maintains that two related bonding experiences of the generation that went off to college in the second half of the 1960s were the Vietnam War and "the almost manic tape-recording of aging relatives," which continued into the 1970s and beyond. She explains the motivation behind the family histories: It was "as if we were starved and wanted to wolf down a chunk of the past, not only to make sure it was there, but to make it our own" (Hampl 1992, 20). During this phase, when she was still technically outside the church, certain images provided orientation on Hampl's journey. These images beckoned from "*back there,*" more a place than a time, Hampl discovered, in her random cocktail-party conversations with Catholics of her generation who were "educated out of it all, well climbed into the professions." She could identify Catholics in diaspora by their disclaimers: "Nobody says, when asked, 'I'm Catholic.' It's always, 'Yes, I was brought up Catholic.' Anything to put it at a distance, to diminish the presence of that heritage which is not racial but acts as if it were" (Hampl 1993, 50).

Hampl and her Catholic acquaintances tried out a variety of metaphors. Catholicism often sounded like a "hopeless congenital condition." The "love-hate lurch" familiar to those brought up Catholic could resemble "having an extra set of parents" or "an added national allegiance" to complicate life and decision-making. In their mellower moments, Hampl and her companions would move beyond the burden and touch upon the wonder and the lingering traces of magic from their childhood: "a strange country where people prayed and believed impossible things." Sometimes an image from that country—even a "broken and incomplete image" or "half-recollected fragments"—captivated Hampl and became a "touchstone." Only other Catholics—and not all of them—could understand how such a signifier functioned: not to tell "the whole truth and nothing but the truth of our experience" but to provide "a version of its swirling, changing wholeness" (Hampl 1993, 50; Hampl 1999, 33–34).

An important touchstone for Hampl was an anonymous parish lady from her parochial-school years at St. Luke's. Hampl crossed her path on countless misty mornings as the lady made her way home from six o'clock mass and she herself walked to school early so that she could practice the piano before classes began. Hampl never knew the lady's name, where she lived within the parish, or even the sound of her voice, but for a while they saw each other often. The woman in her mid-40s, who was dressed in a neutral-colored "librarian's cardigan sweater," looked unmarried to Hampl. She was "homely, . . . plain and pale, unnoticeable" and always walked alone. She paused for traffic; she never quickened her "peaceful gait" to beat an oncoming vehicle.

There was something about her that stayed with Hampl over the years and even served as a kind of beacon leading her back to the world of St. Luke's Parish that she had left in the 1960s, much to her parents' regret. What made the lady so memorable, a touchstone, was the way that she had greeted Hampl, a young girl from the parish school she knew only by sight. "When finally we were close enough to make eye contact, she looked up, straight into my face, and smiled. It was such a *complete* smile, so entire, it startled me every time, as if I had heard my name called out in the street of a foreign city." Somehow, the homeliness of the woman and the "vague" fabrics she wore made her smile all the more memorable and compelling. It was a "brief flood of light" on those misty mornings and left Hampl with a powerful inner conviction: "She loved me. I was sure." In the years of diaspora, Hampl meditated on the woman's smile, puzzling over its source and its power. She knew that the woman was praying; the crystal beads of her rosary occasionally glistened from her pocket (Hampl 1993, 51–52).

As she probed deeper and deeper into the image, Hampl realized that had the woman been a "nun, mumbling the Rosary along Summit," a fairly common sight on that street, she could not have functioned as a touchstone in the same way. It was precisely because Hampl encountered this non-professed woman on Oxford, a quiet side street, that she had been able to recognize the parish lady for what she was: an almost invisible middle-aged laywoman who "prayed without ceasing" (Hampl 1993, 52). In this lingering image from her past, which reached out to her from the strange country she had left, the two Catholic worlds of her girlhood and adolescence, St. Luke's and the convent school, came together. Surely this was the woman in the balcony that Sister Marie Helene was talking about, the modern Mary who pondered all things in her heart. She was real and compelling, even for an urbane, well-traveled, professional woman such as Hampl, who, like the others at the cocktail parties in the 1970s and 1980s, was clinging to the crucial distinction implicit in having been "*brought up* Catholic" (Hampl 1993, 50).

In the latter part of the 1980s, when she was over 40, Hampl married. The night before the wedding, she dreamed of a group of nuns she had never met, singing and smiling and gathering sheaves of wheat: "Very *Sound of Music* nuns, costumes and set design by Cecil Beaton." She ran after them and tried to follow them into a monastery. She could hear the familiar strains of Gregorian chant beckoning. It was as if she was back in study hall with her French grammar, listening to the chanting nuns, "[tak-ing] the bait and going deep with the beauty of it" (Hampl 1993, 13, 63). In her dream, the door slammed behind the nuns and she could no longer hear their music. Then she remembered: "*I can't go in there, I'm getting married.*" A friend who ventured a Jungian interpretation declared it "a heavy dream"; for Hampl it was a "light" dream. It comforted and liberated her, even though she was not entirely sure what it meant. She was sure of the end result: "With the nice inconsistency of dreams, the happy nuns in the adobe monastery left me free not only to marry but to pursue—from a safe distance—this first love. The one I would have winced to call the love of God. But what else is it?" (Hampl 1993, 13–15).

Twenty years after she left the church "in a blaze of contempt," part of an innocent search for experience in the world, Hampl made a systematic effort to find her way back. She started going to mass, praying, and read-ing the Psalms, "marveling as if I had never read a poem before in my life." Her parents were pleased, but her friends needed reassurance. One old friend wanted to hear that she "was just doing research," that Hampl did not believe "all that Catholic stuff." For Hampl, as for Antonia White decades before, returning was not really about belief, not about orthodoxy or orthopraxy. As she began to explore her "big, floppy New Jerusalem Bible," the "Church deconstructed." It was no longer "the imprisoning cell of catechized thought and repressive habit." Instead, it "became, simply, my most intimate past. It returned to its initial state. It became poetry" (Hampl 1993, 13–15).

Hampl instinctively knew that she needed guidance. She could not reenter the church through the same door she had exited. The door no longer existed, nor did the self who had left. An attempt to go to a Latin Christmas mass, replete with smells and bells, a few years before, had had the opposite effect than she had anticipated. ("I thought I would be swimming in nostalgia, but I gagged on the incense as if on a lie.") She found a spiritual advisor, Sister Mary Madonna, "Donnie," a contemplative nun at the San Damiano Monastery in a suburb of Minneapolis. Donnie told her: "Just follow your instinct." One powerful instinct in Hampl, memoirist since girlhood, was the "instinct for wonder" acquired over the years at St. Luke's and her convent school. She thought that she had incinerated it long before with her "burning scorn," but when she took walks in the old neighborhood, she could still sense its presence (Hampl 1993, 16, 34–36).

Donnie, who was only a few years older than Hampl, had entered a community of Franciscan contemplative nuns when she was 17. The two women had lived entirely different lives but found themselves deeply compatible when it came to spirituality. Donnie, no stranger to female Catholic humor and irony, could read Hampl's body language and hear what Hampl sometimes left unsaid. With Donnie's help, Hampl, the compulsive traveler throughout the world and the landscape of her past, planned a pilgrimage that Hampl preferred not to call a pilgrimage.

> "You're going on a pilgrimage," [Donnie] said, meaning to be helpful.
> "No," I said bristling, "I'm just going." Something about the word set my teeth on edge. *Pilgrimage.* I wince at the eau-de-cologne language of spirituality, but the whole world as I first understood it comes rushing back on the merest scent. I still want to embrace it—so, of course, when it dares to draw close, I slap it clean across the mouth. (Hampl 1993, 6)

Even after she has put a few friendships at risk in order to find her way back to the church, the instinct to slap it all away—both the pious words and the values and images clinging to them—remains strong for Hampl. She discovers that she has a low tolerance for certain kinds of piety and certain breeds of perennial pilgrim. Donnie, with her unfailing Celtic irony, knows this and helps her to negotiate through the rough spots. When a Franciscan missionary priest at San Damiano (Minneapolis) tells Hampl "I understand that you praise the Lord with your pen," she cannot help the reflex reaction, which she could only describe as "shame," a recurring experience since her Catholic girlhood. The feeling returned numerous times when she was in the presence of fellow pilgrims at monastic sites all over the globe. It was a kind of violation, "being known without having given permission." Hampl noticed a difference between the way she dealt with this shame before she left the church in her 20s—by filling notebooks with narratives about "a sensitive, daring person misunderstood by a timid Catholic family"—and her approach to the same emotion after her return to the church in her 40s. This time, she examined her memories and experience to see if she could understand what made her ashamed, with the instinctive knowledge that "shame alone was not the end of the story" (Hampl 1993, 38–40).

The pilgrimage that Hampl planned with Donnie's help had several stages: She would "work [her] way up to the loneliness of the monasteries" (Hampl 1993, 16). The first phase was a walking tour, "The Road to Assisi," organized by a serious noncommercialized firm in Cambridge, England. A friend who had taken the tour in the past told Hampl to expect "grown-up Girl Guides," "wiry middle-aged women in culottes" with an extensive knowledge of flora and fauna. Instead, she found herself amid English couples who considered an American Catholic woman rather exotic. Even in this low-key sociable tour, shepherded by an attractive young Englishwoman with impeccable Italian who carefully selected the inns and restaurants, Hampl encountered the recurring shame. She referred to it almost in code, in a manner reminiscent of Antonia White. In moments of insecurity, in unfamiliar environments in the company of intimidating confident strangers, she found herself mentally reverting into a convent-school girl whose selfhood and value always depended on others' assessments of her. She sought primarily to win the approval of others, and in the process she became almost invisible, even to herself. Later she thought back on these scenes, and the shame only increased when she realized her own complicity in these recurring episodes (Hampl 1993, 11, 19, 21, 91).

One of Hampl's goals upon returning to the church was to part company with this phantom schoolgirl self and develop an adult Catholic spirituality in which she could stand confidently on her own. After the walking tour, Hampl spent two weeks living in the Poor Clare monastery of Santa Chiara in Assisi, which took in laypeople as boarders. She was waiting to join a study tour of sites important to St. Francis of Assisi recommended by Donnie, which was designed primarily for Franciscan priests, friars, and sisters. During the interval at Santa Chiara, Hampl stayed in a small single room named for the annunciation. Even the room, with its polished floor and pristine white bedspread, flooded with sunshine and fresh air, had a special spiritual significance. It evoked a powerful memory of an almost identical room in her convent school: the room just outside the cloister. It always struck her as a "perfect" room, and it spoke to her own interior self (Hampl 1993, 89–90). Something about the uncluttered simplicity and practical beauty of the Annunciation Room, combined with two unscheduled weeks spent exploring, writing in her journal, and sketching local scenes as her husband had urged her to do, made Hampl feel mature and self-sufficient. The interval also gave her a sense of distance and perspective with which to contemplate her struggles with shame and her schoolgirl alter ego:

> By the end of the first week I realized that, for once, I wished to be nobody else.... I felt a comfortable distance from my own life as its odds and ends sifted over the weightless days.
>
> The aloof part of my mind . . . had always been there. I was free—always had been free—of the slavish convent-school girl I had been railing at all these years. . . . It was so easy. There was no daughter straining to break free, no mother, no father, no stockade of love and loyalty. No Catholic girlhood to ransack for jokes or outrage.
>
> There was only this mind—the simple room which turned out to be a camera, admitting light; it had been taking its quirky snapshots all along. Everything from the past seemed valuable, yet almost weightless, without the usual attachments of pride or grief, regret or resentment. (Hampl 1993, 108)

The Franciscan study tour came at a perfect time for Hampl. She was ready to explore what coming home to the church could mean to her. It need not be an adjustment, a compromise between who one is and what the church wanted one to be: the dreaded accommodations and abjection that had kept Antonia White out of the church after her encounter with the spiritual fascist in the confessional. Hampl saw how the Franciscans who were taking a break before returning to their strenuous work in Brooklyn, Hawaii, or Malaysia treated Assisi—their shared spiritual home—with an earthy intimacy. It was a real home, a place to eat, drink, joke, and gossip—even about St. Francis and St. Clare—as well as a place to pray. An overheard conversation between two fellow pilgrims who had become her friends, Sister Bridget and Father Felix, stayed with her. Felix had quoted one of the Berrigan brothers, who had called Mother Church a whore, and Bridget's usual smile had given way to a profound sadness. Like Donnie, Felix and Bridget had a wholistic vision of the church; they refused to divide it into segments in an effort to avoid complicity with the bad or to associate themselves with the blameless. This was part of the Franciscan way, balancing activism with acceptance of the reality of human sin, seeing both as parts of religious life. Hampl was beginning to understand that "prayer as focus is not a way of limiting what can be seen; it is a habit of attention brought to bear on all that is" (Hampl 1993, 224).

After her European sojourn, Hampl pleaded with Donnie: "No more pilgrimages. I just take a billion notes. It's like eating too much." Still, a year later, at Donnie's suggestion, she found herself on retreat at Rosethorn, a small Cistercian women's monastery among the redwoods in northern California. Hampl was surprised at how she welcomed this experience, including the tiny cell, the silent vegetarian meals, even the company of strangers she would not have sought out on her own. She had further narrowed down what she was seeking on her spiritual travels. She called it "Our Integrity," or "It," for short. She associated It with her Catholic childhood, not the happiness she had experienced but an awareness of the interrelatedness of all reality—both inside and outside herself—that she had taken for granted. She sought to experience again the impact that It had on her in her childhood when it arrived unbidden, like a sudden silence or a song (Hampl 1993, 202).

As always, she spent much of her time in communion with touchstones from her past. Everything came together for her at an informal service at dawn on the summer solstice. The community offered morning praise to commemorate absent trees, redwoods the sisters and friends had been unable to save from the loggers. She remembered a metaphor from Merton depicting contemplative life: "the virgin instant." She recalled all of her efforts to "wrestle free" from "that old monster, innocence." So much of her life had been devoted to breaking away from her "Catholic good-girl background." She recognized the many methods she had tried: "sex as freedom; books as tactical missiles; the outward mobility, away from the soul, of intellectual life; passionate politics; and a string of wrong romances" (Hampl 1993, 206–207).

Now, at last, she saw a new direction that she had not considered: "to find a *use* for innocence, after all." Standing at dawn in a cluster of women—almost strangers—in sweatshirts and bulky sweaters, commemorating the absent redwoods, she prayed, "*I can't help it, it's how I am.*" She had achieved a new clarity: Prayer was "a plain statement of fact." In her case, her prayer acknowledged the life she had been born to live. She understood that "You don't get to live Life—that thing I feared I was missing. You just live a life." Innocence was beside the point. The innocence that she had sought so strenuously to lose was elusive after all: "an absence, a vacancy" (Hampl 1993, 207–208). Two days later, as she worked in the monastery garden, she recalled Donnie's words about the church and metaphors. The real problem comes "when the church tries to tame the metaphors." Donnie had insisted: "You can't control the images. That's not what they're for. You have to get *in* there with them" (Hampl 1993, 218).

Hampl had spent decades trying to hold at bay the powerful images planted in her imagination during her Catholic girlhood. She was shocked, even ashamed, when certain images, especially those related to innocence and goodness, haunted her consciousness. Donnie was right when she sensed that it all revolved around control and the "vigilance" convent-school girls were urged to cultivate. In an essay entitled "The Need to Say It" in *I Could Tell You Stories,* Hampl is overheard laughing at her former self, as those who come home frequently have occasion to do:

> For years, decades even, I considered it one solid accomplishment that I had escaped the nuns. Result: I spent the better part of five years writing a memoir about growing up Catholic, a book which took me for extended stays at several monasteries and Catholic shrines in Europe and America. The central character of the book: a contemplative nun, the very figure I was determined to dodge. (Hampl 1999, 201)

Donnie finds the cure for Hampl's spiritual malaise. She knows that Hampl needs a homeopathic dose of the religious life to heal the wounds and disperse the ghosts of her intensely Catholic girlhood. When Donnie tells her that she needs to "get in there" and let the metaphors have their way with her, Hampl trusts the nun and her advice. By the third day of her retreat at Rosethorn, Hampl could tell that the process was well underway. When she called her husband from a phone in the hall, she knew that she sounded strange, like "a record playing at the wrong speed." When her husband observed, awestruck, that she was "really in there," she agreed, in her new soft quiet voice, only temporarily a woman of few words (Hampl 1993, 212–213). By the last page of *Virgin Time,* Hampl has come full circle and revisited the Catholic girlhood she has sought so strenuously to escape. Like so many Catholic women in diaspora, she has spiraled back to a new place.

EPILOGUE

What matters is that lives do not serve as models; only stories do that.

—Heilbrun 1988, 37

We define ourselves by the stories that we tell and by those we long to hear. Catholic women—at least those born before the 1960s—have been raised on the lives of the saints, usually carefully packaged for the edifying, appropriately "feminine" lessons that they teach, but when in search of models for real life, Catholic women have turned to different sources. They have immersed themselves in stories about departure and mobility, life in diaspora, the magic of reversals, the power released in the act of naming, and the alchemy of healing broken lives with recycled fragments of the past. They have cherished personal narratives of notorious Catholic bad girls who did not wither up and die when they moved beyond the control of the church but instead recycled images and moments from their Catholic girl-hoods, treasures that remained their talismans and touchstones.

Mary Jo Weaver accurately depicts Catholic women in the pre–Vatican II church as "eavesdroppers" rather than preachers, pastors, and framers of doctrine and policy (Weaver 1995, 3). Weaver is correct in calling attention to the limitations inherent in this role and the historical and spiritual importance of Catholic women's expanding goals and self-perceptions in the post–Vatican II era. Still, eavesdropping is highly underrated. Because Catholic women were reduced to eavesdropping, they became skilled strategic listeners and creative storytellers. Because eavesdropping takes place on the margins, out of the spotlight, Catholic women have explored that frontier and recognized its spiritual potential. Their carefully developed sense of irony, itself a kind of spirituality, a way of being in the world, has its roots in the boundary experience accessible to all Catholic women, even those who remain within the institutional church. The authors examined in this book all recognized the combined power of language and imagination to create and cultivate space for Catholic women to explore new selves that would not be acceptable within the constraints of the Catholic compounds in which they were raised.

Feminist theorist Marilyn Frye asserts: "There probably is really no distinction, in the end, between imagination and courage. We can't imagine what we can't face, and we can't face what we can't imagine. To break out of the structures of the arrogant eye we have to dare to rely on ourselves to make meaning and we have to imagine ourselves beings capable of that" (Frye 1983, 80).

The narratives examined in this book illustrate and confirm Frye's insight. Monica Baldwin was reawakened in her late 40s by an almost-forgotten volume of Malory that had brought passion and wildness into her sheltered, lonely convent-school life. Karen Armstrong smuggled into the convent her vivid recollections of Baldwin's memoir and Audrey Hepburn's performance in *The Nun's Story,* both of which informed her own experience of religious life. Mary Gordon adopted Mary McCarthy as a literary mother precisely because she showed how (and that) one could be Catholic and a bad girl. Antonia White and Mary Daly recognized in Thomas Aquinas the raw materials for new ways of being. Barbara Ferraro and Patricia Hussey wrote their departure narrative in large part to honor the power inherent in the stories of countless unnamed women they encountered in their ministries, stories that gave them the courage—even the mandate—to leave their religious order. At a critical point early in college, Patricia Hampl relied on Walt Whitman as a literary and spiritual mentor. Often, books were the catalysts for these authors' spiraling spiritual journeys, their departures and returns. When, like Hélène Cixous, these women acknowledged within themselves the need to move on, to believe that "there has to be someplace else," they, too, turned to books to provide "routes, signs, 'maps'—for an exploration, a trip" (Cixous 1986, 72).

Those of us who wish to participate in the departure stories of Baldwin, White, McCarthy, Gordon, Daly, Armstrong, Ferraro and Hussey, and Hampl, just as they built their departures on the written works and shared stories of others, are struck—and heartened—by the unfinished quality of their narratives. Like our own stories, they are works in progress, outcome uncertain. Closure, completion, flawlessness, selflessness, even fulfillment—goals proffered to women by well-meaning religious and secular teachers—show themselves to be dead and static, no longer worthy of our desires and exertions. Departure from the rituals and touchstones of Catholic girlhood is never complete. Even the adamant post-Catholics Mary McCarthy and Mary Daly carried plunder from their pasts with them when they left the church behind: memories of mystical moments, intimations of Be-ing and Integrity, a commitment to justice and human dignity originally embraced in a Catholic context. Armed with these treasures, Catholic women have imitated birds and robbers, have found new space on the margins of the church and beyond, and have even sometimes returned to a new church first discovered within themselves, where memories of Catholic girlhood and imaginings of adult womanhood find room to grow.

SOURCES CONSULTED

Published Material

Armstrong, Karen. 1995. *Through the Narrow Gate.* 2nd ed. New York: St. Martin's Press.

Asirvatham, Sandy. 2002. "An Interview with Mary Gordon." In *Conversations with Mary Gordon,* edited by Alma Bennett. Jackson: University Press of Mississippi.

Augustine. 1992. *Confessions.* Translated by Henry Chadwick. Oxford: Oxford World's Classics.

Baldwin, Monica. 1950. *I Leap over the Wall: Contrasts and Impressions after Twenty-Eight Years in a Convent.* New York: Rinehart and Company.

Bannon, Barbara A. 2002. "Mary Gordon." In *Conversations with Mary Gordon,* ed. Alma Bennett. Jackson: University Press of Mississippi.

Barbour, John D. 1994. *Versions of Deconversion: Autobiography and the Loss of Faith.* Charlottesville: University Press of Virginia.

Bennett, Alma, ed. 2002. *Conversations with Mary Gordon.* Jackson: University Press of Mississippi.

Bennett, Jackie, and Rosemary Forgan, eds. 1991. *There's Something About a Convent Girl.* London: Virago Press.

Benstock, Shari. 1998. "Authorizing the Autobiographical." In *Women, Autobiography, Theory: A Reader,* edited by Sidonie Smith and Julia Watson. Madison: University of Wisconsin Press.

Bolen, Jean Shinoda. 1994. *Crossing to Avalon: A Woman's Midlife Pilgrimage.* San Francisco: HarperSanFrancisco.

Bowen, Elizabeth. 1992. Introduction to *Frost in May,* by Antonia White. New York: Penguin Books.

Brereton, Virginia Lieson. 1991. *From Sin to Salvation: Stories of Women's Conversions, 1800 to the Present.* Bloomington: Indiana University Press.

Brightman, Carol. 1984. "Mary, Still Contrary." *The Nation* 238 (May 19): 611–619.

————. 1992. *Writing Dangerously: Mary McCarthy and Her World.* New York: Clarkson Potter Publishers.

Byrne, Patricia. 1989. "In the Parish But Not of It: Sisters." Part 2 of *Transforming Parish Ministries: The Changing Roles of Catholic Clergy, Laity, and Women*

Religious, by Jay P. Dolan, R. Scott Appleby, Patricia Byrne, and Debra Campbell. New York: Crossroad.

Chitty, Susan. 1985. *Now to My Mother: A Very Personal Memoir of Antonia White.* London: Weidenfeld and Nicolson.

———, ed. 1983. *As Once in May: The Early Autobiography of Antonia White and Other Writings.* London: Virago Press.

———, ed. 1992. *Antonia White Diaries 1926–1957.* London: Virago Press.

———, ed. 1993. *Antonia White Diaries 1958–1979.* London: Virago Press.

Christ, Carol P., and Judith Plaskow, eds. 1992. *Womanspirit Rising: A Feminist Reader in Religion.* 2nd ed. San Francisco: HarperSanFrancisco.

Cixous, Hélène. 1976. "The Laugh of the Medusa." Translated by Keith Cohen and Paula Cohen. *Signs: Journal of Women in Culture and Society* 1, no. 4: 875–893.

———. 1986. *The Newly Born Woman.* Translated by Betsy Wing. Minneapolis: University of Minnesota Press.

Cunneen, Sally. 1968. *Sex: Female; Religion: Catholic.* New York: Holt, Rinehart and Winston.

Daly, Mary. 1965. "The Problem of Speculative Theology." *The Thomist* 29: 177–216.

———. 1984. *Pure Lust: Elemental Feminist Philosophy.* Boston: Beacon Press.

———. 1985a. "Autobiographical Preface to the 1975 Edition." In *The Church and the Second Sex.* 3d ed. Boston: Beacon Press.

———. 1985b. *Beyond God the Father: Toward a Philosophy of Women's Liberation.* 2nd ed. Boston: Beacon Press.

———. 1985c. *The Church and the Second Sex.* 3d ed. Boston: Beacon Press.

———. 1985d. "Feminist Postchristian Introduction [to the 1975 Edition]." In *The Church and the Second Sex.* 3d ed. Boston: Beacon Press.

———. 1985e. "New Archaic Afterwords." In *The Church and the Second Sex.* 3d ed. Boston: Beacon Press.

———. 1990. *Gyn/Ecology: The Metaethics of Radical Feminism.* 2nd ed. Boston: Beacon Press.

———. 1992. *Outercourse: The Be-Dazzling Voyage.* San Francisco: Harper-SanFrancisco.

———. 1998. *Quintessence. . . . Realizing the Archaic Future: A Radical Elemental Feminist Manifesto.* Boston: Beacon Press.

Daly, Mary, and Jane Caputi. 1987. *Websters' First New Intergalactic Wickedary of the English Language.* Boston: Beacon Press.

Dohen, Dorothy. 1960. *Women in Wonderland.* New York: Sheed and Ward.

Donohue, Stacey Lee. 1996. "Reluctant Radical: The Irish-Catholic Element." In *Twenty-four Ways of Looking at Mary McCarthy: The Writer and Her Work,* edited by Eve Stwertka and Margo Viscusi. Westport, Conn.: Greenwood Press.

Dunn, Jane. 1998. *Antonia White: A Life.* London: Jonathan Cape.

Ebaugh, Helen Rose Fuchs. 1988. *Becoming an Ex: The Process of Role Exit.* Chicago: University of Chicago Press.

————. 1993. *Women in the Vanishing Cloister: Organizational Decline in Catholic Religious Orders in the United States.* New Brunswick, N.J.: Rutgers University Press.

Estés, Clarissa Pinkola. 1995. *Women Who Run with the Wolves: Myths and Stories of the Wild Woman Archetype.* 2nd ed. New York: Ballantine Books.

Evasdaughter, Elizabeth N. 1996. *Catholic Girlhood Narratives: The Church and Self-Denial.* Boston: Northeastern University Press.

Ferraro, Barbara, and Patricia Hussey with Jane O'Reilly. 1990. *No Turning Back: Two Nuns' Battle with the Vatican over Women's Right to Choose.* New York: Poseidon Press.

Fitzgerald, Penelope. 1987. "Various Women." *London Review of Books* (April 2): 15–16.

Franchot, Jenny. 1994. *Roads to Rome: The Antebellum Protestant Encounter with Catholicism.* Berkeley: University of California Press.

Friedan, Betty. 1983. *The Feminine Mystique.* 3d ed. New York: Dell Publishing.

Frye, Marilyn. 1983. *The Politics of Reality.* Freedom, Calif.: Crossing Press.

Frye, Northrop. 1957. *Anatomy of Criticism: Four Essays.* Princeton, N.J.: Princeton University Press.

Giles, Paul. 1992. *American Catholic Arts and Fictions: Culture, Ideology, Aesthetics.* Cambridge: Cambridge University Press.

Gilligan, Carol. 1993. *In a Different Voice: Psychological Theory and Women's Development.* 2nd ed. Cambridge, Mass.: Harvard University Press.

Gilman, Richard. 1986. *Faith, Sex, Mystery: A Memoir.* New York: Penguin Books.

Gilmore, Leigh. 1994. *Autobiographics: A Feminist Theory of Women's Self-Representation.* Ithaca, N.Y.: Cornell University Press.

Gleason, Philip. 1987. *Keeping the Faith: American Catholicism Past and Present.* Notre Dame, Ind.: University of Notre Dame Press.

Gordon, Mary. 1979. *Final Payments.* New York: Ballantine Books.

————. 1982. "Coming to Terms with Mary." *Commonweal* 109 (January 15): 11–14.

————. 1992. *Good Boys and Dead Girls and Other Essays.* New York: Penguin Books.

————. 1996a. "Hot Dog." *The New York Times Magazine* (May 12): 38–41, 58.

————. 1996b. *The Shadow Man.* New York: Random House.

————. 2000. *Seeing through Places: Reflections on Geography and Identity.* New York: Scribner.

————. 2002. "Women of God." *The Atlantic* (January): 57–91.

Gramick, Jeannine, S.S.N.D. 1986. "The Vatican's Battered Wives." *The Christian Century* (January 1–8): 17–20.

————. 1988. "Catholic Nuns and the Need for Responsible Dissent." *The Christian Century* (December 7): 1122–1125.

Gross, Beverly. 1996. "Our Leading Bitch Intellectual." In *Twenty-four Ways of Looking at Mary McCarthy: The Writer and Her Work,* edited by Eve Stwertka and Margo Viscusi. Westport, Conn.: Greenwood Press.

Halsey, William M. 1980. *The Survival of American Innocence: Catholicism in an Era of Disillusionment, 1920–1940.* Notre Dame, Ind.: University of Notre Dame Press.

Hampl, Patricia. 1992. *A Romantic Education.* Boston: Houghton Mifflin.

———. 1993. *Virgin Time.* New York: Ballantine Books.

———. 1999. *I Could Tell You Stories: Sojourns in the Land of Memory.* New York: W.W. Norton and Company.

Hardwick, Elizabeth. 1993. Foreword to *Intellectual Memoirs New York 1936–1938,* by Mary McCarthy. San Diego: Harvest Book/Harcourt Brace and Company.

Heilbrun, Carolyn G. 1988. *Writing a Woman's Life.* New York: W.W. Norton and Company.

Hollingsworth, Gerelyn. 1985. "Are Nuns Going with a Whimper or a Bang?" *National Catholic Reporter* (March 1): 16.

Hopkinson, Lyndall Passerini. 1988. *Nothing to Forgive: A Daughter's Life of Antonia White.* London: Chatto and Windus.

Hulme, Kathryn. 1956. *The Nun's Story.* Boston: Little, Brown and Company.

Keyser, Les, and Barbara Keyser. 1984. *Hollywood and the Catholic Church: The Image of Roman Catholicism in American Movies.* Chicago: Loyola University Press.

Khouri, Callie. 1996. *Thelma & Louise; and, Something to Talk about: Screenplays.* New York: Grove Press.

Kiernan, Frances. 2000. *Seeing Mary Plain: A Life of Mary McCarthy.* New York: W.W. Norton and Company.

Lee, Don. 1997. "About Mary Gordon." *Ploughshares* 23 (Fall): 218–226.

Maitland, Sara. 1992. Introduction to *The Hound and the Falcon: The Story of a Reconversion to the Catholic Faith,* by Antonia White. London: Virago Press.

Mandell, Gail Porter. 1997. *Madeleva: A Biography.* Albany: State University of New York Press.

Maritain, Jacques. 1966. "The Intuition of Being." In *Challenges and Renewals,* edited by Joseph W. Evans and Leo R. Ward. Notre Dame, Ind.: University of Notre Dame Press.

Mason, Mary G. 1998. "The Other Voice: Autobiographies of Women Writers." In *Women, Autobiography, Theory: A Reader,* edited by Sidonie Smith and Julia Watson. Madison: University of Wisconsin Press.

Massa, Mark S. 1999. *Catholics and American Culture: Fulton Sheen, Dorothy Day, and the Notre Dame Football Team.* New York: Crossroad Publishing Company.

McBrien, Richard P. 1987. Preface to *The Future of Catholic Leadership,* by Dean Hoge. Kansas City: Sheed and Ward.

McCarthy, Mary. 1970. *The Company She Keeps.* New York: Harvest Book/Harcourt Brace and World.

———. 1985. *Memories of a Catholic Girlhood.* San Diego: Harvest Book/Harcourt.

———. 1987. *How I Grew.* San Diego: Harcourt Brace Jovanovich Publishers.

———. 1993. *Intellectual Memoirs: New York 1936–1938.* San Diego: Harvest Book/Harcourt Brace and Company.

McCarthy, Thomas J. 2000. "Communion Without Community?" *America* (July 29–August 5): 6.

McGinley, Phyllis. 1957. "Mary Was an Orphan." *Saturday Review* 40 (June): 31.

McNamara, Jo Ann Kay. 1996. *Sisters in Arms: Catholic Nuns through Two Millennia.* Cambridge, Mass.: Harvard University Press.

Merriman, Brigid O'Shea, O.F.M. 1994. *Searching for Christ: The Spirituality of Dorothy Day.* Notre Dame, Ind.: University of Notre Dame Press.

Milhaven, Annie Lally. 2002. "Mary Gordon." In *Conversations with Mary Gordon,* edited by Alma Bennett. Jackson: University Press of Mississippi.

Morris, Pam. 1993. *Literature and Feminism: An Introduction.* Oxford: Blackwell Publishers.

Morton, Nelle. 1985. *The Journey Is Home.* Boston: Beacon Press.

Mudge, Alden. 2002. "A Sense of Place: Looking Into the Life of Mary Gordon." In *Conversations with Mary Gordon,* edited by Alma Bennett. Jackson: University Press of Mississippi.

Neal, Marie Augusta, S.N.D. de Namur. 1985. "American Sisters Now." In *Where We Are: American Catholics in the 1980s,* edited by Michael Glazier. Wilmington, Del.: Michael Glazier.

"Nuns: The Battered Women of the Church?" 1984. *National Catholic Reporter* (December 11): 25.

Occhiogrosso, Peter. 1987. *Once a Catholic.* Boston: Houghton Mifflin Company.

Pieper, Jeanne. 1993. *The Catholic Woman: Difficult Choices in a Modern World.* Los Angeles: Lowell House.

Silk, Mark. 1988. *Spiritual Politics: Religion and America since World War II.* New York: Simon and Schuster.

Smith, Tom. 2002. "A Conversation Between Tom Smith and Mary Gordon." In *Conversations with Mary Gordon,* edited by Alma Bennett. Jackson: University Press of Mississippi.

Stanley, Liz. 1992. *The Auto/biographical I: The Theory and Practice of Feminist Auto/Biography.* Manchester: Manchester University Press.

Stourton, Edward. 2000. *Absolute Truth: The Struggle for Meaning in Today's Catholic Church.* New York: TV Books.

Tillich, Paul. 1936. *On the Boundary.* New York: Charles Scribner's Sons.

Tyler, Anne. 1997. *Ladder of Years.* New York: Ivy Books.

Weaver, Mary Jo. 1993. *Springs of Water in a Dry Land: Spiritual Survival for Catholic Women Today.* Boston: Beacon Press.

———. 1995. *New Catholic Women: A Contemporary Challenge to Traditional Religious Authority.* 2nd ed. Bloomington: Indiana University Press.

White, Antonia. 1950. "Smoking Flax: The Story of a Reconversion." *The Month* (August): 114–130.

———. 1954. "Antonia White." In *Born Catholics,* edited by Frank Sheed. London: Catholic Book Club.

———. 1992a. *Frost in May.* New York: Penguin Books.

———. 1992b. *The Hound and the Falcon: The Story of a Reconversion to the Catholic Faith.* London: Virago Press.

[201]

————. 1993. *The Lost Traveller.* London: Virago Press.

Williams, Margaret, R.S.C.J. 1978. *The Society of the Sacred Heart: History of a Spirit 1800–1975.* London: Darton, Longman and Todd.

Wills, Garry. 1972. "Memories of a Catholic Boyhood." Chapter 1 in *Bare Ruined Choirs: Doubt, Prophecy, and Radical Religion.* Garden City, N.Y.: Doubleday and Company.

Unpublished Material

America Magazine Archives. Special Collections, Georgetown University Library, Washington, D.C.

Mary McCarthy Papers. Special Collections, Vassar College Libraries, Poughkeepsie, New York.

INDEX

abortion: Catholic policy on, 149;
Ferraro and Hussey study
Catholic church's policy on,
147–148; Ferraro speaks to Sisters
of Notre Dame about, 150;
McCarthy and, 43; *New York
Times* advertisements about,
132–133, 143–146, 148, 151–152;
White and, 41, 43, 159, 162. *See
also* Mario Cuomo; Geraldine
Ferraro; Ted Kennedy; Parental
Notification Bill; Sacred
Congregation for Religious and
Secular Institutes; Vatican 24
abstinence, xvii
abuse: childhood sexual, 42; marital
rape, 39; of power by nuns, 35; of
power by priests, 110, 137. *See
also* "Nuns: The Battered Women
of the Church"
alchemy, 93, 97, 194
alcoholism, 69, 113–114
Annie Wright boarding school
(Tacoma), 58
anti-Semitism, 172
Aquinas, Thomas. *See* St. Thomas
Aquinas
Archaic Future, 80, 95, 99, 100, 103
"The Architecture of a Life with
Priests," 72
Armstrong, Karen: breakdown of,
128–129; difficulties with convent
life, 118–125; education of, 126,
128–129; family life of, 113–114;
joins convent, 114–117; leaves

convent, 130–132; parents
oppose decision to join
convent, 5, 117; parents' plans
for, 115; post-convent life, 111;
reads Baldwin, 5–6, 113, 194;
work outside convent, 109,
126–127; writes memoir,
111–112 (*see Through the Narrow
Gate*)
atheism, 56–61, 136, 159, 171
"Autobiographical Preface," 84, 95, 97,
104
Autobiographics, 4
*Awful Disclosures of the Hotel Dieu
Nunnery in Montreal,* 3–4, 109

Baldwin, Monica: decision to enter
cloister, 11–12; difficulties with
cloister life, 10, 12, 118, 121; post-
departure life of, 7–8, 13–26, 29,
63, 131, 194; and use of humor,
xxiv; and writing as healing,
xviii–xix, 1; writings of, 2–7, 81,
113 (*see I Leap over the Wall*). *See
also* Cornwall; Sir Thomas
Malory; *Morte d'Arthur*
Bare Ruined Choirs, 59
Barnard College, 71, 76–77, 168–169,
172, 176, 183
battered women, 32–33. *See also*
"Nuns: The Battered Women of
the Church"
Beauvoir, Simone de, 44, 104
Be-ing, 80–84, 88–94, 98, 100, 102,
105, 194

psychiatry, 61; Freudian, 43, 158; Jungian, 21–22, 163, 187
puberty, 15, 40, 114
Pure Lust, 80, 87–89, 91, 100, 105

Quakerism, 159
Quintessence, 18, 80, 92, 100, 103, 105

Radical Feminism, 79, 82–84, 87, 89, 92, 94–95, 96–99, 102–103, 105, 154, 171
rape, 41
Raymond, Janice, 90
Re-membering, 85, 89, 91, 93, 97
Roehampton Convent of the Sacred Heart, 31–34, 36, 38–39, 41–43, 51, 76, 155–158. *See also* Lippington
A Romantic Education, 177, 185
Rosethorn, 191–192
Ruether, Rosemary Radford, 137

sacraments: absolution, 160, 179; communion, 35, 61, 160; confession, 64, 71, 73, 126, 160. *See also* Catholic ritual
Sacred Congregation for Religious and Secular Institutes (SCRIS), 110, 144–151. *See also* "Essential Elements in the Church's Teaching on Religious Life"; *New York Times* advertisements; Vatican 24
Sacred Heart, 45, 55, 164
St. Athanasius, 53
St. Augustine, xxvi–xxviii, 7, 10, 37
St. Benedict Center (Cambridge), 53
St. Blaise's Day, 179
St. Clare, 190
St. Cyprian, 52
St. Francis of Assisi, 190
St. John of the Cross, 51
St. Lidwine of Schiedam, 7
St. Luke's School (St. Paul), 178–179, 182, 186–188

Saint Mary's College (Notre Dame), 85–86, 93
St. Patrick's Cathedral, 75
St. Paul's School (London), 33, 156, 180
St. Peter's Basilica, 136
St. Stephen's Parish (Minneapolis), 52; parish church, 48, 50; parish school, 48–49, 50–51, 54–55, 59–60
St. Thérèse of Lisieux (Little Flower), xxiv–xxv, 24
St. Thomas Aquinas, 37, 85, 87–88, 93–95, 99, 159, 163, 194
Ste. Anne de Beaupré, 47
same-sex affairs, 157
San Damiano Monastery (Minneapolis), 188
Sandinistas, 143
Santa Chiara (Assisi), 189
Santayana, 42, 159
Sayres, Dorothy, 11
scholasticate (London), 126, 129–130
Seeing through Places, 68, 168–169
separatism, 82, 95
The Seven Storey Mountain, 10
Sex: Female; Religion: Catholic, xvii
sexuality, 64
The Shadow Man, 68, 74–76, 169, 173, 175, 177
shock therapy, 47
Shriver, Margaret, 47–48, 50
Shriver, Myers, 47–48, 50
Sister Catherine Hughes, 144. *See also* Sisters of Notre Dame de Namur
Sister Madeleva, 86
Sister Marie Augusta Neal, 109
Sister Mary Madonna (Donnie), 188, 191–192
Sisters of Notre Dame de Namur (SND), 133–139, 142, 144, 148–152
Slaves of the Immaculate Heart of Mary, 53

DEBRA CAMPBELL was born in Buffalo, New York, where she was a student at the Convent of the Sacred Heart (Nottingham) for eight years before attending Mount Holyoke College. She is Professor of Religious Studies at Colby College in Waterville, Maine. She co-authored *Transforming Parish Ministry* (1989) with R. Scott Appleby, Patricia Byrne, and Jay P. Dolan and has published articles in *Signs, Commonweal, CrossCurrents, Church History,* and *The Catholic Historical Review.*

DATE DUE
